Madame Proust

Madame Proust

A BIOGRAPHY

Evelyne Bloch-Dano

Translated by Alice Kaplan

THE UNIVERSITY OF CHICAGO PRESS | *Chicago & London*

EVELYNE BLOCH-DANO is the author of many books, including a prize-winning biography of Emile Zola's mother and a novel, *Le Biographe*. ALICE KAPLAN is the author of, among other books, *French Lessons, The Collaborator: The Trial and Execution of Robert Brasillach,* and *The Interpreter.*

The University of Chicago Press, Chicago 60637
The University of Chicago Press, Ltd., London
© 2007 by The University of Chicago
All rights reserved. Published 2007
Printed in the United States of America
Originally published as Madame Proust, © Editions Grasset & Fasquelle, 2004.

16 15 14 13 12 11 10 09 08 07   1 2 3 4 5

ISBN-13: 978-0-226-05642-5 (cloth)
ISBN-10: 0-226-05642-2 (cloth)

LIBRARY OF CONGRESS CATALOGING-IN-PUBLICATION DATA

Bloch-Dano, Evelyne.
    [Madame Proust. English]
    Madame Proust : a biography / Evelyne Bloch-Dano ; translated by Alice Kaplan.
        p. cm.
    Includes bibliographical references and index.
    ISBN-13: 978-0-226-05642-5 (cloth : alk. paper)
    ISBN-10: 0-226-05642-2 (cloth : alk. paper) 1. Proust, Marcel, 1871–1922—Family.
2. Proust, Jeanne Weill, 1849–1905. 3. Novelists, French—20th century—Family
relationships. 4. Mothers of authors—France—Biography. 5. Proust family.
I. Kaplan, Alice Yaeger. II. Title
    PQ2631.R63Z544813 2007
843'.912—dc22
[B]

                                                        2006101401

To my father, Robert Bloch

At every moment I thank you for thinking of me
as you do and for making my life so easy,
a life that would be sweet if only I were entirely well.

Marcel Proust to his mother, September 12, 1899

CONTENTS

Marcel Proust's *In Search of Lost Time* begins famously as the young narrator waits for his mother's goodnight kiss. The attachment Marcel feels for his mother is so central to the meaning of *La Recherche,* and Proust's own life so closely tied to his great work, that Proust's mother may well be considered the most influential mother figure in modern literary history and Proust himself the leading "mama's boy" of the canon.

That mother, Jeanne Weil Proust, is the subject of Evelyne Bloch-Dano's biography, which is at once the touching life story of an extraordinary woman; a cultural history dealing with issues ranging from French-Jewish assimilation, anti-Semitism during the Dreyfus affair, homophobia and medicine, Parisian high society and spa culture; and a rich, focused reading of Proust's work through the lens of the maternal relationship. Bloch-Dano writes much of her book in the style of fiction, re-creating intimate scenes and dialogue. But *Madame Proust* is anything but fiction: Almost every detail, almost every quoted word or phrase is taken directly from the writings of Jeanne Weil and Marcel Proust.

One of the pleasures of reading *Madame Proust* is the opportunity to immerse oneself in Proust's language—his correspondence and his publications, especially *A la Recherche du temps perdu* and its semiautobiographical precursor, *Jean Santeuil*. Whenever possible, I have used existing translations of these texts so that the curious reader can go back to the sources.

For *A la recherche du temps perdu*, I've quoted from the Viking/Penguin translations, which have given the English-language Proust a whole new lease on life. The appearance of a new translation, or rather a series of translations by different translators, to replace the classic Moncrieff has been controversial. For those curious about the polemic, I recommend "'Proust's Way?': An Exchange" in the April 6, 2006, issue of the *New York Review of Books*. Readers familiar with the older Proust translation will note that even the title has changed face: *Remembrance of Things Past*, with its echo of Shakespeare, has been replaced by *In Search of Lost Time*, closer to the original French.

Finding existing translations became a little more complicated when it came to quoting from Proust's letters and lesser-known texts. Philip Kolb edited all of Proust's correspondence, which was published in France in twenty-one volumes. Kolb also published a selection of letters in English; I've quoted from those translated letters whenever possible, referring to them under the title *Marcel Proust: Selected Letters*. I've also quoted from George Painter's collection, *Marcel Proust: Letters to His Mother*. Otherwise I refer to the French edition of the *Correspondance de Marcel Proust* and the translation is my own. Proust's novel *Jean Santeuil* was translated in the 1950s by Gerard Hopkins, though the French text was later reedited, and that new edition contains many passages that aren't included in Hopkins's text. I quote from Hopkins whenever possible. Proust's *Contre Sainte-Beuve* is a posthumous collection; various French editions have included and excluded different essays. I've quoted both from translations by Sylvia Townsend Warner and John Sturrock. From time to time, I've also relied on Euan Cameron's excellent translations of Proust's letters within his translation of Jean-Yves Tadié's definitive biography of Proust.

For readers who want to know more about the life and times of Marcel Proust, Evelyn Bloch-Dano's bibliography at the end of this volume offers an excellent introduction to some of the major social and cultural histories as well as to significant work on Proust, much of it available in English. There are several recent Proust biographies available in English: Jean-Yves Tadié's definitive *Marcel Proust*, with its expert scholarly attention to Proust's literary development; William C. Carter's lively narrative, *Marcel Proust: A*

Life; and Edmund White's *Marcel Proust,* a tour de force in 160 pages. All are highly recommended.

A final note on a single word: I've kept the French word "Israelite," which rings strange to an American reader and has been avoided by some of Proust's English translators. It was the word used in polite French society for "Jew": Evelyne Bloch-Dano describes its use and special meaning in fascinating detail. There's no real equivalent in English, although I noticed, driving through an old neighborhood in Durham, North Carolina, a cemetery whose metal entry gate reads "Hebrew Cemetery"; "Hebrew" must have had the same kind of resonance for early twentieth-century southerners as "Israelite" had for turn-of-the-century Parisians.

Alice Kaplan

Part One

Part One

A Daughter to Marry

At the Weils', dinner was always served at seven o'clock sharp. At ten to seven, Nathé Weil would put his newspaper aside and pull his watch out of his waistcoat pocket. At two minutes to the hour, he would stand up, and the others would move toward the table. But on a particular July evening in 1870, his son Georges still wasn't home. His wife, Adèle, disappeared into the kitchen. Dinner was ready. The broth from the *poule au pot* was simmering on the stove. The grated horseradish was ready on the table. Adèle returned and peered out the window of the dining room, which, like the other rooms in the apartment, looked out over the courtyard. There was no chance of seeing Georges come in from the street, but if she craned her neck, she might catch sight of him at the entrance to the building before he vanished into the stairwell, grabbed the walnut railing, and bounded up the two flights of stairs.

Adèle sat down and exchanged glances with her daughter Jeanne, who had looked up from her book when her mother walked in. The two women understood one another. Nathé Weil's principles allowed for no exceptions; they were as inflexible as the Ten Commandments and the nearly six hundred biblical rules that the family had long ceased to observe. All in all, Adèle's situation suited her romantic nature. She had merely placed her passions elsewhere. A smile floated on her face.

"He won't be long," she announced calmly. She knew her son. The young lawyer had forgotten what time it was while chatting with a friend. He was probably running to get home.

"I certainly hope so. In any case, we're eating in three minutes," Monsieur Weil responded, consulting his watch yet again.

Jeanne was back in her book, sitting in her favorite spot near the window. All you could see of her was a mass of brown hair gathered into a chignon and a few strands of loose hair on the nape of her neck. Her white summer dress showed off her ivory profile. A rather prominent nose, a strong chin, a full mouth (she bit her lips as she read)—everything about her indicated a strong personality. Her ripe beauty was already that of a woman. Her black eyes with curly lashes, under her thick brows, were focused on her reading. This pre-dinner scene didn't concern her. It had happened a hundred times. Georges would show up at the last second, still out of breath. He would utter a few words of apology and make a joke to put everyone at ease. His father would scold him for appearances' sake, and everything would be forgiven until the next time. Jeanne's own turn would come later, and on a much more serious subject. The door opened at the third chime of the clock, just as Nathé was standing up to head into the dining room.

At seven o'clock precisely, the Weil family gathered around the table, and Philomèle brought in the soup tureen.

The Weils had plenty of reasons to worry in 1870. Despite the plebiscite in May, the French knew that their empire was far from flourishing. The ailing emperor was in a fog from all the medicine he was taking. He scarcely seemed aware of the danger threatening France. The queen of Spain had abdicated, and the Spanish throne was likely to revert to a member of the Hohenzollern dynasty. The ambitions of Wilhelm, reinforced by his clever chancellor, Otto von Bismarck, knew no bounds. Wasn't it his dream to unify Germany and Prussia?

Perhaps more than others, Adèle and Nathé Weil were sensitive to the kinds of tensions that preceded a war. Though both Parisians, they came from those border regions that always suffer more than most places in times of war. The Weil family had left Alsace at the beginning of the nineteenth century. Adèle's mother, Rose, had lived in Paris after her marriage in Metz, and her father, Nathan Berncastel, born in Trèves, had become a French citizen. Still, the prospect of a conflict between Prussia and France recalled antagonisms from long ago. Never had Nathé's patriotism been so pronounced, so vigorous. He had served as a national guardsman in 1828, and any threat to France was intolerable to him. He was proud of his brother Alphonse, a unit commander in the infantry. Military careers among Jews were rather infrequent. How could it be otherwise, since they had only acquired the right to citizenship in 1791?

Nathé Weil had other, more material reasons to worry. Wars were never good for the stock market. He was a partner in a brokerage firm. And he had a daughter to marry.

Jeanne had turned twenty-one on the twenty-first of April, and despite her respect and love for her parents, she had thus far refused to bend to the kind of arranged marriage that had long been traditional among families of her kind. Her maternal grandfather had married off one of her aunts to a cloth merchant at Flers, in the Orne, and the other to Moïse, Nathé's half-brother, an architect at Beauvoir. Were her mother and aunts happy? The question never came up. Twenty-one was the age by which girls were established in their new families. Not a month went by without some marriage broker soliciting her father or some well-intentioned aunt playing the go-between with her mother. However much they sang the praises of this or that wealthy young Jewish man, Jeanne didn't want to marry a banker or a stockbroker or a lawyer, or even an engineer like her cousins, who attended the Ecole centrale. So why should she accept a suitor suggested by her father? Because Nathé was her father, whispered a little voice within.

"You're the one who should have gone into law," her lawyer brother sometimes teased her. It was true that if Jeanne had been a boy, she would have earned a degree. She knew Latin and spoke fluent English and German. Like her mother, she was an excellent pianist. She shared her passion for books with her parents and her brother. She loved to deepen her understanding of the world. At the Weils' there was always discussion and debate. And that alone distinguished them from traditional bourgeois families, in which girls grew up like force-fed geese bred only for marriage.

"But whose career could possibly rival Monsieur Proust's?" Nathé asked. At the age of thirty-six, Proust held an advanced medical degree and was the director of a clinic. Considered one of the bright lights of French medicine, he was already an uncontested authority in his field. Nathé's voice boomed as he described how, the year before, the government had entrusted the young doctor with an official mission to Russia, Persia, and Turkey. And he was a good-looking fellow, an imposing presence with his graying beard. "A real *goyish* patriarch," Georges quipped. "Right, he's no *yid*," Nathé shot back; on occasions like these he always seemed able to recall the few words of Yiddish left over from his childhood. Philomèle came in to clear away the plates and the soup tureen. With the arrival of the *meshore,*[1] the table was instantly silent.

No, Adrien wasn't Jewish, Nathé continued. But Jeanne wouldn't be the first one in the family to marry a Christian. Her mother's cousin had had a church wedding, hadn't she? And her cousin's father, the great Adolphe Crémieux, who had done so much for the Jewish people, had discovered one day that his wife had converted behind his back, along with their two children. And on the Weil side, only this past January 3, hadn't Jenny, Uncle Moïse's daughter, married François Boeuf, a law professor whose last name made it clear that . . .

Yes, but Uncle Adolphe was a Freemason, and Moïse too, Georges interrupted. Nathé pointed out that he was far from a practicing Jew himself. He only went to synagogue on the High Holy Days; he laid a pebble on the tomb of his father, Baruch, on the anniversary of his death; he recited the Kaddish without understanding the words, but that didn't prevent him from listening to the Lent sermons at Notre-Dame. The Catholics are smarter than we are, he claimed. They're far superior to us. Of course, for centuries, the Jews have had no choice other than to remain loyal to the beliefs of their ancestors and to marry among themselves. But today? For God's sake, we're not in the Middle Ages anymore!

Jeanne was silent. She knew that underneath it all, things weren't that simple for her parents. She even guessed that when they were alone, they discussed the issue at length. Could they really break with tradition? Nathé wondered. And what would his half brother Godechaux, an authority in the Jewish community, have to say? And his brother Louis? After all, Georges had been circumcised and had had his bar mitzvah, according to tradition. As for Adèle, she wanted only one thing: her daughter's happiness. A good doctor would look after her. And Dr. Proust was becoming an expert in the fight against cholera. She would always remember that her dear Jeanne had been born a few days before the terrible epidemic of 1849 and that she had feared for her daughter's life for weeks. If she hadn't been a rational thinker, a product of the Enlightenment, Madame Weil might almost have seen the hand of destiny here. As for feelings, as long as her daughter didn't dislike the man—the rest would come with time!

Jeanne was ready to admit that she didn't dislike Adrien Proust. She even felt that she might be able to love this quiet man with his gentle ways. He was serious, hard-working. But she knew so little about him. Nathé had been the first to meet him a few months earlier, at the home of one of his colleagues on the rue Mogador, a stockbroker whose older brother was a doctor, like Adrien. Dr. Proust lived nearby, he had come to the Weil home as a neighbor and friend, Monsieur Weil had a daughter, and the two had been introduced to each other. Her father would not make her marry against her will, Jeanne knew. But he had been thinking about the marriage contract for quite some time. Marriage was a serious matter, and he loved his daughter.

And Jeanne? Had she ever even been in love? The kind of passion you read about in books is one thing, marriage is another. Like Jane Austen's heroines, caught between "sense and sensibility," Jeanne leaned toward sense. She knew she could share her life with this man, start a family with him. Something even told her she would be happy, despite all their differences. But she would have to leave her mother, be a wife in turn, have children. But then, what would become of the children? That was the real question for her and, she suspected, for her parents as well. They were living in France, a Catholic country, and in those rare mixed marriages they were familiar with, it was always the majority religion that dominated. The Proust family was very devout. Adrien's grandfather even supplied the votive candles for his parish. A Weil marrying the descendant of a man who sold votive candles! Jeanne knew that her parents would not tolerate her converting and marrying in church. Was she herself capable of doing so? Wouldn't it feel like a betrayal? No one was more loyal than she, and her loyalty excluded any deceit. She would never convert, she was certain of it.

She lowered her eyes and stared at the plate that Philomèle had just set before her. Its green border was decorated in flowers and gold wreaths, its center with the image of an Andalusian couple. Georges had always preferred the picture by Horace Vernet representing the port at Le Havre. The dinner service came from grandfather Baruch Weil, a manufacturer of fine china. Jeanne smiled. When they were little, they used to fight over the plates on holidays. Like her parents she was and would always be a French Jew, perfectly integrated into the society that had once welcomed her ancestors. But, as she probably already realized, however liberal and freethinking Adrien might be, their children would be raised Catholic, as "real" Frenchmen, descendants of a landed family whose name appeared on the parish registers of Illiers, the Prousts' little town in Eure-et-Loir. Of course they had no fortune. Why else would Virginie, Adrien's mother, have agreed to this marriage? She had done so, of course, with pursed lips and only on the condition that the children . . .

Jeanne was wealthy enough for the two of them. She had a generous dowry, and a brilliant career awaited Adrien Proust. She had no doubt of that. It pleased her to think that their children would belong fully to the culture she loved, that they would spring from the same soil that had nourished Racine, George Sand, or her beloved Madame de Sévigné. Or nearly. The process of assimilation begun by her parents would be complete. Dr. Proust's children would never have to fear rejection. They would be no different from others.

The young woman glanced at the painting on the wall across from her. As long as she could remember, it had always been there. It was a scene from the Bible, the work of a minor Flemish painter, Franken the Younger: Esther the Jew preparing to marry Ahasuerus, the Persian king. Jeanne smiled. She had found her Ahasuerus.

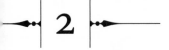

2

Monsieur Proust
and Mademoiselle Weil

Dr. Proust was certainly good-looking. With an athletic build, a high fore-head, a slight wave in his hair, brown eyes, a salt-and-pepper beard, and full lips, he was a man to inspire confidence. He stood up straight, yet wasn't stiff; he held his chin up; he had the gentle gaze of the near-sighted and a benign expression. He was obviously aware of the young woman looking at him with her dark eyes. Her half-smile didn't fool him. He knew women.

Leaning against the fireplace, his hands in his pockets, he held forth, and Jeanne listened. From time to time, she glanced at her mother. But Adèle's expression was impenetrable. She was daydreaming. Nathé was holding a glass of cognac in his hand, sipping it like a connoisseur. From time to time, he'd insert a question: "And after Moscow?"

"After Moscow, we traveled in *kibitka*, miserable carriages made of wood and wicker. What a difference from the luxurious trains that had taken us out there! You needed a strong back. It was quite a relief to cross the Caucuses and the plateaus of Iran on horseback. We followed the caravan route: rose at three in the morning, rode until ten, took a break, and rode again until six or seven in the evening. A tough journey!"

"And after that?"

"After that we arrived in Tehran for a reception given by the king of Persia . . ."

The king of Persia! Jeanne couldn't believe her ears. "The king of Persia?" she murmured. Adèle smiled. "And did he speak to you?"

"Of course he did! The shah even gave me some rugs."

The rest of the journey was lost in the meanderings of geography. They had returned through Turkey, where Dr. Proust was received in Constantinople by the grand vizier Ali Pacha, who named him an officer of the Order of Medjidie. But Jeanne wasn't listening anymore. Who cared about Ali Pacha! She was back in Persia, with the king.

━━━◆••◆━━━

Born in March 1834, Adrien Proust, after a dazzling debut as a pathologist, switched to the field of epidemiology under the supervision of Professor Antoine Fauvel, general inspector of public hygiene. In 1866, cholera had once again wreaked destruction. In a few months, the death toll stood at more than eleven thousand. Adrien was convinced that certain rules of public hygiene were mandatory and that it wasn't enough to deal with the epidemic on a case-by-case basis. This was a revolutionary thesis. In 1869, at the recommendation of Professor Fauvel, the ministers of agriculture and commerce sent Dr. Proust on a government mission to evaluate the quality of Russian sanitary installations on the southern border, to verify that the measures set up during the last conference at Constantinople were being implemented, and to work on public health policy with the authorities in Persia. He had returned certain of one thing: cholera came from the East but followed the paths of communication. To fight it effectively, it was essential to organize systems of defense as close as possible to the place where the epidemic has originated and to make sanitation measures—he was insistent about this—the number one priority from then on.

The former scholarship student from the Collège de Chartres had an inquisitive mind, both skeptical and passionate about the progress of science. His was the era that saw the birth of modern medicine. The obligatory Latin thesis had just been abolished; Claude Bernard had published *An Introduction to the Study of Experimental Medicine*.[2] Adrien Proust was an ambitious man. He loved to write. He wasn't afraid of taking risks, and in his own quiet way he was courageous. His government mission had enabled him to envisage a career in public health. And in the course of this one official trip, he had become a quasi-official figure, welcomed in places where a grocer's son would never have dared to tread. His career was taking off.

Jeanne knew nothing of this. She saw a man who was sure of himself, solid, his bearing proud but not pompous. He was reassuring. She was a quick study, and she noticed something a little naive about him, which amused her. So different, she could already tell, from her own father. Nathé was a domestic tyrant; Adrien had a kind of serene authority. Nathé was a man of stern principles; Adrien was far more relaxed in his. Nathé was frugal to the point of stinginess; Adrien loved comfort and socializing. Nathé hated to travel; Adrien loved to. The Law on one side; Reason on the other. Of course, Jeanne discovered these differences only little by little, but she was far too intuitive not to have sensed them quickly. You can love your father and still marry a man who is nothing like him.

Following his courtship, Adrien sent a friend to ask for Mademoiselle Weil's hand, as was the custom. Nathé had already gathered his information and questioned the doctor about his career prospects. The deal was made among men.

Adrien Proust was living on the cusp of two eras. During the Third Republic, the best physicians were certainly part of the elite, welcomed in the best society, but even then, no one wanted a doctor living in their apartment building.[3] And back in the Second Empire, the attitude toward doctors was far from positive. Most of them, like Adrien, came from modest backgrounds in the provinces. Why would the son of a wealthy Parisian be interested in such a long and difficult training, followed by such an uncertain future? They were better off going into the law—the choice made by Jeanne's brother Georges. Adrien had been through hard times; he had experienced the bohemian ways of students in the Latin Quarter, boardinghouse meals, draft beer in cheap bars, all-nighters. He'd also experienced hospital wards, medical student pranks, dance halls, one-night stands, fancy clothes like the velvet jacket he wore in the photograph he had taken by Nadar in 1870, the year he met Jeanne. He had moved up to Paris, where he knew no one. His widowed mother lived with him as he began his studies, but then she returned to Illiers. He passed every competitive exam, wrote articles while pursuing his clinical work, opened a private practice in addition to his work at the hospital. He worked constantly, driven by a belief in his vocation and a fervent desire to succeed. He was a talented man, conscious of his gifts and what they required of him, flexible enough to know how to garner protection and build a valuable network of contacts. Head physician at the Center for Social Services at the age of twenty-two; holding an advanced medical degree at twenty-eight; chief clinician at thirty-two, having passed the rigorous state exam that qualified him to teach medicine—he'd garnered every honor. But although his income was comfortable, he had no personal fortune.[4]

Nathé had taken stock of his future son-in-law. Professor Proust would provide his daughter with respectability and security—the best possible long-term investment for a second-generation French Jew. Monsieur Weil also knew that in order for Adrien to succeed in his career, to establish himself, and to live in a manner appropriate to his position, he needed money. Marrying a young woman with a large dowry was the only solution.

Jeanne was a catch. She wasn't lacking in suitors: she was young, beautiful, cultured, intelligent. With perfect manners, she made an ideal companion for a doctor who wanted to succeed. She knew how to manage a household, entertain, be a helpmeet to her husband. And she was rich, which for a talented man devoid of capital or the hope of any was far from negligible. On the one side, then, was education and a fortune; on the other, success and a promising future. Their union would open wide the door to the grande bourgeoisie, which would otherwise have remained closed both to the self-made man and to the Jewish heiress.

Which is why Mademoiselle Weil's dowry had been the object of such meticulous care on the part of her father. It showed that Nathé had understood the true worth of his son-in-law and was serious about this marriage. Dr. Proust was not a newcomer fresh from the provinces. He had already earned a position in society. The highest authorities of the empire recognized his merits. His republican, secular values and his profession were guarantees for the future, in case of a change of regime. Nathé had weighed these advantages carefully. In 1870, being Jewish was a handicap. Monsieur Weil was offering his daughter a passport to society.

Besides a trousseau worth 8,000 francs, Jeanne brought 200,000 francs to the marriage—a hefty sum, which still didn't preclude her right to an inheritance from her parents.* Adrien's net worth, certainly not negligible, couldn't compare with his fiancée's.[5] Nathé, as a former stockbroker, therefore took every precaution to protect his daughter. Each spouse would be responsible for his or her own debts. Only revenue from investments made in the name of Jeanne Weil, the future Madame Proust, would be part of their common property. A clause stipulated that the dowry itself had to be used for reliable investments—real estate, national bonds, or stock in the Bank of France.[6] These investments would be allowed only if they were formally accepted by the future wife, with the authorization of the husband. In the event the marriage were dissolved, she would have the right to recover the entire amount of her dowry, as well as anything that had come to her by way of inheritance or gifts.[7] But as a precaution, her future husband had negotiated a clause for himself: in the event of her death, he would receive an annual stipend of 6,000 francs for the remainder of his life.[8]

The contract was duly signed at the home of the bride's parents in the presence of the notary Cottin and a number of witnesses: Jeanne's brother Georges, her uncle Louis Weil and his wife, and two of her friends, Madame and Mademoiselle Houette. On Adrien Proust's side, there were no witnesses.

Religion had certainly been an issue for both families. For the Weils, the marriage broke with two centuries of Jewish tradition, which was why Jeanne never would convert.[9] Mixed marriages were still rare. A young Jewish man could have as many affairs with Christian women as he wanted, but when the time came, he was to take a young Jewish bride. This would be Georges's story. For women, conversions and marriages outside the faith were even more unusual. This marriage represented a choice and a commitment. Nathé Weil's strong desire to assimilate—and perhaps his anxiety, given the political situation—was also part of the equation. War was looming. The contract was signed on August 27, 1870. The marriage itself would take place on September 3.

On the Prousts' side, can we even imagine what a Jewish daughter-in-law must have meant to a pious widow from a small town near Chartres in 1870? Had Adrien's mother, Virginie Proust, née Torcheux, ever set eyes on a Jewish person in her entire life?

A note on money: 1 franc in 1901 was the equivalent of 3.2 euros or $4.04 in 2006, calculated according to relative purchasing power.

But Jeanne was as far from the ghetto as Adrien was from his village. They didn't practice their respective religions or even believe in God. She had "profound faith in reason alone"; he was "an irrational positivist." Like any number of his colleagues, Dr. Proust was an atheist and a materialist. In 1882, when called to testify at a trial, he had refused to take an oath under the crucifix.[10] So Adrien and Jeanne didn't have a church wedding. The young Jewish woman and the grocer's son from the Beauce met on the threshold of a secular bourgeoisie that the Third Republic would elevate to the pinnacle of society. Each, in his and her own way, dreamed of integration. Money and success were the two keys. They would cross the threshold together.

While they did not combine a "total of two equivalent dowries," their union certainly appeared to be "the association of two mutually attractive social situations," in the image of the parents of Jean Santeuil, the character in Marcel Proust's first, unfinished novel.[11] Was there also an attraction between the two individuals? Nothing obligated Mademoiselle Weil to marry Dr. Proust. It was a marriage of convenience, surely, but a marriage from which feelings were not absent. They respected each other, enjoyed each other's company. As for their deepest feelings, who can ever tell?

"A love-match, that is to say a marriage based on love, would have been considered as a proof of vice," Marcel would write years later about the milieu in which his mother grew up.[12] He added, however: "Love was something that came after marriage and lasted until death. No woman ever stopped loving her husband any more than she would have stopped loving her mother."[13]

3

Very French Israelites

> There is no longer anyone, not even I, since I'm not able to get out, who visits the little Jewish cemetery along the rue du Repos where my grandfather used to go every year, according to the ritual he never understood, to place a pebble on his parents' tomb. MARCEL PROUST[14]

At the intersection of the road to Strasbourg and the road to Obernai, surrounded by grapevines and fields of flax, the little town of Niederenheim lay hidden behind its walls. A fort, a clock tower, outskirts, and a town, a main street wide enough for carts and cattle to pass: with its half-timbered, thatched-roofed houses, its fountain, and its church steeple, Niederenheim—Niedernai in French—looked like a hundred other Alsatian villages. Or almost, because in the heart of this village was the Judengasse, the street for Jews, and on it was a synagogue and a rabbi's residence.

The Landsberg family had reigned over Niedernai since the Middle Ages. Back then, the peasants, crushed by taxes, revolted against the *droit de corvée* and the presence of Jews in their village. For centuries the Jews were at the mercy of feudal lords who could expel them whenever they liked. Louis XIV finally granted them his royal protection in exchange for a levy. But they also had to pay taxes to the lord in charge of the *Judenschirmgeld*, or *taxe de la manance*. From year to year, the registry books were carefully kept up to date. On thick yellowing paper, the litany of names and sums unfolds; each new name corresponded to an arrival or a marriage; here and there, a stroke of the pen indicated a death, its date noted in the margin.

On this list appears Jeanne Weil's paternal great-great-grandfather, Moyse Weyl (later spelled Moïse Weil), who died on May 2, 1758.[15] His name also appears on several marriage contracts in Niedernai and the surrounding area. Moyse Weyl was a rabbi or, more precisely, a *commis rabbin*, someone who was supposed to assist the titular rabbi.[16] Lazare Weyl, Jeanne's paternal great-grandfather, and Baruch, her grandfather, were also born in Niedernai. Her ancestors, probably from Germany, had stopped in this little town in the Bas-Rhin and put down roots there at the beginning of the eighteenth century, perhaps even earlier. Like most Alsatian Jews, they were poor and from rural backgrounds. Attached to their ancestral customs and their faith, they had a long history of persecution, expulsion, and massacre.

In 1784, Louis XVI issued his *Lettres patentes*, whose twenty-five articles legislated the lives of Alsatian Jews. From then on they were authorized to rent out land; and factories, banks, and businesses were open to them. Syndicates or *parnossim* were authorized to represent them to the community. At the same time, Louis XVI ordered a census of the Jews in Alsace, which, in the absence of any government records of Jews before 1792, is the most complete source we have today.[17]

Lazare Weyl, the son of Rabbi Moyse Weyl, appears on that census as the "head of the ninth family of Niedernai" along with his wife Reichel and their three children: Baruch (five years old), Bluemel, and Delté. A villager, Jeanne's great-grandfather spoke Judeo-Alsatian, a form of Yiddish strongly inflected with German, and he only wrote Hebrew. He wore the beard and pointed hat that were typical of Alsatian Jews. Ten years earlier, at age thirty-two, he had married, as shown by the marriage contract: "Lazarus Weyl son of the late Moyse Weyl with Reichel Bloch daughter of Goetschel Bloch and the late Bluemel of Niedernai. Dowry 350 florins ketouba 550 florins."[18] The *chadchen*, or marriage broker, had introduced the two young people: no union could come to pass without him. The conditions were carefully debated and put in writing. Reichel's dowry was small, but Lazare was scarcely any richer than she.[19]

Baruch, their oldest son, was born in 1780. Lazare and Reichel Weyl lived like all the other Jews in the village.[20] While some stayed in the Judengasse, others set up households where their activities took them. Prominent on that street was the Jewish Inn, frequented by the Nathan brothers; Abraham Jacob and Barach Hertz, the butchers; Joseph Franck, the horse trader; Jacques Heim, the tailor; and sometimes Abraham Bloch, a cattle merchant from Rosheim. It was Jacob Nathan, with his bold handwriting, who signed all the civil registers as a representative of the syndicate.[21] Most of the Jews from Niedernai were peddlers who went from village to village, carrying their merchandise on their backs.[22]

At Leiser Lévy's Jewish cabaret, there was little drinking and lots of talking. Amid smoke from their long pipes, the men discussed, closed deals, told jokes, laughed, swore, raised their voices, quarreled. News spread. The atmosphere was almost as noisy as at synagogue, where all the congregants prayed out loud, mulled about, and greeted one another from both sides of the *chulle*.[23]

The days were punctuated by prayers; the years, by the holidays celebrated at the synagogue and at home. Every Friday night, Lazare went to services while Reichel prepared dinner. After reciting the *kiddouch*,[24] the family sat down to eat around the white tablecloth. The *milchtig*[25] was separated from the *fleischtig*;[26] no meat and diary products were allowed in the same meal. "You shall not eat the kid in the milk of its mother," says the Law. No pork, no fish without scales or fins, no game. Meat had to be slaughtered according to ritual and emptied of blood. These rules didn't bother them, for it had always been that way, though breaking them would have caused extreme distress. But Riechel's *knepfles*[27] were light as snowflakes. For Purim, the children dressed up as Esther and Ahasuerus and feasted on fritters; at Shavouot—the Gentiles' Pentecost—they ate cheesecake. On the preceding Shabbat, at synagogue, they always commemorated the martyrs of the Crusades and the Black Plague. Despite the sweet but ephemeral odor of peace, they would never forget the bitter taste of earlier persecutions.

We don't know how Lazare Weyl made a living. We do know that, toward the end of the century, he left Niedernai and his native Alsace with his family.

◄••••►

For several years, French philosophers had been taking an interest in the Jewish question. In 1787, the Royal Society of Arts and Sciences of Metz invited essays from its members on "the means by which the Jews in France might become more useful and happier." Most of the papers proposed improving the status of the Jews by recognizing their civil and political equality. The Abbé Grégoire titled his paper "Essay on the physical, moral and political regeneration of the Jews."[28] The notion of human "regeneration" would be one of the great ideals of the French Revolution.

But as early as July 1789, violent demonstrations broke out in Alsace, once again directed against the Jewish population. Hundreds of Jews fled to Mülhausen and Basel. The Jews of Paris, for their part, demanded citizenship; the Jews in the east followed suit.

It wasn't until the final hours of the National Constituent Assembly, on September 27, 1791, after an overwhelming vote, that the Jews of France obtained citizenship.[29] From then on, they could come and go, live where they wanted, practice whatever trade they desired. They were citizens like everyone else, with no restrictions.

A page had turned definitively. The Jews entered the history of their country. Still, a stroke of the pen cannot erase centuries of enslavement, humiliation, and persecution. The "regeneration" would take years.

◄••••►

By this time, Lazare and Reichel Weyl had already left France. In 1788, their second son, Cerf, was born in Bürgel, in the principality of Isemburg, south of Frankfurt.[30] The Jews enjoyed a privileged status there and were able to settle freely. They constituted almost one-quarter of the population.[31] Not far from Bürgel was a porcelain factory, in Höchst am Main, operating from 1750 until 1796. That may have been where Baruch learned his skill. In France as well, factories had been multiplying since the discovery of beds of white clay in Saint-Yrieux, and there was a huge demand for artisans from Germany who knew the secret of making Chinese porcelain. Among them were many Jews.

We find a trace of the Weils again in 1799, in Fontainebleau, where a Jewish community had established itself about fifteen years earlier.[32] The first to settle there were peddlers, attracted by the town's location. But the bulk of the community arrived when Jews from Alsace, reacting to the Terror and the collapse of the revolutionary treasury, fled west, away from the instability.

Baruch, Lazare's eldest son, was nineteen and full of ambition. For twenty years, he forged his destiny in a swift ascension to privilege. First he acquired a porcelain manufacturing plant founded four years earlier by Jacob Benjamin.[33] That same year, Benjamin sold him an interest in the Hôtel de Pompadour so that he could start his own factory. He appointed his father as director.[34] On October 27, 1800, at age twenty, he married. His bride, Hélène, was only thirteen and a half. Her father, Moïse Schoubach, was a member of the local elite, a merchant, and the president of the philanthropic Society of the Last Duty, one of the fraternal organizations in charge of watching over the dead and dealing with burials.[35] After their marriage, the couple left Fontainebleau for Paris.

Within a few years, Baruch Weil had become rich and powerful. He presided over a family of eleven children born to two spouses. Starting at age eighteen, Hélène fulfilled her role to the utmost, bearing five children: Merline (1804), Mayer (1805), Godechaux (1806), Benjamin (1807), and Moïse (1809). Two years after the birth of her last child, Hélène died, aged twenty-four. The paternal family of Baruch Weil's second wife, Marguerite (Sarah) Nathan, was originally from Trèves, but the young woman had been born in Lunéville. Among her maternal ancestors she could claim Lion Goudchaux, a horse dealer who, with his brother Lazare, financed the rise of the duc de Lorraine. One of the descendants of her great-great grandfather would become famous: his name was Karl Marx.[36] Thus Marcel Proust and Karl Marx were distant cousins. Born in Trèves (like Nathan Berncastel), Marx, whose father converted to Lutheranism, is another example of assimilated Jewry in the nineteenth century.

Marguerite thus had the task, at age twenty-seven, of raising the children from her husband's first marriage, along with the ones to whom she gave birth. In the years that followed, from 1814 to 1923, she bore Nathé, Jeanne's father; Lazare, who would be called Louis; Adélaïde (Adèle); Salomon; Abraham (Alphonse); and Flora. Baruch had certainly respected the biblical precept "Go forth and multiply."

There was no stopping this avid worker. In 1802, he opened his first store in Paris, Au vase d'or, at 101, rue du Temple. He owned another warehouse nearby, on the rue Chapon. The store was transferred in 1809 to 23, rue Boucherat, where the whole family was already living. Then it moved to the

rue de Bondy—now the rue René-Boulanger—in a neighborhood inhabited by industrialists and Jewish financiers during the Empire. Later, Baruch
joined forces with his younger brother Cerf and opened a new store in the
Galerie de l'Horloge—the current Boulevard des Italiens—a fashionable district. He also owned a luxury boutique in the Passage de l'Opéra.

Baruch manufactured goods destined especially for decorators and for ex-
port. He knew how to take advantage of the craze for porcelain: the eighty-
six cups he produced for the merchant Flandin in 1802 are a veritable catalog
of the decorations then in vogue. An industrialist and a quick-witted man
of the trade, he was also a progressive. His factory employed eighty-four
people. In 1822 he had a gas kiln constructed with the latest technology, at a
time when coal-burning kilns had only just begun to replace wood.[37]

The Alsatian was proud to count the duchesse de Berry, the Dauphine,
and the duchesse d'Angoulême among his clientèle. In 1820, he obtained a
license from Louis XVIII for a new kind of enamel, and seven years later—a
supreme distinction, very rare at the time for a Jew—he was decorated with
the cross of the Légion d'honneur by Charles X at the Exposition des Arts et
Manufactures.[38] The Musée national de la céramique at Sèvres then acquired
several pieces of porcelain from Fontainebleau made in Baruch Weil's factory: a plate, a large coffee pot, a cup for hot chocolate, and a bowl for milk.
The bowl was destroyed in the March 1942 bombings, and the cup was put in
storage at another museum in Vierzon; the white coffee pot and white plate
are still languishing among the thousands of pieces piled up in the glass cases
in the basement storage area of the museum. Until recently, no one had ever
seen Baruch Weil's porcelain but only his red-stenciled trademark. The two
white pieces of porcelain conserved in the museum at Sèvres, and a catalog
photograph of two plates, their green borders decorated with gold flowers,[39]
give us a glimpse of the work done by Jeanne Weil's grandfather. Through
these objects, Baruch speaks to us—a distant echo of *In Search of Lost Time*.

These plates, decorated with people and genre scenes, evoke those used
for serving petits fours described by Marcel Proust's narrator: "the *Arabian
Nights* side plates which had once afforded such a variety of entertainment
to my aunt Léonie, depending on whether Françoise brought her one day
Aladdin and His Wonderful Lamp or, on another day, *Ali Baba* or *The Sleeper
Awakes* or *Sinbad the Sailor Taking Ship at Basra with All His Riches.*" To which
Proust adds: "I wished I could see them again, but my grandmother did not
know what had become of them; and in any case she believed they were
just vulgar old plates, which had been bought locally."[40] No one knows if

such plates existed at Illiers. But I am certain that at Uncle Louis's, or else at Grandfather Nathé's, some of these decorative plates from the family factory remained.

The indefatigable Baruch Weil also became a fixture in the Parisian Jewish community. After Napoleon passed through Strasbourg on his return from Austerlitz, he was convinced that he needed to deal with the Jewish problem. So he ordered a meeting of his government and convoked a "General Synagogue of the Jews" in Paris. The assembly took place in July 1806, bringing together 111 members of the Jewish elite from every province. They were given a questionnaire designed to evaluate the Jews' attachment and loyalty to the Empire.[41] Napoleon also decided to hold a Grand Sanhedrin. Its work created three decrees, all dated March 17, 1808. The first two established "consistories" according to administrative "departments" and headed up by a Central Consistory. For the first time in their history, the Jews of France were united by a single organization, recognized by the state.[42] The delegates to the General Synagogue would be called to this body, resulting in a veritable oligarchy.[43] Baruch Weil was a member. He was an active participant in the creation of the first Consistory of Paris, joined the Central Consistory in October 1819, and remained a member until his death.[44] In addition, he administered circumcisions and assumed other responsibilities on behalf of various religious organizations.[45]

Meanwhile, he got the government to appoint his father to head up the Jewish community in Fontainebleau as a supervisory commissioner. Marguerite played her own role in the community by helping to found a school for girls, where she worked with the ladies on the school committee, also from elite families—the sisters, mothers, or wives of businessmen involved in Israelite institutions: the Worms of Romilly, the Rodrigues, the Halphens, the Cerfbeers, and, of course, the Rothschilds.

Active, ambitious, scrupulously honest, but also somewhat uncouth and rigid, Baruch Weil was not liked by everyone. According to his contemporary Michel Beer, "he has the haughtiness of an arriviste without education, but is beyond reproach as a merchant and in his private life, and if his piety is a little showy, at least it is sincere."[46] The judgment seems severe when we consider the pamphlet that Baruch had printed in 1827.[47] Did he use the services of an editor? Probably. But his ideas, influenced by utopian ideals of Saint-Simon, reflected his enterprising spirit. In his plea for a free market, he took on the mantle of defender of national pride.[48]

Baruch Weil didn't become a French citizen until the age of ten. Although his father could only write in Hebrew, Baruch's religious faith was matched only by his desire to integrate and his appreciation for the country that had granted him the same rights as other citizens. "The Israelite is obligated by all means to lament his country's misfortunes and to applaud its prosperity," stipulated one of the articles of the Grand Sanhedrin. "Regeneration" was making progress.

————

Who knows what the future might have held for Baruch Weil? He died at the age of forty-eight, on April 8, 1828. He was buried in the Père Lachaise cemetery, where Hélène is said to have been the first person listed on the register of Jewish tombs. It was the same cemetery on the rue du Repos that his great-grandson Marcel Proust used to visit until, to his sorrow, illness no longer allowed it. The name Baruch and those of his descendants can still be found there, though barely legible.

His death was probably quick and unexpected, for he left his estate in disorder. On May 1, Marguerite, the legal guardian of his six minor children, gathered her relatives and friends before a justice of the peace in order to create a family council[49] charged with naming a joint guardian and authorizing her to accept the inheritance on behalf of the children to whom she had given birth: Nathé (14 years), Louis (11), Adèle (10), Salomon (7), Alphonse (5½), and Flora (4). The relatives chosen by Marguerite Weil for this important task formed a veritable clan. Michel Goudchaux was named joint guardian. Familial, sentimental, financial, and community interests were closely linked.[50]

Baruch's factory disappeared, but his powerful personality left its mark on the family. Jeanne's grandfather was the first Weil to have come of age a free man, the first to reap the benefits of economic opportunity, the first to make his way into society. He was exemplary of the Jewish elite at the start of the nineteenth century: a pioneer and the founder of a dynasty at the service of his community and the French nation.

————

Nathaniel Berncastel, Jeanne's maternal grandfather, was originally from Trèves, where his father, Mayer Nathan, had been a merchant. Mayer had been the representative from the Saar in the "General Synagogue" appointed by Napoleon. Nathaniel began his own career in the offices of the Saar prefecture.

Twenty-two-year-old Nathaniel Berncastel arrived in Paris one day in 1813, in the middle of the war against Prussia.[51] The young man started a business in hardware, porcelain, and watches in the neighborhood near the rue du Temple. His brothers and sisters, some of whom would join him later, remained in Trèves.[52] Nathaniel—now known as Nathan—soon ran a flourishing enterprise. Seven years after arriving in France, he married Rose (Rachel), the daughter of Marx Silny, an embroidery manufacturer from Metz. Nathan and Rose set up their household at 31, rue Vieille-du-Temple.

With the fall of the Empire, the Saar was under Prussian rule again. Nathan wanted to be a Frenchman. In January 1826, he filed a request for naturalization at the town hall for his arrondissement. It took him two years to acquire it. On December 19, 1827, a royal decree finally conferred French nationality to Jeanne's maternal grandfather.

Nathan's wife, Rose, belonged to an old family from Metz that can be traced back to the seventeenth century.[53] The Silnys belonged to the Jewish bourgeoisie of Lorraine who, since Louis XIV, were considered vital to the economy—their trade in grains and horses made them the principal suppliers to the army. But Rose's father, Marx Cahen, was a man of modest means who only wrote Hebrew. Her mother, Gutché Kanstadt, born in Mayence, was much better educated. She had no choice but to work alongside him, and when they later ran into difficulties, her family assisted him financially. They had five children. In 1824, Amélie (Fradché), Rose's younger sister, married a young lawyer with a promising future: Adolphe Crémieux, one of the most prestigious figures of his time in both national and Jewish life.

Adolphe ("Isaac" until he took a French name) was the son of a silk merchant from Nîmes. He himself was born in Chinon. Admitted to the bar at twenty-one, having excelled in the examination, he soon became famous for his refusal to take the Jewish oath or *more judaico*.[54] The young man managed to get the courts of Nîmes and Aix to stop using the oath, and he proposed his services to any rabbi who refused to go along with this infamous ceremony. Refusals multiplied, and Crémieux had cases all across France. This episode illustrates Adolphe's qualities of generosity, courage, astuteness, and popularity.

When he became a lawyer for the Court of Appeals in 1830, Crémieux took to defending the opposition press, all the while maintaining good relations with Louis-Philippe. The year 1840 saw the outburst of the Damas scandals. Jews were arrested.[55] A delegation, made up of the British philanthropist Sir Moses Montefiore, the Orientalist Salomon Munk, and Crémieux, obtained the prisoners' freedom and an official retraction by the Ottoman sultan of the accusation of ritual crime. The return of their mission was triumphant. In 1842, Adolphe Crémieux became one of the first Jewish members of the Chamber of Deputies. In 1843, he was appointed president of the Jewish Consistory: "We are honored to belong to the Israelite sect; we are Jewish French citizens," he proclaimed proudly in the Chamber.[56]

Current events placed Jeanne's great-uncle at the forefront of public life. He participated in the 1848 revolution and became minister of justice in the provisional government. He abolished the death penalty for political crimes, imprisonment for indebtedness, and any use of the pillory.

One of Crémieux's colleagues in government was another friend of the Weil family, Michel Goudchaux (1797–1862), the children's former guardian, who was now minister of finance. This banker, a fervent defender of the French republic, argued for the nationalization of railroads and the creation of workers' cooperatives. He proposed a proportional tax on inheritance and income, free and obligatory education for workers, and workers' rights to take loans and receive benefits. After December 2, 1851, Goudchaux devoted all his time and his personal fortune to the exiles from the 1848 Revolution living in London and Brussels. He asked to be buried in a common grave. Thus, the two first Jews who rose to official functions in a French government were part of Jeanne's family background.

What would Uncle Adolphe have amounted to without his Amélie, whom wagging tongues nicknamed "the red mother"? She fought all his battles; she was his confidante, his muse, and his companion. The way they met is described in detail in one of Amélie's letters. Rose, already married to Nathan Berncastel, was living in Paris, and it was she who secretly contacted a *chadchen* for her younger sister. This matchmaker, bragging about his clientele, mentioned a young lawyer—probably too good a catch for Amélie. But Rose described her sister in such a flattering light that the matchmaker agreed to speak to the young man, who immediately traveled to Metz and fell madly in love with Amélie. "I've never met a more likable man," Amélie confessed to her sister, "even among Catholics!" That was saying a lot. Forty-five years later, Adolphe wrote to his wife: "You know how Jews are required to love their good Lord. Hello, my dear little Lord."[57] Their correspondence reflects their exceptional relationship. The man's ugliness was legendary, yet everyone who met him fell for his charm, if disagreeing with Amélie, who thought him handsome.

Adolphe's passion for his wife was probably what made him avert his gaze from an act whose consequences must have weighed heavily on this tireless defender of the Jewish cause: the secret conversion of Amélie and her children. It was all the more shocking in that he had just taken a stand against another conversion. He resigned his position in the Consistory as soon as he learned about it.

When were Amélie and her children, Gustave and Mathilde, baptized? A yellowing piece of paper torn into four pieces, buried at the bottom of a file in the French National Archives, answers this question. It's a baptismal certificate for Mathilde, drafted by the parish priest of Mortefontaine, a village near Senlis. The godmother was none other than the Baroness of Feuchères, the same baroness seen by the poet Nerval as an amazon on the lawns of the Château of Mortefontaine.[58] Amélie's decision to convert is puzzling, for she knew how much suffering it would cause the man she loved. In 1853, when her daughter Mathilde was married to Alfred Peigné at the Saint-Roch parish, Adolphe sadly signed his name at the bottom of the religious document.

Amélie Crémieux's salon was a meeting place for an elite of political liberals and literary romantics—Lamartine, Victor Hugo, Lamennais, Odilon Barrot, George Sand—but also for followers of Saint-Simon such as Rodriques, or Freemasons such as Gambetta, Carnot, Arago, Jules Simon, or Charles Floquet. As Grand Master of the Scottish rite, Adolphe didn't keep his membership in the Freemasons a secret.[59] In the large apartment on the rue Bonaparte, furnished Troubadour style, you were likely to meet Alexandre Dumas or Eugène Sue as well as Princess Mathilde, whom Swann would introduce to the young narrator of *In Search of Lost Time*.[60] Adolphe and Amélie were passionate lovers of music and theater. Rossini, Meyerbeer, Chopin, and the soprano Pauline Viardot were among their guests. The lawyer used to ask the legendary actress Rachel to recite her lines—she called him Papa. Amélie and her sister Rose, Jeanne's grandmother, were excellent pianists. One of Adolphe's first gifts to his fiancée was a complete set of Mozart. An Erard piano came later.

Nathan and Rose Berncastel, Jeanne's grandparents, had three children: Amélie (1821), Adèle (1824), and Ernestine (1830). Adèle, Jeanne's mother— the inspiration for Marcel's grandmother in *In Search of Lost Time*—was very attached to her aunt Amélie and uncle Adolphe. Adèle's father, Nathan, was successful enough in his business to have been appointed "census elector" as of 1842.[61] He was a stern, authoritarian character. He wouldn't allow his wife, Rose, to go to Nîmes to attend her beloved sister's wedding. She was afraid of him. Was he "such a bad father" as Marcel Proust claimed?[62] The two Silny sisters spent a lot of time together. A little older than her cousin Mathilde, Adèle was a frequent visitor to the Crémieux salon throughout her youth. She shared their tastes in art and literature and transmitted these to her own daughter, Jeanne.

Adèle's milieu was thus more sophisticated than that of the Weils, who seemed like nouveaux riches compared to the Berncastels and the Silnys. The Weils' rough edges, their piety, their whole way of life, were about to make an alliance with the older money and more polished manners of a family linked to the inner circle of power, where culture and politics played an important role.

Baruch Weil and Nathan Berncastel in the business world, Marguerite and Rose through the school committee, Michel Goudchaux and Adolphe Crémieux through politics, the Weil and Crémieux brothers through Freemasonry: there were already multiple connections between the Weils and the Berncastels. A first marriage had united the families—that of Moïse, Nathé's half brother, to Adèle's older sister Amélie. There was probably no need of a marriage broker for the union of Nathé and Adèle.

The marriage contract signed on December 6, 1845, the same day as the civil ceremony held in the town hall of the tenth arrondissement of Paris, indicates that their fortunes were well matched.[63] On May 17, 1851, Ernestine, the third Berncastel sister, was married at age twenty-one, like her sisters, to Samuel Mayer, a cotton merchant with a business in Flers, in the Orne region.[64]

As for Adèle's feelings in those "distant days when her parents had chosen a husband for her,"[65] to whom did they matter? Feelings not withstanding, a long conjugal life was about to begin for Nathé Weil, a stockbroker with a caustic wit, and Adèle Bernstein, a romantic young woman.

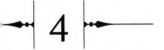

4

At number 40 *bis*

May 1849: corpses were piling up in the stench and the horror. There were 20,000 deaths in Paris, more than 110,000 in France, the cholera epidemic was spreading across Europe, and there were predictions that it had reached America. Some insisted that you had to avoid water, others that you must wash your hands as often as possible. What to do? A little girl named Jeanne had just been born to the household of Nathé and Adèle Weil.[66] The rue du Faubourg Poissonnière, where they were now living, usually such a vibrant neighborhood, was a death zone; there were rumors that the working-class areas were the most vulnerable, and some of the bourgeois were even leaving Paris for their safety. Where were they supposed to go? was all Nathé would say, shrugging his shoulders. Nothing in the world would force him to sleep away from home.

Nathé Weil was a strange fellow. Authoritarian, quick-tempered, sarcastic, yet generous: until his death, Jeanne's father played the patriarch. Like all patriarchs, he assumed he would be respected, listened to, obeyed. His was a stock role that men of his era—and, let's admit it, especially Jewish men—adhered to without giving it a second thought. So his family listened to his opinions, feared his anger, laughed at his jokes, asked him for money, served him first at meals—none of which kept them from thinking as they liked.

His face looked severe, perhaps because of the lines around his mouth and his piercing eyes. Yet his lips were full. His hair was thick, his curls resistant to a comb. His beard, too, encircling his chin beneath shaven cheeks, would have spread shamelessly if he hadn't trimmed it. Impeccably dressed, he wore a stiff collar, a dickey, a black suit coat with wide lapels. He had presence, exuded confidence, and though slight of build, appeared robust. He looked as if he belonged to the Third Republic rather than the Second Empire. Yet he was born in 1814.[67] He lived through monarchies, revolutions, the end of one empire, and the course of another.

At his side was his wife, Adèle, with her fine, almost sharp features and her free spirit. She waited out his tantrums—she was used to them from her own father. A good, sensitive, and discreetly tenacious little woman, she wasn't bothered by her husband's irascibility.

Nathé Weil's caustic nature came through clearly in his brief exchange with the mayor of the ninth arrondissement, when he was attempting to reconstitute his papers along with those of his wife and his daughter. Like thousands of Parisians, he had to furnish proof of his identity after the various town halls in Paris had been burned by members of the Commune.

Wednesday, September 10, 1873

Sir,

I regret not having found you in your office; I therefore take this opportunity to leave you the papers you officially requested that I leave with you in order to reestablish my official status, there being a number of documents missing from my files, for which a simple declaration ought to suffice. At the Stock Exchange they gave me nothing but trouble, so I simply left, hoping for your kind intervention.

I repeat, I have no supporting documents to furnish—and your office has had the nerve to ask me to produce a certificate from the Chief Rabbi, a request based on the idea that there must be some official document from religious initiation ceremonies that only he could furnish—but religious initiation for a daughter is an innovation begun barely fifteen years ago! Our Chief Rabbi has nothing and cannot be involved here—

Allow me to rely on your influence and protection so that I might avoid a new round of errands and procedures, and please, Sir, accept the expression of my gratitude along with the distinguished and devoted sentiments of

Your humble servant,

Nathé Weil[68]

For readers of Marcel Proust, Nathé is the grandfather in *In Search of Lost Time,* and Monsieur Sandré in *Jean Santeuil.* Quick-witted Monsieur Sandré, who smokes his pipe while he surveys the room "with slow haste," in whom old age still struggles with "a vehement temperament."[69] The following letter written by Marcel at age seven and a half is quite revealing of the tutelary figure incarnated by Nathé Weil:

My dear grandfather,

Forgive me for my sin since I ate less than usual I cried for a quarter hour after that I was weeping

I beg your pardon

Pardon father who must be honored and respected by everyone

Robert sends you his love

Your Grandson Marcel

Adieu my grandfather[70]

In the Weil family, there was plenty of love among parents and children, brother and sister.

Georges, Jeanne's older brother, was the first grandchild born to the Berncastel and Weil families. His maternal grandfather, Nathan, and his uncle Louis on his father's side went solemnly together to register him at the town hall.[71] According to Jewish custom, he was given the first name of his deceased grandfather, Baruch. Jeanne and her brother grew up together, lived next to each other, and died a few months apart, from the same illness that had taken their mother. Georges lived with his own mother until her death, like his nephew Marcel, and only married afterwards, at the age of forty-four. Between Adèle and her children, the bond was tight to the point of fusion. She and her daughter were almost like one person.

"I know another mother who counts herself for nothing, who has wholly given herself over to her children," Jeanne once wrote to her son Marcel, quoting Madame de Sévigné and comparing her to Adèle.[72] She might have said the same of herself.

━━◂•••▸━━

Jeanne is sitting on a little chair at her mother's feet. Night is falling, but there is still enough light to read. She loves the twilight, which brings them closer together. Soon, however, they will have to light the lamps. They can hear the clock pendulum swinging and from time to time a door being closed at the end of the hall. The little girl wears a dark, somewhat austere dress. Just two bands of white, stitched above the hemline, brighten the bottom of her skirt; embroidered pantaloons peep out from below it. Her hair, braided into a crown, frames a thin, serious, almost contemplative face. Madame Weil has an open book on her lap, of which the girl is particularly fond. She already knows how to read, but no music can replace her mother's voice. As Adèle reads, she rests her chin on the palm of her left hand. Her own brown hair, braided into a crown around her oval face; her high cheekbones; her small bust and narrow waist; the pleats of her black dress, fastened at the neck with a cameo; her pearl earrings—her whole appearance indicates a simplicity that has as much to do with her taste for what is natural as with her sense of beauty. The child sits with her elbows on her knees and her chin in one hand, just like her mother, looking up at her in adoration.

━━◂•••▸━━

Jeanne lived in the maternal orbit. Her father occupied another planet, which belonged to men. It was unclear what became of him when he left the house. He went to work, Mama said. That was a place where women weren't allowed. Even Georges didn't know exactly what went on there. The world of fathers was mysterious.

Nathé's world in particular. There was something vague about his profession. He was a *runner*, a broker who operated on the sidelines, dealing in the free market of stocks and shares not registered with the Stock Exchange. The stockbrokers had a monopoly in the pit. The runners operated outside, under the columns of the Exchange building, and they dealt with brokers via a bunch of assistants and messengers who shuttled back and forth between them. They were both the official stockbrokers' competitors and, at the same time, their clients, sometimes their partners..

This world is the one depicted in Zola's novel *Money*, inspired in part by the memoirs of Ernest Feydeau, a contemporary of Jeanne's father.[73] Feydeau describes the swarm of people in the pit, the continuous rumble of voices, the barking stockbrokers, the hellish commotion from one o'clock to three, the back and forth of the assistants, the blue smoke of the cigars, the frock coats, the quick trades, the shouts, and then, gradually, silence until the next day. Nathé was probably clever enough to earn a lot of money and frugal enough to keep it—unlike the brokers Zola tells us about in his notebooks: "This whole world of the Stock Exchange goes in for pleasure, eating, carousing, and gambling at the track."[74]

In 1945, Nathé described himself as retired from the Stock Exchange, with a private income. But retired didn't mean indolent. In the 1850 census of Paris Jews, he is listed as a merchant. Later he appears to have been associated with a broker named Ramel, then another named Blin, at 18, boulevard Montmartre.[75] Nathé's career had unfolded during the July Monarchy, a period of vigorous industrial and financial expansion, when many people grew rich very quickly. James de Rothschild wrote in 1840, "I go to see the King whenever I want. [. . .] He completely trusts me, listens to me, and takes into account what I tell him."[76] Even though banking was only beginning to be modernized and the methods for "mobilizing" savings were still traditional, the Paris Stock Exchange saw the number of listed stocks rise from 38 in 1830 to 260 in 1841 and continue to rise in the years that followed. Of course these figures seem small to us. But in *In Search of Lost Time*, Charles Swann's father, a stockbroker who is a close friend of the narrator's grandfather, "must have left four or five million" to his children.[77] Nathé Weil, too, managed to build a fortune and make it bear fruit.

Antoine Haas, the father of the elegant Charles Haas, who partially inspired the character of Swann, was an auditor for James de Rothschild and a powerful figure in the establishment; in 1828 he was considered one of the fifty most influential Israelites in Paris.[78] Gustave Neuburger, the husband of Laure Lazarus, Jeanne's cousin, was also a director at the Rothschild bank. His brother Léon, married to yet another cousin, Claire Weil, worked for the same bank.[79] But Nathé was the only man in the Weil family who belonged to the world of finance. In a family in which everyone took a different path, he was the only one to have chosen a profession stigmatized as typically Jewish.

Even Zola, who certainly could not be considered an anti-Semite, noted that "probably half of the men working at the Bourse were Jews. [. . .] Fasquelle, Busnach, and the others give me the impression that French brains are repelled by the abstract nature of the operations." And he added: "It's a Jewish profession, you need a certain kind of brain, the aptitude of the race."[80] Like Charles Swann's father, Nathé Weil practiced a "Jew's profession."

By making the intimate friend of the grandfather in *In Search of Lost Time* a "broker's partner with a rather large fortune" whose "Jewishness was scarcely noticeable because he only associated with Catholics and gave everyone who was curious the desire to ask him if it was true that Jews were required to eat live children on certain days,"[81] Proust gives us valuable insight, albeit with humor. In the mid-nineteenth century, could a person be Jewish and practice a Jewish profession, yet mask the fact by only spending time with Catholics? Such was the ambition of Nathé Weil, who was far less involved in the life of the Jewish community than his father and his older brothers had been. But whether he liked it or not, he still had countless ties to that community.

First of all, the neighborhood where he lived: Nathé Weil was born and grew up on the rue Boucherat (now the rue de Turenne). Next he moved to the rue Hauteville, in the tenth arrondissement. This long, narrow street that led from the Church of Saint-Vincent de Paul to the Boulevard Bonne-Nouvelle became, with his marriage, a family fiefdom. His future in-laws, Nathaniel and Rose Berncastel, lived at number 18; back in 1845, they were already living at number 57 when Nathé and Adèle moved to number 43, a few houses down the street. His brother Louis lived at number 33, a bit farther down. Rue de Paradis, rue des Petites-Ecuries, rue Richer, rue du Faubourg-Poissonnière (to which the Weils moved just before Jeanne's birth), rue de la Boule-Rouge (where Jeanne's maternal grandmother spent the last years of her life), rue de Trévise (where her mother grew up): this was the heart of the Jewish district where, even now, kosher grocers, synagogues, fur and pelt businesses, glass and mirror shops, and bookstores indicate a lively and long-established community. Today, North African Sephardic Jews have replaced Eastern European Ashkenazi Jews, who themselves had taken the areas vacated by Jews from Alsace and Lorraine and from Germany.

The same push toward the western part of Paris coincided with social mobility: Baruch moved near the Place de la République, Nathé to the Faubourg Poissonnière; Jeanne lived with her husband and children on the boulevard Malesherbes, then on the rue de Courcelles. As for Louis Weil, Jeanne's uncle, having made his fortune he bought a building at 102, boulevard Haussmann, on the other side of the Grands Boulevards, as well as some property in the suburb of Auteuil. Belonging to a neighborhood was a sign of success. The great-aunt in *In Search of Lost Time*, "the only rather vulgar person" in the family, was offended because Swann, who could easily have lived on the boulevard Haussmann or the avenue de l'Opéra, made his home on the quai d'Orléans, an address she thought shameful. "Well, Monsieur Swann! Do you still live next door to the wine warehouse, so as to be sure of not missing the train when you go to Lyon?" she managed to say every New Year's Day when this perfect gentlemen came calling with his gift of *marrons glacés.*[82]

So the Weils lived in one of those "squalid areas"[83] so alien to the narrator of *In Search of Lost Time* but not to the author, since his beloved Mama had lived there and he himself had visited his grandparents there. Proust made number 40 *bis* the home of Uncle Adolphe, except that he located it on the boulevard Malesherbes (where his own parents lived); it was in fact the home of Jeanne's parents until their death. The family used to refer to the apartment as "40 *bis*," without the street name. Shorthand for a clan and a way of life, 40 *bis* designated the Weils just as in *In Search of Lost Time* it designated the great-uncle:[84] "Some of Mama's cousins would say to her, in the most natural way, 'Ah, we can't have you on Sunday, you're dining at 40 *bis*.' If I was going to visit a relative, I was advised to go first of all to '40 *bis*,' so that my uncle would not be offended that we had not begun with him."[85]

But 40 *bis* was also part of an old residential neighborhood that was turning industrial, living off its artisans, a stone's throw from the Grands Boulevards and its theaters. Clothing stores such as Au Petit Saint-Antoine or the Comptoir général du vêtement rubbed shoulders with the Bazar des comestibles, a grocery that stretched all the way to the rue d'Hauteville, or later, L'Alcazar d'hiver, quite fashionable during the Second Empire. A foundry, small metallurgy plants, or a glassworks were echoed by factories a few blocks away on the rue du Faubourg-Saint-Denis that produced radiators, "English-style metal buttons," or cotton thread.

This was the environment where Jeanne was raised, and the contrast between the Weils' fortune and the relative modesty of their surroundings is striking. From all appearances, they had none of the splendor of the Crémieux salon or the quantities of gold that Jewish stockbrokers were supposed to enjoy. Solid habits of frugality controlled their purchases. They had a cook, a valet, and a chambermaid. Nothing in their home was ostentatious or even expensive. Nathé Weil preferred saving his money to guarantee his children's future: good schools for his son, a substantial dowry for his daughter.

———•···•———

An architect, a stockbroker, an industrialist, a military man, a bailiff, a banker—Moïse, Nathé, Lazare, Abraham Weil, Benoît Cohen, and Joseph

Lazarus—the sons and sons-in-law of Baruch Weil all achieved success, each in his own way. Five of them came from the Alsace, one from Holland. These men lacked the gaiety of the idle scions of the aristocracy; they didn't know how to enjoy life without thinking about wealth. They climbed the ladder of French society through work, stubbornness, and ambition. They give us a faithful image of the first generation born to French citizenship. They spoke and wrote in French; they lost their fathers' accents, which Balzac had found so amusing. They were Parisians, yes, but they were Jews, and it was by that yardstick that they measured their success: Godechaux Weil, the first Jew to become a bailiff; Moïse Weil, architect for the city of Beauvais;[86] Alphonse Weil, an officer decorated with a papal medal and the cross of the Légion d'honneur. Alphonse, a bachelor who received such fine evaluations from his superiors, spent his entire career as an accountant in the army. Although he couldn't even ride a horse, he participated in the African and Roman campaigns to defend the Papal State.[87] The Weils were Israelites living in France, but they were not yet Frenchmen who happened to be Israelites, much less ordinary Frenchmen.

Not all of them were involved to the same extent with the Jewish community. Also changing in their generation were attitudes toward religion. Baruch Weil found a successor in his eldest son Godechaux, Jeanne's uncle. Twenty-two years old at his father's death, Godechaux was already playing a role in Jewish institutions. Liberal Jews, unlike the conservatives, were in favor of adapting their religion to modern society. They hadn't yet decided how far to go. Should they blend completely into French society? Should they conserve the main aspects of Judaism and adapt these to modern life? Liberal Judaism, as Godechaux Weil understood it, proposed a middle path between assimilation and the shelter of rigid traditions.

This debate intensified during the nineteenth century because, for the first time, there was a real chance for Jews to integrate into French society. For the first time, young Jewish men could go to the same schools and plan on getting the same jobs—at least in theory—as their non-Jewish friends. Many were tempted to free themselves from the shackles of religion, from any markers of belief. They preferred to be called "Israelites"—a term deemed more neutral, less tainted by centuries of anti-Semitism. From there to renouncing their origins and trying to erase any mark of their identity was only a small step, which some of them took: a conversion movement was triggered by Nicolas de Ratisbonne and Benjamin Drach, son-in-law of the chief rabbi Emmanuel Deutsch.[88]

It so happened that Benjamin Drach had been the tutor of Baruch Weil's elder sons, Godechaux in particular. Hiring him as tutor (well before his conversion) was proof that Baruch wanted to give his children the best possible education. Drach was a serious scholar, later a renowned Orientalist, who had come from Alsace, where he had been a tutor. When he converted in 1823, he shocked the Jewish community.[89]

Godechaux Weil, using the pseudonym Ben Lévy, wrote a book called *Saturday Mornings* that became a best-seller in the French-Jewish world. He was editor-in-chief of the leading organ that favored integration, the *Archives israélites*, a liberal magazine created in 1840 to celebrate its readers' success in French society. He also proposed founding a worldwide organization for the purpose of defending Jewish rights. He was fifteen years ahead of his time. The Alliance israélite universelle was finally born in 1860, thanks to Adolphe Crémieux.

Godechaux's professional success was no less striking, since he abandoned the fine china business to become a bailiff for the Tribunal de première instance in the Seine region. It was he who convinced his close friends the Rothschilds to play a major role in Jewish welfare, vital for a community in which there was still so much poverty. The image of the Rothschilds was tied in large part to this philanthropic activity.[90]

Uncle Godechaux, nearly as prominent in the Jewish community as Adolphe Crémieux, was a witness to the marriage of Jeanne's parents. He died in 1878. His wife, Frédérique Zunz, born in Frankfurt, lived at 36, rue d'Enghien until 1897. Visiting Aunt "Friedel" was one of the New Year's Day duties that Jeanne demanded of her sons.[91]

Another major player in Jewish institutions was Benoît Cohen, Jeanne's uncle by marriage. He had emigrated to France from his native Amsterdam at a very young age, and was married to Merline, Baruch Weil's eldest daughter. After working in the porcelain business with his father-in-law, he held positions of financial responsibility in an insurance company. But his main focus became the administration of Jewish welfare organizations. His fate, too, was linked to that of the Rothschilds, for he became the first director of the Hospital for the Indigent on the rue Picpus, the future Rothschild Hospital.[92]

Beginning with Baruch and continuing down to his sons and sons-in-law, a dynasty was built that played a major role in Jewish institutions, to which it had numerous family, community, and professional ties. At the same time, the Weils were gaining entry into French society. Integration and a weakening of religious practice went together for many French Jews. This development was less a calculated one than a social necessity, of which the Weil family offers a perfect illustration. But the attachment to certain rituals and traditions only grew stronger. Belonging to the Jewish community was measured by fidelity, and marriage within the faith was one of the only remaining touchstones of that fidelity. Nathé Weil, like Moïse, his half brother (two of whose daughters married non-Jews),[93] made another choice, that of assimilation. Jeanne's marriage marked the accomplishment of that process. It had taken three generations.

5

Mother and Daughter

On a July evening in 1864, a crowd gathered at the doors of the Comédie-française. All of Paris was talking about the new production of Racine's play *Esther*. The critics were divided. But everyone was dazzled by the audacity and sumptuousness of the production. The actress Maria Favart charmed the most reticent spectators: her simple approach made her a more touching Esther than Rachel, Uncle Adolphe's protégée, who, in taking the role twenty years earlier, had been called an "Oriental houri." At exactly 8:15 P.M., when the curtain rose, the stage set prompted gasps of admiration from the audience. Arcades, draperies, veils, low couches, enormous feather fans, exotic plants in ornate vases, and rich fabrics endowed Esther's chambers with luxury worthy of *A Thousand and One Nights*. At the back of the stage, you could just make out the outlines of the doors to Ahasuerus's palace.

The costumes matched the décor, transporting the audience to the kingdom of Persia, embracing Assyria and Egypt. With their black beards, red and blue tunics, and gold and silver crowns, the male characters moved slowly, as regal as the heroes on bas-reliefs. In the second act, winged monsters and bird-headed gods appeared at the foot of the immense colonnades of Ahasuerus's palace. It was a barbarian Orient unfolding in all its splendor, a baroque backdrop for Racine's classical text. The young woman kneeling at the foot of a monarch who was holding out his gold scepter toward her seemed to have come straight out of a Gustave Moreau painting. After the intermission, when the curtain rose on Esther's gardens, the audience was transfixed. Only a critic as sour as Francisque Sarcens could find fault in so much delight. Gigantic cedars inclined their boughs over kneeling sphinxes, allowing a glimpse, behind them, of the towers of the city of Suse. The enthusiastic audience cried out for an encore of the final chorus: "He's appeased, he pardons . . ."[94]

There were fifteen evening performances and an additional free matinee on August 15.[95] It's hard to imagine that fifteen-year-old Jeanne would have missed the century's most famous production of *Esther*, the play "that Mama loves best."[96]

To save her people, Esther must hide her true origins without ever denying them—she became one of the great symbols of Marranism, the secret Judaism practiced in post-Inquisition Spain.[97] If heroic, Esther was hardly intrepid. Only because of pressure from Mordecai did she end up taking action. She lived under the yoke of two authorities—that of her uncle and that of her husband, the king. As a harem wife, her only weapons were her beauty and her intelligence. Far from resisting the king or transgressing his law, she knew how to use him to achieve her goals. "A Jewess who became a Persian Sultan," she was capable both of casting an illusion and of maintaining her identity. Her role as mediator depended upon the covert power she held over the king. Love played no part whatever. She served the king according to his commands. She fulfilled her duty.

Esther was a character who intrigued Jeanne Weil throughout her life. Racine's tragedy, commissioned by Madame de Maintenon for the young ladies of Saint-Cyr, was part of the education of any cultured young woman. "Imagine that after the first performance of *Esther*, Madame de Sévigné writes to Madame de La Fayette to tell her how much she regretted her absence": this was the essay question given to Gisèle, one of Marcel Proust's "young girls in flower," to qualify her for her certificate of studies.

Adèle had certainly read Jeanne the letter from Madame de Sévigné, her favorite author, who in fact attended the fifth performance of *Esther* at Saint-Cyr. The marquise's correspondence was almost like a secret language for Adèle and Jeanne. Madame de Sévigné's own love for her daughter, her curiosity, her lucidity, her sense of humor, and her irony all served Adèle and Jeanne, through their common penchant for quotation, to communicate their own feelings toward each other. Like the marquise, the two of them and, later, Jeanne and her son Marcel, refrained from any overt expression of their tender feelings: "Another great friendship, my dear child, might be made from all the feelings that I hide from you."[98]

Jeanne was already familiar with Maria Favart, who played Esther. For six months Favart had been performing in a play inspired by George Sand's *La Petite Fadette* at the Théâtre des Variétés and then in a work by Musset, the Weil women's favorite poet, at the Comédie-française.[99] So Racine, Madame de Sévigné, George Sand, Musset, the authors most beloved by Jeanne and her mother, were all implicated in the 1864 production of *Esther*. Two Classicists, two Romantics. Together they give us a sense of the young girl's culture and the development of her taste. Adèle Weil's role was formative.

For Madame Nathé (just as for "Madame Amédée" in *In Search of Lost Time*, to whom Proust gave the rare first name of Bathilde, inspired by Dumas's drama), intellectual and artistic values mattered most, along with a deep passion for what was natural. Adèle had no use for conventions; she disdained prejudice and society's opinion. Proust is thought to have combined his mother's traits with his grandmother's in creating the character of Madame Amédée. The grandmother's fiery, emotional, exquisitely sensitive nature—so pure she was almost naive—is certainly based on Adèle and not on her daughter. Her rationalism, counterbalanced by her idealism, came straight from the milieu she inhabited, full of progressive thinkers. In *In Search of Lost Time*, the narrator's grandmother even has socialist leanings, since she presents Saint-Loup, a supporter of the People's University, with original letters by Proudhon that she has purchased—the same Proudhon that Adèle Berncastel met at her uncle Adolphe Crémieux's apartment.

Freethinking and a taste for art, rejection of high society and a love of nature: nothing about Adèle was frivolous. These characteristics made Jeanne's mother an original who wasn't always understood by those around her, if we are to believe Proust's portrait of her and the few mentions of her in letters.[100]

"Madame Amédée is always as different as she can be from everyone else," remarks Françoise, Aunt Léonie's cook in *Swann's Way*, with a touch of bitterness. There is reason to believe that Adèle, in much the same way, was an original. Passionate about the theater (it was his grandmother who took the young narrator of *In Search of Lost Time* to see La Berma in *Phèdre* for the first time), cultured, a member of several private lending libraries, a reader of Latin and German, she was also very much taken up with the great outdoors and healthy living.

Marcel's grandmother's eccentricity and commitment to health are a source of embarrassment for the narrator of *In Search of Lost Time*. At Balbec, annoyed because the closed bay window of the Grand Hotel was depriving her grandson of fresh air, she "surreptitiously opened one of the windows, which had the effect of blowing away the menus, newspapers, veils, and caps of the other people having lunch."[101]

This whimsical grandmother also causes the narrator's father to worry: he "foresaw that her idea of a tour designed for intellectual benefit would turn into a series of missed trains, lost luggage, sore throats, and disregard of doctors' orders."[102] After all, she believes that the higher the artistic component, the more interesting the site, whether a view of Florence or a trip following in the footsteps of Madame de Sévigné. Reality and practical matters don't matter: who cares if Florence no longer looks as it did in Renaissance paintings, or if traveling to Balbec by a seventeenth-century route is inconvenient.

Certainly, Madame Amédée is distinctly nonconformist. She shocks her son-in-law by planning to present her seven-year-old grandson with Musset's poems, Rousseau's *Confessions,* and George Sand's feminist novel, *Indiana.* She has to return them to the bookstore and exchange them for Sand's pastoral novels. Even if we don't take this anecdote literally, we can imagine that Adolphe Crémieux's niece introduced her daughter to books other than those deemed proper for young ladies and that she aimed to nourish the vibrant intelligence she must have sensed in Jeanne.

Adèle Weil's personality had a profound affect on her daughter. Young Jeanne was brought up mainly by her mother, as was the custom. She was very close to her, and remained close to her for her entire life. In two photographs most likely taken the same day, the photographer had them strike the same pose, their hands resting against the back of a chair over which a curtain was draped. Adèle is wearing her usual enigmatic smile; Jeanne is staring intensely at the camera. She is serious. They must have told her to look straight at the camera and not move. She's a little rigid, and seems to be holding the curtain like a child hanging onto her mother's skirts.

What kind of education did Jeanne receive? In the absence of any records, we can only hypothesize. She probably took what were called "short courses," private school classes in which young ladies from good families learned a few of the rudiments of general culture.[103] Near the Weils' apartment on the cité de Trévise was a school for young ladies that Jeanne, and even Adèle before her, might well have attended: the "Methodical Course in Primary Education," founded by David Lévi Alvarès in 1820. His school was extraordinarily successful, and its reputation spread from Paris to the provinces. Alvarès's method consisted in dividing the task of education between the schoolteacher and the mother. Some of his schools involved as many as four hundred mothers. The students saw the teacher only once a week for six months. (In spring and summer, these young ladies, just like the perfect little girls described by the comtesse de Ségur, followed their parents to the countryside.) Their mothers participated in classes and then became teaching assistants. The actual learning depended upon them. Alvarès's basic principle was the use of reason. The goal of his teaching method, quite innovative, was to make the child active.

His clientele came from the Faubourg Saint-Germain and the Chaussée d'Antin, an "aristocracy of money, finance and high commerce." The main subjects taught were grammar, "the art of speaking and writing well"; cosmography; physical, political, and commercial geography; history; natural history; and elementary physics. The students, one inspector observed, were particularly well informed about their era and were as familiar with Jules Favre, who had just been elected to the French Academy, as they were with Taine and his *Essay on the Fables of La Fontaine.* "We are strenuously opposed to the idea of creating bluestockings," the director insisted, and he was just as opposed to "salon dolls." A report on the school made it clear that the majority of Alvarès's students were Catholic—which of course precluded any bias.[104]

Neither classical nor modern languages were offered. Latin, reserved for boys, was purposely excluded from any official schooling for girls. Jeanne could only have learned Latin through private lessons or from her mother, since Adèle would have had no hesitation in exposing her daughter to what was then considered the ultimate in pedantry for a woman.[105] We recall that in *In Search of Lost Time,* the young narrator tries to write to his grandmother in Latin. He also studies German with her.

The Weil children must have benefited from the services of a "Miss" to teach them English, a language they both knew well. As for their knowledge of German, that was no surprise, since their maternal grandparents and their mother still spoke it. The daily use of two languages was rather rare at the time and constituted a quite unusual pedagogy, due both to the family background and to the personality of the woman in charge of her children's education.

One of Proust's notes for *Jean Santeuil* suggests yet another possibility: "Mme Santeuil university student. Prize ceremony. Put elsewhere."[106] The similarities between Madame Santeuil and Jeanne Proust, and more generally between *Jean Santeuil* and the life of its author, have long been recognized.

Although lycées were opened to girls in 1880, universities, with a few exceptions, were not accessible to women before 1918. When Victor Dury, the minister of education, set up his project for secondary education for girls in Paris, the courses were administered by an association headquartered at the Sorbonne. Classes were held at the Sorbonne from 1867 to 1870. Those who chose to do homework and to take exams—both optional endeavors—were eligible for the medals given out at a solemn prize ceremony. The empress herself, despite the accusations of anticlericalism and Saint-Simonism directed against the ministry (which ultimately put an end to the experiment), enrolled her nieces. The classes at the Sorbonne enrolled some two hundred students, accompanied by their mothers, who were far less disciplined than their daughters.[107]

Among the teachers at the Sorbonne there was only one woman: Marie Pape-Carpantier, who later founded the Pape-Carpantier primary school. Her curriculum was based on "duties incumbent upon women by virtue of nature and reason." The first part of the course, concerned with personal hygiene, had all that Adèle Weil and the future wife of Dr. Proust could wish for: nutrition, cleanliness, breathing (in particular the dangers of corsets, shoes, and belts that were too tight), gymnastics, and sanitary measures in the home. A class in morals—the first right of women is "the right to be respected"—and one on household management as well as notions of civic education rounded out the syllabus. Whether by chance or out of respect for an educator she knew, when Jeanne Proust sent her son Marcel to primary school, she chose the Pape-Carpantier.

"Neither a bluestocking nor a salon doll": Jeanne Weil, like Adèle and Rose, Amélie and Ernestine, before her, was raised to be a young person of culture and a marriageable heiress. She received more intellectual nourishment than was customary; thanks to her constant dialogue with her mother she acquired the habit and the taste for such nourishment, and she transmitted the need for it to her son. If she had been born fifteen years later, she would have pursued higher education. Instead, her family was happy enough to get her married at the same age her mother and her aunts had been married.[108] Like Esther, she was about to wed "the foreigner" they had chosen for her.

Part Two

6

A Change of Regime

Jeanne Weil's marriage to Adrien Proust was celebrated on Saturday, September 3, 1870, the day after the French were defeated by the Prussians at Sedan. The entire Weil family was present, but none of the Prousts attended—not Virginie, Adrien's mother; not Jules and Elisabeth Amiot, his sister and brother-in-law; nor any of the Proust cousins—even though Illiers was less than a hundred kilometers from Paris. The political situation certainly made travel difficult. An invitation had nonetheless been sent by the Weils to Illiers.[1] Dr. Proust's medical colleagues, however, honored the occasion with their presence. Was Dr. Dieulafoy, famous for his theatrical lectures, among them? Professor Fauvel was probably there. Jeanne entered the large room in the town hall of the tenth arrondissement on her father's arm. After the exchange of rings, she must have thought of the Jewish ritual of the broken wineglass, signifying an indestructible union.

There was something incomplete about the civil marriage, devoid of any religious ceremony. What was missing was the lyrical quality of eternal vows. But that was an illusion, for in the absence of legal divorce, the marriage was indissoluble. Jeanne made the transition from her father's tutelage to her husband's, promising to obey him. The mayor called on the witnesses. Sixty-two-year-old Dr. Gustave Cabanellas signed first, followed by Georges, Jeanne's brother. Then came Adolphe Crémieux, her great-uncle and, last, Gustave's brother Charles, a fifty-five-year-old stockbroker. The choice of the aging Cabanellas brothers as witnesses was probably due to their role in introducing the young couple at their apartment at 5, rue de Mogador. A doctor and a stockbroker may well have plotted the marriage. Jeanne left the town hall on her husband's arm, surrounded by a small group of guests.

The hostilities, the rumors of surrender, the instability of the regime and the threat of foreign occupation weighed heavily on all of them. Napoleon III had declared war against Prussia on July 19. The result was not long in coming: by August, Prussian troops had entered France and a state of siege was declared. At the beginning of that month, Dr. Proust was sent on an inspection tour of the border troops. He returned well informed and with no illusions about the turn of events. The marriage contract was signed as soon as he returned, on August 27. Who knew what might happen?

All males between the ages of thirty and forty were drafted into the National Guard. Uncle Alphonse was at the front. The massive mobilization, the appointment of Bazaine as supreme commander and Trochu as military governor of Paris, had prevented neither the growing number of strategic mistakes nor the final debacle. After a desperate battle, the emperor had surrendered and been taken prisoner. Eighty-three thousand French soldiers had fallen into enemy hands.

By nightfall of the Prousts' wedding day, news of MacMahon's defeat and the emperor's imprisonment was confirmed and circulated in Paris. The newsstands were teeming with people. Crowds formed on street corners. On the boulevards, large disorganized gangs waved flags, crying "Long live defeat! Long live Trochu!" At 10:30 P.M. several thousand people assembled on the boulevard des Italiens and the boulevard Poissonière, a stone's throw from the Weils'. The neighborhood was erupting. In front of the Théâtre du Gymnase, policemen drew their weapons. There were arrests. The crowd dispersed.

Jeanne refused to see these events as bad omens; she wasn't superstitious. But Adrien was a high-ranking civil servant, a physician at the Central Office who had been sent on an official mission; he had just been decorated with the cross of the Légion d'honneur by the empress Eugénie herself, who had been appointed regent at the start of the war.

Adolphe Crémieux, Jeanne's great-uncle, had excused himself quickly from the marriage ceremony, along with his wife Amélie, after tenderly kissing his great-niece. The next day he was appointed minister of justice in the National Defense Cabinet. Having spent time with the Bonapartes and having even helped draft Louis Napoleon's platform for the presidential election, he had quickly joined the opposition. After the coup d'état, Crémieux was put in prison. To his great chagrin, he spent the night of December 2, 1851, in prison, far from his darling Amélie. It was his wedding anniversary: he never forgave Napoleon III, and from then on, he celebrated his anniversary on October 10, the date of his engagement.

Upon his release, he decided to abandon political activity. He involved himself in a new cause—founding the Alliance israélite universelle. Despite urging from the opposition, he refused to run for deputy in 1863, was nonetheless elected in Paris in 1869, but gave the position to his former secretary, young Gambetta.

Now history had caught up with him. He was seventy-five years old. A month later, after retreating to Tours with a government delegation, he was suddenly appointed minister of war. He was not successful in this position, however. Whether due to good-heartedness, weakness, or opportunism, the valiant Adolphe Crémieux said yes to everyone: in the midst of a debacle, this was not an asset. He lodged with his wife and granddaughter at the archbishop's palace in Tours. Amélie could satisfy her penchant for good works by visiting the wounded. The archbishop was delighted and thanked her warmly.

On August 24, 1870, Crémieux signed the historic decree that remains attached to his name: he made Algeria into several administrative departments whose citizens could elect their own parliamentary representatives. And he made it possible for Algerian Jews to become French citizens through naturalization.

———•••••———

Jeanne found herself pregnant a month after her marriage, in a Paris under siege, where the people were growing hungrier by the day. Prussian troops held the city. From their apartment on the rue Roy, near the Eglise Saint-Augustin—a new and wealthy neighborhood, into which Adrien had been keen to move, quite different from the tenth arrondissement, where Jeanne had grown up—you could hear cannons firing near Saint-Cloud and Auteuil. The worst part was the hunger. Despite all their connections, the couple suffered like the rest of the Parisians. First, horsemeat replaced beef, and Jeanne found its bloody flesh nauseating. But soon, for lack of horsemeat, people started to devour anything that moved: they ate donkeys, dogs, and cats, and those who were lucky got buffalo, antelope, and kangaroos from the zoo at the Jardin des Plantes. The Voisin Restaurant served elephant sausage. Once people had used up their ration tickets for portions of salted, inedible meat, once they had eaten the last jars of boiled mutton and boiled beef that they'd purchased in September for an exorbitant price at Corcelet's, they had to face facts: nothing was available. A single baker, Hédé, still sold white bread and croissants on the rue Montmartre in Paris, not far from Jeanne's parents. The price of food was staggering, the lines interminable. Eight *sous* for a small turnip, seven for a few onions; no butter, no milk, no cheese; and as for potatoes, you needed solid connections to get any at all, at 20 francs a bushel. It was a wretched diet for a pregnant woman. No proper nutrition, no light—you couldn't even find candles—no heat. Hunger, cold (December 1870 was bitterly cold, with snow flurries and ice), and fear prevailed. That's how it always was in wartime. During the first months of her pregnancy, Jeanne lost weight instead of gaining. She was gripped by constant anxiety.

She was afraid. She feared for her parents, until her father, who hated travel and never left Paris, finally decided to abandon the rue du Faubourg-Poissonière for Etampes, a safer place for his wife. Adèle was terrified, but she wanted to stay with her daughter. She remembered her own pregnancy during the 1848 Revolution. The parallel was striking. Who knew if there wouldn't be another uprising? But Nathé insisted. They left, and it was with a heavy heart that Adèle left her pregnant daughter. This was their very first separation. The Weils got out just in time. On November 27, 1870, the gates of Paris closed. Jeanne also feared for her brother Georges, when, in March, the Commune drafted all males between eighteen and forty years of age. And she feared most of all for Adrien, who continued to go to the Hôpital de la Charité, where he practiced. One day he was nearly killed right on the street by an insurgent's bullet. Jeanne was six months pregnant. What a terrible start for their married life. But she would never have considered leaving her husband's side. Adrien feared a new outbreak of cholera, the scourge that followed disasters. He also worried about his loved ones. It was impossible to get any news of family members living outside the capital. Thanks to a postal balloon, Adrien managed to send a note to a friend in Tours, inquiring about his mother's safety. The Prussians had captured Châteaudun. Had she remained in Illiers? Had she taken refuge in Tours? He begged his friend to reply by carrier pigeon, however much it cost.

After the surrender at the end of January 1871, Paris began to get supplies. Wilhelm I had been proclaimed emperor of Germany in the Gallery of Mirrors at Versailles, next to the bust of Louis XIV, and his troops had paraded down a deserted Champs-Elysées, flanked by the Parisians' closed shutters. There was total chaos, and the measures taken by the Commune, which had seized power in March, were threatening. The government had retreated to Versailles, and everyone was expecting a standoff. Now danger was at the Weils' door. They spoke of moving to Auteuil, as they did every year, to the house belonging to Jeanne's uncle Louis Weil, who had lost his wife Emilie in November, at the beginning of Jeanne's pregnancy. But they had to wait. The little town of Auteuil, once a haven of greenery and tranquillity, had suffered badly: short of food, bombarded, cut off from Paris during the siege, ransacked, it had even been occupied for a few days by the Prussians. All that was left of the boulevard Murat were ruins. In January, German grenades started to fall on the rue Boileau and the rue La Fontaine, the street where Louis's house, number 96, was located. In April, the soldiers in Versailles had fired their own grenades from the Mont Valérien: some houses were completely destroyed.

But Paris itself was hardly more peaceful. On April 21, 1871, Jeanne celebrated her twenty-second birthday in apocalyptic conditions. Cannon fire was endless. Hearses sped along the boulevards, their flags flapping. A grenade hit the Arc de Triomphe. The threat was coming nearer. Gaping holes opened up on the avenue de la Grande Armée and throughout the neighborhood. At every street corner stood men and women, baggage in hand, trying to escape from Paris as discreetly as possible. But where was there to go? In early May, Auteuil was still being bombed. Edmond de Goncourt's house on the boulevard de Montmorency was hit. The sidewalk was littered with tree limbs, sections of train tracks, sewer covers twisted by the force of the explosions. Nothing was left of the rue d'Auteuil, the town's main street, but smoking ruins.

When the bloody week of May 21, 1871, arrived, marked by unbelievably violent fighting between the soldiers at Versailles and members of the Commune, Jeanne, despite her courage, feared for her own survival. Paris was an inferno. The flames could be seen for miles. Grenades were exploding underfoot, from the Tuileries to the Faubourg Saint-Honoré. The rue Royale was on fire. From the sky, fragments of charred paper rained down like soot: ledgers and French administrative records, burned by insurgents in the town halls. Jeanne begged Adrien not to leave the building. He reassured her, but went out anyway. There had never been a greater need for doctors. For months, ambulances had been crisscrossing the city, carrying soldiers in retreat. And now there were thousands of corpses, dying men, wounded men, members of the Commune and troops from Versailles, savagery against savagery. In his quiet way, Adrien defied the danger. Jeanne trembled. What did she know of this older man, her husband? They hadn't even had a chance to live together in peacetime.

The repression of the Commune was ruthless. Arrests and summary executions bred terror among the people of Paris. "I will be merciless," Thiers had promised. He was true to his word. But by June, the bourgeoisie was breathing more easily. Adrien could finally take Jeanne to Auteuil. The streets had begun to be cleared. Louis's grounds had been ransacked, but the house itself was undamaged. They were just in time. Marcel was born on July 10, 1871.

Mother and Son

Marcel almost died at birth. Jeanne delivered the child in Uncle Louis's spacious house at Auteuil. Mercifully, her mother had returned from Etampes and was able to be by her side. The maids fretted and prepared large basins of water; Dr. Proust had insisted on clean sheets and linens. Applying what had only just been learned about avoiding sepsis, he insisted that the midwife wash her hands before touching Jeanne. She looked at him as if he were out of his mind, muttering as she did his bidding. Who was he to tell her how to deliver babies after all these years?

From the moment of his birth, it seems, Marcel caused his mother anxiety. It took extra care and vigilance to keep him alive, to feed him. Jeanne's relationship to her son was marked by this early worrying. Did the anguish of the war, the shortages, the violence of the conflicts, the destruction, the noise of the grenades make Jeanne herself more nervous? Possibly. The birth may have been long and difficult, as is often the case for a first child. His family feared the worst, and having avoided the worst, they gave little Marcel the benefit of constant care—a benefit that was also a burden.

On July 13, Adrien, Nathé, and Louis Weil went to the town hall in the sixteenth arrondissement to sign the birth certificate; the boy was named Valentin Louis George Eugène Marcel Proust. As was customary, in giving the child so many names his parents tried to honor everyone: Adrien's deceased father and Marcel's godmother, maternal uncle, and future godfather.

Religious tradition dictated that the baptism should take place within three days. On August 5, 1871, a good three weeks after his birth, the child was baptized at the Church of Saint-Louis d'Antin. We don't know whether the Weil family attended the ceremony. The Prousts, once again, were conspicuously absent, even though the war was over, the roads clear. What must Jeanne have felt during this symbolic rite that admitted her son into the bosom of the church? Was she relieved to spare him a circumcision, always an ordeal for a mother? Perhaps she conceived of the baptism less as a sacrament than as a simple formality, the key that gave Nathé Weil's grandson full access to French society, the certificate that qualified him as normal. While the practice of their own religion isolated the Jews, Catholicism was practically a requirement in a France, where there was as yet no separation of church and state. Baptism, the catechism, Holy Communion, Mass, meatless Fridays were all social as well as religious rituals.

Jeanne and Adrien Proust, both atheists, gave in to the demands of the bourgeoisie without any sort of spiritual commitment. Baptism was the first phase in a future they hoped would be bright. Next would come First Communion, grade school, a good lycée, advanced studies, the right marriage. The path to social success was clear.

They chose as godfather a man named Eugène Mutiaux, who may have been related to the Weils since he lived on the rue d'Hauteville with the rest of the family. The godmother, Hélène Louise Houette, a friend of Jeanne's, lived in their new neighborhood on the boulevard Malesherbes. Thus the certificate of baptism that Marcel Proust discovered one evening in 1916, in a drawer of his little table, sums up a part of Jeanne's history, the move from the Faubourg Poissonnière to new districts of the bourgeoisie.

The neighborhood that the young woman had discovered since her marriage was indeed different. The rue Roy, where her husband had settled on

September 1, 1870, connects the rue La Boétie to the rue Laborde, a stone's throw from the Place Saint-Augustin. A brand-new neighborhood, airy, with Haussman-style buildings presenting their bourgeois facades along broad, tree-lined avenues and around the squares. Dr. Proust set great store by hygiene and wanted to live in accordance with his principles. He affirmed that "new houses give off quantities of fresh air and light, the two most powerful antibacterial tonics we know." Around the corner, the Parc Monceau, swarming with children at play with their hoops, offered expanses of green grass, rare plants; uniformed maids pushed elegant baby carriages along the wide footpaths.

Night and day, Jeanne watched over her fragile infant. He was considered "nervous." Even as a baby, Marcel was sensitive, emotional. He loved to snuggle up against his mama's knees, hide his head against her bodice. She rocked him, cuddled him, reassured him with her gentle voice. She created a soft, cushiony world for him, a nest he later evoked with nostalgia in his unfinished novel *Jean Santeuil.* When it was cold out, she rubbed his feet in her hands, not too lightly because he was ticklish. His uncle Louis knew all about this; later, he got devilish pleasure in tickling the little boy, who considered it torture. Sometimes Jeanne would wrap his feet in a little knitted shawl, softer than anything he'd ever felt.

Adrien worked all day. Chief physician at the Hospice Sainte-Périne in Auteuil, he was appointed service chief at the Hôpital Saint-Antoine in late 1873. When he was home, he shut himself up in his study and wrote. He had meetings at the ministry. He went out at night and was soon appointed temporary physician for the Opéra-comique. In those days, fathers weren't much interested in babies. Babies belonged to their mothers. But Adrien Proust was a doctor, and his sensible advice bore fruit. Marcel developed from a skinny little creature into a beautiful child with blond curls and big black eyes like his mother's. Those curls certainly caused problems. Uncle Louis, a practical joker, couldn't resist sneaking up behind Marcel and pulling them. The child, terrified, would start to scream. Though Jeanne knew it was just friendly teasing on the part of a widowed uncle who had no children of his own, she couldn't bear her child's fear. One day they'd have to cut off the curls. But it was too soon. Just as it was too soon to put away his baby dress.

In August 1872, Jeanne's cousin Hélène (nicknamed Nuna) was married. Hélène was the daughter of Nathé's half-brother Moïse Weil and Adèle's sister Amélie Berncastel (known as Mother Weil). Hélène had two sisters, Jenny and Claire, and the three young women were so beautiful that they were known in their hometown of Beauvais as the Three Graces. Jeanne loved Hélène very much. This marriage brought the two cousins even closer together, since Hélène, like her sister Jenny, married a non-Jew. Camille Bessières, a great-nephew of a Maréchal d'Empire but lacking a fortune, was in the insurance business.

A few weeks after this marriage, Jeanne learned she was pregnant again. She had a son; now she hoped for a girl. With a few months' difference, there would be the same age span between her two children as between Georges and herself. She loved her mother too much not to want a girl. But on Saturday, May 24, 1873, she gave birth to a beautiful, robust boy, his mouth as round as a cherry. He was named Robert Emile Sigismond Léon Proust and baptized in turn.

In total contrast to Marcel, with his fragility and nerves, Robert seemed to grow without any help. Yet the two brothers looked alike. And to accentuate this resemblance, they were dressed alike, as was the custom in bourgeois families. In keeping with the century that invented the Child King, the two little Prousts delighted everyone. "The child and its mother are no longer relegated to the woman's apartments as in the past. The child is shown while still an infant. Parents proudly present the child's nurse. It's as if they were on stage, making a great show of their production," wrote Goncourt in his diary.[2] Marcel and Robert were dressed alluringly; they were taken to the photographer, looking like little princes, to immortalize their growing up and their indestructible union. Jeanne took her two children to a photographer on at least four different occasions. From 1876 to 1887, these photos allow us to follow the development of the fraternal couple.

Marcel is five, Robert three. They are perched on an armchair. The younger brother is wearing a sleeveless white blouse over a skirt of broderie anglaise. White socks, laced boots. His hair is darker and curlier than his brother's, whose own combed-back hair and bangs reflect the light. Robert is leaning slightly toward Marcel, who has wrapped one arm around his little brother and has taken his hand. Marcel is wearing a pastel dress with a white collar and lace-trimmed sleeves. All is as it should be. The two brothers love one another tenderly. As their body language shows, the big brother is protective of his little brother; the pose is as classic as the one of a baby lying on his tummy.

In the second photo, the difference in their size has diminished. Robert is

growing fast! They are still standing side by side, the younger brother leaning slightly against his older brother. Both are dressed in Scottish costumes,
long jackets with tails, white collars and pockets, gold buttons. Robert is
sulking with the look of an imp who's been forced to stand still. The two
brothers are still in skirts: the little boy's is white, the older boy's matches
his jacket. Yet he is already nine years old, the age by which boys normally
wear short pants. It looks as though Jeanne wanted to emphasize their resemblance, as if the two boys were being treated as twins. There was nothing feminine in the mentality of their era: the passage from dresses to pants
marked a certain stage in a boy's maturation—it meant he had reached the
age of reason (seven years). To stop wearing a skirt meant you were a big
boy, a little man. Every time he wore the Scottish costume, the older boy
was back at his brother's level. In this photo, which was passed around the
family and marked a stage in the boys' development, Marcel was demoted to
the age of the skirts, dressed as a little boy. The stiff way he holds his hand—
which looks either affected or tense—indicates his discomfort.

By now the boys are about twelve. (If Marcel is fourteen, as the date on
the photo would indicate, he looks very young for his age.) They look almost alike, though Marcel's hair has grown darker and is neatly parted, distinguishing it from Robert's curly mop. This time, Marcel is standing to the
right side of his brother and Robert is perched on a pedestal, which makes
them look about the same height, with a slight advantage for Robert.

In the last photo, the metamorphosis is complete. We see two rather
awkwardly built adolescents wearing high laced boots, their hair cut short
for school. Robert is standing, his hat in his hand, slightly stooped, with the
manly look of his father. Marcel is sitting on a bench, his legs crossed, his
chin resting on his fist—a mannered version of his grandmother's pose. The
difference between the two brothers is striking. They are in the process of
becoming themselves.

What is obvious in all the photos is the elegance of these young bourgeois boys, the care taken by their mother to erase any difference between
them. A maniacal care, revealing her will to demonstrate the equal treatment given to both. A worry of all good mothers, who know their behavior
is watched carefully by their children.

But when you are the older sibling, being treated the same as the younger,
or seeing the younger treated as you are, means a loss of privilege. Equality is the worst thing of all. When the older child in question is someone as
sensitive and "nervous" as Marcel, the mother needs a great deal of subtlety,

tenderness, and fairness to reassure him without giving in, to show him affection without hurting the younger one's feelings, to love both without inciting jealousy, and to ensure that they love each other.

Jeanne had a lifetime to work out such an ambitious agenda. And in the end, she achieved her goal. The two boys did love each other.

8

Summers at Auteuil

It was more than habit: it was a way of life.[3] From early May and usually until August, the season for patronizing spas or moving to the countryside, the Weil family stayed at Auteuil. In 1857, Uncle Louis had purchased his country house at 96, rue La Fontaine. His button business, the first in Paris, was flourishing.[4] Fancy decorative buttons; uniform buttons; buttons made of silk, porcelain, agate; English-style metal buttons (he was the exclusive supplier of Sanders and Sons); sleeve buttons of the kind that Céleste Albaret admired on her dear Monsieur Proust; and religious medals—all of these combined to make him a rich man. An honorary member of the customs board, a member of the Comptoir d'escompte, a chevalier of the Légion d'honneur, Louis Weil saw his fortune grow even larger with his marriage. Emilie Oppenheim, whom he married in Hamburg in 1844, was a banker's daughter. This union, however, didn't inhibit Uncle Louis: a connoisseur of beautiful women, he would invite them to his Parisian pied-à-terre. He was the model for Uncle Adolphe in *In Search of Lost Time*, at whose house the narrator first met "the lady in pink." But we will return to these ladies in pink who so delighted certain men in the family.

Uncle Louis, now widowed, opened wide the gates to his Auteuil property. Jeanne had been going there with her parents since her own childhood and wouldn't miss this summer visit for anything. For at Auteuil she was reunited with her parents and her cousins.

Let us imagine a day in May 1878. The armchairs on the boulevard Malesherbes were draped in white covers. Auguste, Uncle Louis's coachman, drove the horse-drawn carriage to Paris to pick up Jeanne and her sons. Immaculate in his livery, his whip crossed in front of him, he stood at attention in front of the carriage, waiting for his passengers. The trunks had already left with the chambermaid. Adrien had taken the omnibus to the hospital, as he always did; he would join his wife that evening. Jeanne traveled with her two young boys. Marcel was seated by her side; he had a slight cold. Robert insisted on sitting next to Auguste; and with a little luck, he'd get to hold the reins. He would be turning five in a few days, and for once, Mama gave him permission. They took the avenue du Bois. The chestnut trees were in bloom.

Auteuil, on that spring day, looked very much like a village. Closed all winter, the country houses had opened their shutters. Here a gate was painted in haste, there a chambermaid polished a copper bell. Green shutters, latticed gates, climbing rose bushes, linden trees, and front lawns made a kind of operatic décor. Lawyers, businessmen, wealthy merchants, and successful investors owned country houses here. It was stylish countryside, a stone's throw from Paris, and had served in the past as a retreat for Boileau, Racine, and Molière. You could get there by a local train that stopped at the Porte d'Auteuil, by omnibus, or by the Auteuil-Saint-Sulpice tramway. Or you could even, as Jeanne sometimes liked to do, take a bateau-mouche down the Seine, disembarking at the Quai d'Auteuil. The scent of lilacs filled the air. Ivy and Virginia creeper climbed up the walls. This was Jeanne's image of the countryside—at least until she got to know Illiers, her husband's native village. A country setting for Parisians, with no bad smells, no boredom, no poverty, and plenty of sophistication. The Auteuil house was the essence of happiness for Jeanne, a place where her world came together in large gatherings around the dinner table and in conversations under the trees at nightfall. Relieved of the burden of managing her own household, even though, as time went on, she increasingly assumed the role of mistress of the house at Auteuil, she had time to read—the lending library on the rue de Passy furnished books for the entire family—and to spend more time than usual with her children.

Louis Weil had purchased his house from an actress, Eugénie Doche, who had become famous when playing Marguerite Gautier in *La Dame aux Camélias*. Rumor had it that Louis and she had been intimate. The huge house, with its twenty-nine windows, had two main stories as well as a third, attic floor with mansard windows. It was built in the middle of a large lot that connected the rue La Fontaine to the rue de la Source. A stable for two horses and a coach house for two carriages had been added near the entryway. In 1876, Louis built an additional wing for the Proust family: two rooms on the first floor and two on the second. Jeanne planned to make the mansard room on the third floor into a study for the children. They could hang engravings and reproductions of works of art, like Giotto's allegories—Charity, Envy, and Justice—which Swann gives to the narrator as a child in *In Search of Lost Time*. With its toilets, its baths, its bedrooms, its billiard room on the ground floor, there was space in the house for the whole Weil brood. Although some of them came and went during the summer, Sundays brought all of the cousins together in a Jewish version of the Countess of Segur's *Holidays*.

On any given Sunday, Jeanne's cousins Jenny, Hélène, Claire, and her favorite, Laure, would arrive with their husbands, François Boeuf, Camille Bessières, Léon Neuburger, and Gustave Neuburger. (Léon and Gustave were brothers, and both were bankers at Rothschilds.) Laure's parents, Adélaïde and Joseph Lazarus, were also invited. And, of course, Nathé and Adèle were present as well.

The children ate lunch with their nannies. For dessert, there was cream cheese with strawberries. Marcel loved to smash the strawberries and mix them up until he had a kind of soup the same color as his favorite cookies.[5] There were plenty of young children: Marie, Henri, Jacques, Noémie, Pauline, Louise, Mathilde—not to mention Marcel and Robert, the younger one rushing around and playing the fool. The oldest cousin was eight. The babies—Jeanne, Amélie, and André—took naps. A few years later, Albert, Pierre, and Georges would be added to the group.[6] So many cousins, whose laughter, tears, fighting, and horsing around resounded throughout the house at Auteuil.

Three or four years later came fishing expeditions and long walks. The cousins would tramp upstairs to change their shoes. Marcel, reading in his bedroom retreat, would try to escape. He was then ten years old, deep into *Captain Fracasse,* his favorite book. Jeanne knew how much he valued his solitude. She protected him, pretended he wasn't feeling well, that he needed to rest. Ahasuerus didn't wish to see anyone—an empathic lie from a mother who knew from the beginning that her son was different. He loved contact with other people, but on his own terms, and when it suited him. And he had been subject to violent mood swings since his early childhood. Marcel thought the cousins were going to drag him out of his room. He fled up into his uncle's office, locked himself in. They knocked on every door. Where was Marcel? His uncle sent his little cousin Pierre to get him: "Look for him carefully, tell him to come down." The child did as he was told. But when he knocked on the right door, Marcel opened it, put his finger to his lips, and whispered "Shush." Pierre docilely went back down and announced: "I couldn't find him. He's gone out."

Without making it obvious, Jeanne rarely let her elder son out of her sight. She was never wholly without worry, as if at any moment he might disappear or die. She had been afraid of losing him at birth, perhaps even during her pregnancy, and Marcel seemed to have absorbed that maternal fear into the very core of his own being. Whatever Jeanne did, the memory of her original fear was indelible, imprinted like a matrix that engendered a thousand insignificant everyday worries. This was the dark side of her love for him, a threat that she fought with all the force of her rationality. How could she know whether this fear stemmed from her maternal instinct or from her son's personality? Their anxieties fed on each other, forming an inextricable knot. The son played on them and also suffered from them. Things that didn't bother other children got to him immediately. The least rough gesture, a sharp word, and he was in tears. Yet at other times he would slide down the banisters and race around the garden, shaking his head like a horse or holding out his arms like a seagull skimming the waves. It worried Jeanne to death: What if he fell into the pond? Or swallowed a fruit pit? Seeing something bulging in his cheek, she rushed to his side: "What's that you've got in your mouth?"[7] He stopped in a sweat, out of breath, his coat covered with wet lilac petals. "It's nothing Mama!" She wiped his face and helped him catch his breath. She gave him a drink of cool water, telling him, "Don't drink too quickly!" "Me too, I want water! With cocoa!" came Robert's cry; he was always thirsty and arrived at a gallop. And the little boy gulped his water, looking over his glass at his brother. Jeanne, pensive, watched her sons join their cousins, who were playing cards under the trees.

Fresh in her blue muslin dress tasseled with braided straw, the young woman walked through the living room, its shutters closed to keep out the heat, and into the pantry where the cider had been put to cool. Throughout, the décor was Second Empire. It was, in Marcel's later opinion, "completely lacking in style." Uncle Louis had purchased this luxurious home fully furnished. Valentine Thompson, one of the little cousins, would describe it as "a strange house, way out of fashion, with an unfashionable garden,"[8] full of massive, dark mahogany furniture, shiny blue satin drapes, mantelpieces of Siena marble, mirrored armoires that smelled of soap, canopy beds curtained in raw silk—nests of dust that left Marcel gasping for breath. Every spring, the child suffered from hay fever. The countryside wasn't good for him. Jeanne had a small, wrought-iron bed placed in his room that he could use when it was too hot to sleep in the big bed. "The flame of the night light of Bohemian glass, in the shape of an urn, which hung from the ceiling by little chains"[9] looked like a sacred object from the synagogue, transformed into an everyday accessory.

In the dining room with its odors of Swiss cheese and apricots, the walls were covered with ornamental plates. Waiting for lunch, the family entertained themselves by reading the sayings on the plates, a light-hearted homage to grandfather Baruch.

"I don't know about you, but I'm ravenous!" Uncle Louis proclaimed.[10] Gustave Neuburger, whose only known vice was gourmandise—as evidenced by his round belly—nodded in agreement. They could hear the rattle of hot plates in the pantry. The new cook was busy. Would she last long? Auguste served as coachman, butler, and valet for Uncle Louis; his wife did the laundry, and their daughter helped with the cleaning. Jealous of his territory, this very devoted servant could not stand having any other domestics in the house. Yet they needed a cook. Auguste arranged things so that none of them lasted very long. Uncle Louis was taken in, but not Jeanne: she finally figured out the mystery of the cooks who served lukewarm leg of lamb and curdled or over-salted gravies. Auguste held back the dishes on purpose, or salted them secretly. Should they deny themselves the perfect servant, or change cooks yet again? This "pantry drama" was the backstage for many bourgeois households and a subject of endless anecdotes for the Weil family.[11]

The grownups took their places around the table. Uncle Louis presided. The tableware gleamed—white napkins, china from Saxe, solid crystal glasses. The knives, "following the most vulgar custom," were propped on "little glass prisms" that cast "peacock eyes . . . as wonderful as the stained-glass windows . . . of Reims cathedral," according to Marcel, the aesthete, writing later with some exaggeration.[12] It was a classic Sunday lunch, a menu for Parisians in the country, with its baked eggs, filet of beef with béarnaise sauce and fried potatoes, strawberry mousse. "These strawberries are exquisite," Jeanne declared. "Yes, they're genuine wild strawberries," replied Louis "in the impartial tone of one who does justice to his children when they have been a success, or to his cook, when she has been especially clever with a dish."[13] And he added, optimistically: "This time we've got a real jewel." Conversation never lagged, laughter abounded. Sometimes the decibel level rose because Nathé and Louis always disagreed, and each was stubborn. As for Gustave, despite his great wealth (he was Alphonse de Rothschild's right-hand man), he hated society and couldn't tolerate the least show of vanity. He was a calm introvert who liked to say: "When you go on vacation, there are generally two trains, since the service is doubled: the first train is for fools; the second one is for reasonable people who travel comfortably while the people on the first train are jammed together; and both trains arrive at the same time."[14]

The Weils had an excellent sense of humor, though it sometimes turned sarcastic or even malicious. With the exception of Jeanne, whose sense of repartee was unsurpassed in the family, the women usually got the worse of it, especially Adèle: "She had brought into my father's family so different a mentality that everyone poked fun at her and tormented her," her grandson would write.[15] The teasing wasn't cruel, and Adèle put up with it, though with a touch of sadness. Who knows if the needling hurt her feelings or not? It certainly shocked Marcel, who adored his grandmother. As in every family, each member was expected to play his or her role. Adèle was the expert on hygiene and health. She believed only in the benefits of nature, and in any kind of weather she roamed the garden paths, disturbed by the lack of taste shown by Gaillard, the new gardener, who wanted to align everything symmetrically and lacked, according to her, all feeling for nature. To the citified Weils, there was something a little silly about her passion. Even Jeanne, so close to her mother, only admired flowers after they'd been put in vases. When Uncle Louis had huge bouquets of hawthorn and snowballs cut for her to take back to Paris, she threw them out as soon as he turned his back, to the dismay of Marcel, who thought this was mean.[16]

Nathé too was the butt of jokes. He refused, so they said, to leave Paris for a single night. In the evening, he would leave before anyone else and return to the Faubourg Poissonière to sleep. Watching the trains pass over the viaduct with "a mixture of astonishment, pity, and terror," he wondered how people could be crazy enough to enjoy traveling.[17] Was he a Parisian to the core, or simply phobic? He once pushed his obsession to the point of traveling to and from Dieppe in the same day in order to sleep in his own bed. Nathé's journeys were part of family legend.

Once the meal was over, Eugénie served coffee out in the garden, on the wrought-iron table in the shade of the chestnut tree. Adrien, exhausted by the week's work, slipped away to take a nap. Nathé poured himself a little glass of cognac, to his wife's vexation. Jeanne, having abandoned her book, daydreamed, fanning herself in her wicker chair; Laure worked on her embroidery; Gustave and Léon sat apart on the green bench to smoke. The conversation died down. Only an occasional remark to no one in particular broke the heavy silence that followed summertime meals. The sweet peas close to the doorway looked pale in the midday sun. Around the pond, the pink blossom of the hawthorn was drooping a little. At the neighboring house, owned by a painter named Cot, apple-tree blossoms were starting to scatter. Mauve *Vergiss mein nicht* (forget-me-nots)[18] nestled beneath the white lilacs.

The Weils formed a clan, close and interdependent. They couldn't imagine getting along without one another, sharing joys and hardships alike. Their marriage contracts, their identity papers, their wills offer mounting evidence of this closeness, as if the members of the clan literally bore permanent witness for one another. The cohesion of the group dates back to an era when Jews, separated from mainstream society and its institutions, had no resources outside the family group. The more powerful this group, the greater the individual's protection. The more marriages there were among them, the less their assets were disbursed. The system reached its peak in the richest families: Rothschilds married their own cousins. Alliances took place between clans. The Weils were allied with the Neuburgers, the Berncastels with the Anspachs. Each newcomer was absorbed by the clan. Adrien's meager provincial family counted for very little beside the numerous, lively, and affectionate Weil relatives. He was assimilated, an in-law. He found his place in the group and maintained good relations with his father-in-law. By marrying Jeanne he had made a tacit agreement that served both his ambition and his peace of mind: to be an "outside ingredient" in the Weil family, yet someone his wife couldn't do without. Jeanne saw her father, her mother, and her brother every day. She never left them and would never leave them.

With her dowry, she might have joined one of the most powerful Israelite dynasties, but in that case she would have shifted from one clan to another. Thanks to her marriage, she entered less into her husband's domain than he did into hers. The usual process was inverted. The family she founded with Adrien developed in the bosom of her own. Auteuil, where both sons were born, was the family cradle.

In 1897, Louis Weil's heirs put his house on the market. It soon disappeared under the pickaxes of the public works developer who bought it, and the new opening onto the avenue Mozart dismembered the garden. It would have been naive not to realize that the site would be used for an apartment building. Later it became a bank, as happened to 102, boulevard Haussmann, Louis's Parisian residence, where his great-nephew Marcel was later to live. A new street, the rue George-Sand, now bordered the former garden, intersecting with the rue La Fontaine across from the rue des Perchamps. With Adèle, Nathé, and Louis no longer living, Georges and Jeanne had sacrificed their childhood memories. Sadly, they bade farewell to Auteuil.

But an echo of those summer days can be heard in the pages of *Jean Santeuil* that gave birth to the most famous passages of *In Search of Lost Time*. Combray is still called Illiers or sometimes Eteuilles. From Auteuil to Eteuilles, from Jeanne to Jean, from *sans*-Auteuil to Santeuil, there's but a small step, years of maturation and crystallization, and pages of writing. We now know that Marcel took "the little wing opening onto the garden that had been built for my parents behind it," "the lively sound of the fountain," the hawthorns, the lilacs, and the pink chestnuts from Auteuil; transported by involuntary memory, they come to life through the madeleines dipped in lime-blossom tea and mingle with images of his visits to Illiers. Other details aren't as clear: the specialists hesitate. Illiers? Auteuil? Each place has its partisans. The roast goose? Probably from Auteuil, since it's a traditional Alsatian dish. The roast lamb and peas? I'd vote for Illiers. But what about the way the cook slaughtered the chicken? There was something very kosher about the way she split the chicken's neck under the ear instead of wringing it.[19] Not to mention the hawthorns, the most sensitive topic of all. By making his memories of Auteuil part of the material for Combray, merging them into his memories of Illiers, Marcel has made them forever vibrant and indivisible.

Rather than resuscitating a place that had disappeared, he preferred to reinvent a house that still existed: the house at Illiers. But part of the magic of Combray comes from Auteuil: the essence of days forever lost; the memory of Mama, splendid in her summer gown; the band of cousins; the hedges; the poplar tree on the rue des Perchamps; the pink chestnuts; the hawthorns in a circle around the pond; and, forever, the stormy nights, "the smell of invisible, enduring lilacs."[20]

And, especially, the infinite sadness of a goodnight kiss . . .

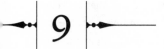

9

The Goodnight Kiss

For the young mother Jeanne, the stages in her sons' upbringing were well laid out. Children had their place in the life of a bourgeois family, but their situation was governed by rules and customs that went unquestioned. Indeed, the children's development could be measured by codified benchmarks: swaddling clothes for the infants, then a gown that made changing diapers easier; bottles, then pureed baby food; around age seven, a boy began to wear short pants instead of dresses, as if to differentiate him from babies and little girls. Before that, his curls would have been cut, another important rite of passage. A boy acquired his individuality by distinguishing himself from all that was feminine. Jeanne saw these stages as progress. Yet her optimism was occasionally mixed with the feeling that she was somehow losing her babies, that in growing older her sons were growing away from her. And while Robert went through his first stages energetically, hastening, like many younger brothers, to catch up with an older male sibling, things were very different for Marcel.

He continued to be beset by mysterious terrors. The fear that someone would pull his hair continued even after his curls had disappeared. He was plagued by recurrent nightmares. Often he would wake up at night and bury his head under the covers to protect himself. What for other children was a simple visit to the barber became, as he later described it, as dramatic as the earth "before or after the fall of Chronos." His hair was cut short, but his dreams always threatened to take him back "into an annihilated world where he lived in fear of having his curls yanked."[21] That fear was tied to the fear of the dark, of solitude, of abandonment—nighttime feelings that made going to sleep the most painful part of his day. At night, Marcel sank into primordial anguish. "But his childhood struggled desperately at the bottom of a well of wretchedness from which nothing could release him," he wrote of his character Jean Santeuil, adding that the pains of childhood are the worst of all because we don't understand their causes.[22] This sadness "inseparable from himself" didn't prevent him from experiencing joy. But it explains his constant need for his mother, the only person capable of helping him deal with that anguish.

Jeanne at first tried to reassure her emotional child, showering him with affection, kisses, and comforting words. When he was sick, she stayed at his bedside and read to him for hours. Her voice calmed him, and he could fall asleep peacefully in her presence. But the child wasn't sick all the time, and there was a little brother who also wanted Mama's attention; Marcel was growing up and needed to be "reasonable."

When I was still a child, no other character in sacred history seemed to me to have such a wretched fate as Noah, because of the flood which kept him trapped in the ark for forty days. Later on, I was often ill, and for days on end I too was forced to stay in the "ark." Then I realized that Noah was never able to see the world so clearly as from the ark, despite its being closed and the fact that it was night on earth. When my convalescence began, my mother, who had not left me, and would even, at nighttime, remain by my side, "opened the window of the ark," and went out. But, like the dove, "she came back in the evening." Then I was altogether cured, and like the dove "she returned not again." I had to start to live once more, to turn away from myself, to listen to words harder than those my mother spoke; what was more, even her words, perpetually gentle until then, were no longer the same.[23]

Although this passage from Marcel Proust's first book, *Pleasures and Days*, probably refers to a somewhat later period in his childhood, it gives us a good overall sense of the relationship between Jeanne and her son, his efforts at separation and periods of regression, and his return to the curved hull of the ark, a magical maternal universe unto itself, drifting in the perpetual night of the unconscious.

Jeanne realized that her son's demands were becoming more and more difficult to satisfy. Giving in wasn't doing him any good. There was something excessive about his fits of tears, about his fervent kisses and the way he stayed glued to her—she saw this clearly. Nathé, whose principles were strict, criticized her weakness. Adrien accused her of turning Marcel into a girl. He's a boy, for God's sake! "We don't want to mollycoddle him [. . .]. My husband and I are so anxious that he should grow up to be a manly little fellow," says Madame Santeuil.[24] Something about her use of "we" doesn't ring true. What's more, on the very next page of *Jean Santeuil*, she renounces those principles.

They had to be tougher, stricter with schedules, and had to stop putting up with Marcel's flights of fancy, Dr. Proust believed. But bringing up children was a woman's job. Adrien Proust wanted tranquillity when he got home from work. He involved himself with his sons only incidentally, in crises or when his peace of mind was threatened. Like many fathers, no doubt, he saw only a small part of things because he was rarely at home, and when he was there, his wife avoided tiring him with household details.

It was up to Jeanne to educate Marcel in the literal sense: to "lead him out" of this well of wretchedness, out of his frantic dependence. How could she not have been divided between her love for her child and the need to help him grow, to help him get through those time-honored stages that would make him a man? She believed that only willpower would allow him to overcome his own nervous disposition. They needed to develop his willpower. Take heart, little wolf, courage! But it also took all her strength not to give in to him, to resist the fits of weeping that tore at her heart, not to let herself be locked in a prison of passionate love. How should she set limits when he was asking for the fourth, fifth, or tenth time for a kiss she had already given him? When he clung to her just as she was leaving his room? When he squirmed on his bed and screamed so loudly that he was bound to wake his little brother, sleeping in the next room? When he stared at her with his big black eyes, so like hers? A part of her wanted to detach him from herself, and she knew she must; another part responded with all her strength to this swallowing up, and she drowned with him in this seamless love, continuing to nourish him from the umbilical cord that made her live according to his rhythms, made her watch over him, guide him, direct him.

We can't understand Jeanne unless we recognize an ambivalence that she would never entirely master. Mother and son were united by a complex bond that the years would only tighten, making any separation impossible. Jeanne's life was a long struggle to put a little distance between herself and her son, to render him capable of living without her—yet she was unable to detach herself, anxiety being the very ground of her love for him. A few months after Jeanne's death, Marcel wrote these revealing words to Maurice Barrès:

> Our entire life has been but a preparation, hers to teach me how to manage without her when the time came for her to leave me, and so it has been ever since childhood, when she refused to come back over and over again to say goodnight to me before going out for the evening, when she left me in the country and I watched the train take her away, and, later on, at Fontainebleau, and even this summer when she went to Saint-Cloud, I would find any excuse to telephone her—at all hours of the day. Those fears, which could be defused by a few words spoken over the telephone, or by her visiting Paris, or by a kiss, how powerfully they afflict me now when I know that nothing can ever allay them. And for my part, I often tried to persuade her that I could live quite well without her.[25]

"Our entire life," wrote Marcel. How could he have said it better? This "training" started in his childhood and didn't stop until Jeanne's death. She died with this worry, believing him even more vulnerable, even less able to cope with life, than he actually was. In the same letter, Marcel, in response to a remark by Barrès, denied being the person his mother loved best: "It was my father, though she loved me infinitely all the same." It would be a mistake not to take these words literally. They set out admirably the terms of what must have been his mother's dilemma (and his own, of course): "But while I wasn't in the strict sense the person she loved best, and the idea of *having a preference among her duties* would have made her feel guilty, and it would have hurt her to see me draw inferences where she didn't want them, she did love me a hundred times too much."[26]

All the elements of what must have been Jeanne's dilemma are here: a woman caught between her duties as a wife and as a mother. But is "duty" the right word? Wouldn't it be more accurate simply to say "love"? Jeanne Proust: a hostage to love, caught between a son who was too demanding and a husband who didn't demand enough.

———•···•———

Sleep was the moment where the impossible separation was most intense. On five different occasions, Marcel Proust put words to the goodnight kiss.[27] As time passed, he elaborated the scene, enriching it with notations, parentheses, metaphors, characters; it became ever more fictional, filled with a deep truth that the novelist gathered from the sources of memory. This truth didn't lie in biographical details but in the essence of a lived experience, which he captured with increasing success. By juxtaposing these fictional transpositions, combining them, mixing them together, noting their differences and their similarities, we can approximate what must have been the mother's perception and behavior, without losing sight of the fact that these texts reflect Marcel's own vision, refracted by the act of creation. But this vision is crucial. It reveals the texture of a conflict that was as much the mother's as the son's. And in the story of this conflict, the most intriguing character may not be the one we expect.

———•···•———

When her sons were little, Jeanne, like many mothers, would go to their bedrooms and kiss them goodnight. The goodnight kiss, being tucked in, the candle blown out (or the light turned off) is a ritual for children throughout the world, including babies like Robert who fall asleep peacefully as soon as they close their eyes. For Marcel, the kiss was much more than a gesture of love or comfort. It was the life force that allowed him to face the evil powers of the night and overcome his fear of death, "the tender offering of cakes which the Greeks fastened about the necks of wives or friends, before laying them in the tomb, that they might accomplish without terror the subterranean journey and cross, without hungering, the Kingdom of the Shades."[28] He compared this kiss to the Communion wafer, as though it carried within it the sacred substance of the maternal body. Waiting for the kiss was proportionate to his anguish: incommensurable. Nothing could fill this bottomless well except the presence of his mother, a single, totalizing presence. On some evenings, all Jeanne had to do was bend down and kiss him, and he would calm down and fall asleep. She could then leave quietly and go back to her husband. But at other times she was so susceptible to the violence of her son's need for her that she had to tear herself away from him. To leave him was to abandon him. She tried to reason with him, to make him ashamed. In vain. There were no limits. And because she knew how he suffered in letting her go, she occasionally gave in and gave him another kiss before fleeing.

Even more heartrending were those evenings when guests came for dinner. The children would eat first and come to the table to say goodnight before going upstairs to bed at eight o'clock. Jeanne knew how important the goodnight kiss was for her older son. Sometimes, to have a little more time with his mother, Marcel asked for a walk around the garden before the arrival of the guests. He would follow the path leading to the monkey puzzle tree. Jeanne's garden smock occasionally got caught on one of its branches. The child would tug on her arm, drag his feet, compel her to pull him along, so assiduously was he putting off the fateful moment when he would have to leave her. Adoringly, he would kiss her hand with its fragrance of soap.

But at other times, when the doorbell rang, Nathé, the grandfather, would grumble with "unconscious ferocity" that "the children look tired, they need to go up to bed." Marcel was about to kiss his mother, but Adrien, backing up his father-in-law, would urge: "Yes, go on now, up to bed with you; you've already said goodnight to each other as it is; these demonstrations are ridiculous!" Jeanne said nothing. She let the children go, and went to greet her guest—in *Jean Santeuil* it was a physician, Dr. Surlande; in *In Search of Lost Time* it was Swann. She fulfilled her role as mistress of the house.

One night in July 1878, in Auteuil, surrounded by the scent of rose bushes, the family was eating at the garden table—lobster, salad, pistachio and coffee-flavored ice cream, and chocolate cookies. The butler passed around the finger bowls, then the coffee. The children were upstairs. From time to time, Jeanne looked up at Marcel's window. His candle was out, so he must be asleep. But he couldn't be. Her suspicion was well grounded. Soon the window lit up. And here we have two versions: first the one in *Jean Santeuil*, the simpler of the two, the one that frames the narrative. Then the story in *Swann's Way*.

The child tries to convince Augustin to take a note to his mother. Augustin refuses to bother her. Madame Santeuil happens to be giving Dr. Surlande an outline of her educational theories and her plans for her son's future—whatever he might become, let him not be a genius—when a little blond head appears: "Mama, I want you for a moment." A moment! Madame Santeuil rises, excuses herself, and, despite the protests of her father, goes upstairs to her son, with her husband's support: "If she doesn't go up, he'll never get to sleep and we'll be a lot more disturbed in an hour's time." She kisses Jean, who calms down, but when she's about to go downstairs to rejoin the company, he bursts into tears, in total despair. Annoyed, but resigned, the mother sits down at his bedside, abandoning her principles and any hope of seeing him master his emotional outbursts. Jean "doesn't know what's the matter with him, or what he wants," she explains to Augustin. By relieving the child of responsibility for the state he's in, she makes him incapable of overcoming his nervous condition. He has turned into a sickly child. She has lost. She knows it.

In the much more elaborate version in *Swann's Way*, other elements come into play. Françoise, the maid, slips a message to Mama, who refuses to give in. "Tell him there's no answer." After dinner, coffee is served outdoors, in the moonlight. When Swann has left, the parents exchange a few words about the dinner. The wife isn't sleepy; the husband goes upstairs to undress. She stays downstairs, bides her time, pushes open the green lattice door that leads from the vestibule to the staircase, asks Françoise to help her unhook her bodice. Then she walks upstairs toward the master bedroom, candle in hand. She has scarcely reached the landing when an apparition throws itself upon her, a little boy who will be seven in two days, not quite the age of reason. Her surprise gives way to anger. "Go to bed." The dramatic tension reaches its climax when the father in turn appears at the stairwell, a quasi-Prudhommesque, quasi-biblical figure in his nightshirt and the pink and violet Indian cashmere shawl that he ties around his head to prevent neuralgia. Panic. Then comes the child's attempt at manipulation: he virtually blackmails his mother so that she will follow him into his room. But she snaps at him: "Run, run!"

It's the father who turns the situation on its head. Although he is supposed to be the tougher of the two, he now suggests that the mother go in with her son. She protests timidly, in the name of her principles. We can't let him get into the habit. But the father goes even further: "There are two beds in his room; go tell Françoise to prepare the big one for you and sleep there with him tonight." And he adds, as a parting shot: "Now then, goodnight, I'm not as high-strung as the two of you, I'm going to bed."[29] In using the plural, "the two of you," he equates mother and son as fragile beings of the same type.

By introducing the father into the story, giving him a major role, Proust restores Adrien's role in the relationship that united Marcel to his mother. If this scene represents the failure of the rite of passage that should have enabled him to go to sleep like a big boy—like a man?—it is because his father gave up on him, didn't force him to surmount his fears. The father's sudden indulgence is an abandonment or a sign of indifference. My mother and my grandmother, wrote Marcel, "loved me enough not to consent to spare me my suffering, they wanted to teach me to master it in order to reduce my nervous sensitivity and strengthen my will."[30]

We're struck by the mother's passivity, her docility. Torn between the desire to strengthen her son—a role that should have been the father's—and submission to her husband's will, she obeys her husband. Proust compares his father to "Abraham [telling] Sarah she must leave Isaac's side."[31] There he confuses—perhaps deliberately—Sarah, the lawful wife, with Hagar, the servant with whom the patriarch had a son, Ishmael. This slip allows Proust to make his point: the father sends his wife to his son's side, just as Abraham sent Hagar into the desert with Ishmael. By opening the door to Marcel's room, the father closes his own: "Now then, goodnight, [. . .] I'm going to bed."

This is why the scene seems to me to reveal the complexity of everything at play between Jeanne, Adrien, and their son, beyond the novel. Could it be that she was so much a mother because they were no longer fully husband and wife? The question is worth asking.

The narrator's mother—let's call her Jeanne—also gives in to her emotions as she tries to stop her son's crying: "There now my little chick, my little canary, he's going to make his mama as silly as himself if this continues. Look, since you're not sleepy and your mama isn't either, let's not go on upsetting each other, let's do something."[32] Clad in her blue-flowered bathrobe, she sits down at his bedside in the cretonne armchair, holding a book with a reddish cover: George Sand's *François le Champi,* the story—and here we see Proust's genius—of an incestuous love between a child and his adoptive mother. "Sometimes—though rarely—in my childhood I knew the feeling of rest without sorrow, of perfect calm. Never did I know it as on that night. I was so happy that I didn't dare go to sleep," Marcel would write many years later.[33] Finally, he does fall asleep.

When he awakens, his mother's bed is empty. Jeanne has risen quietly, leaving a little note on the table: "When my little wolf wakes up, he should dress quickly, Mama is waiting for him in the garden." The sun is already high in the sky when the shutters are opened. Jeanne looks up and smiles.

The rose bushes and the nasturtium are climbing all along the house up to the window of his room. The gardener is watering the sunflowers. It's a beautiful summer day.

It's generally agreed that the scene of the goodnight kiss crystallizes episodes that must have occurred over and over in different times and places. Significantly, Proust situates the scene just before the child reaches the age of seven. He never would reach the age of reason. Jeanne often read to her son at night. Continually defeated, she finally admitted that Marcel was not responsible for his nervous temperament. But she persisted in battling what she called his "lack of willpower." She never gave up educating him. She knew that one day he'd have to go to sleep without her.

And Robert? Robert slept like an angel.

A Small World

The train slowed as it approached the station. Across the fields, you could already see the steeple of the church and "the woolly gray backs of the gathered houses."[34] "Come, gather up the blankets, we're here!" hollered Adrien, revived by the country air of his native village.[35] Already? Jeanne, for whom distances were always a mystery, was surprised. She was ready in no time. The bags were assembled, the blankets folded, the children dressed. The stationmaster's nasal voice rang out: Illiers! Illiers! Two-minute stop. The compartment door opened directly onto the platform. Gathering her skirts, Jeanne walked down the steps, holding Robert by one hand. Marcel followed. Adrien, who had calmly folded his newspaper, brought up the rear. The trunks were carried down. "Uncle Jules is here, I see him!" shouted Robert. They felt the gusts of an icy wind. Jeanne checked to make sure that Marcel's overcoat was buttoned. Easter fell early that year, in late March.

Arriving on Thursday evening, the travelers hurried toward the horse and buggy that awaited them on the other side of the tracks. It wasn't far from the brand-new station to the rue du Saint-Esprit, where Uncle Jules and his wife Elisabeth lived, but this evening they were delighted not to have to walk. Until 1876, you had to get off the train at Chartres and cover the remaining twenty-five kilometers by carriage. Now you could transfer right from the Paris-Bordeaux line. The carriage took the avenue de la Gare, following the rue de Chartres before crossing the Place du Marché. Adrien's mother, Madame Virginie Proust, could look out onto the market square from her narrow window. But it was too late to visit her, Jeanne decided. The children were tired. Adrien agreed.

Here they were, at the corner of the street, number 4: three steps led up to a slate-colored house. In the hallway, the cook, Ernestine Gallou, was awaiting the Parisians in her stiff, white Breton coiffe. A roaring fire in the living-room hearth welcomed them. Jeanne helped Robert to take off his coat. Marcel looked around, delighted. In the dining room with its dark furniture and stained-glass windows, the round mahogany table was already set. On the sideboard, Uncle Jules had placed a decanter of old wine. Dinner was served early in the provinces. In honor of the Parisians, Ernestine had prepared the kind of celebratory meal usually reserved for Sunday supper: omelet, potatoes, chicken with peas, and smooth, not-too-thick chocolate cream, Adrien's favorite dessert. Adrien went upstairs with Jeanne to greet Aunt Elisabeth. The children would go up the next morning; it was important not to tire her.

Was it the ample meal or the journey? The little ones were rubbing their eyes, and Jeanne too was overcome with fatigue. She went to the kitchen to remind Ernestine that Marcel needed a hot water bottle in his bed, "not just hot water, but boiling, so that he can't bear his hands on it: or that the top end of his bed must be made very high, almost uncomfortable—I'm sure you remember that—so that he can't possibly lie flat even if he wants to, four pillows, if you can spare four; it can't be too high."[36] Ernestine understood. She was the only one, Jeanne claimed, who knew exactly how to prepare a hot water bottle with water that was actually boiling, or how to make truly hot coffee. Her forbidding character was the other side of her perfectionism. And for Madame's Parisian family, her character softened with a thousand attentive gestures, signs of affection that proved her devotion.[37]

Robert could barely make it up the stairs; his eyes were already shut. The rooms had an indefinable provincial charm, exotic from Jeanne's point of view: deep beds, thick with quilts and bedspreads, made up with fine linen sheets and pillow cases; crocheted antimacassars on armchairs upholstered in stamped velvet, drapery in three layers, so thick that it was almost impossible to open the windows. What was strangest to her was the profusion of religious objects, banal for most people but part of a universe foreign to her: the crucifix with its blessed palm for Palm Sunday, the image of the Savior above the dresser, on which, between two vases, a clock in its glass bell and some sea shells were displayed, and the prayer stool she regarded with both suspicion and respect. The address itself, rue du Saint-Esprit (street of the Holy Spirit), gave her the same feeling. Nowhere else did she feel as foreign as in Illiers, especially the first night, when she had to go to bed under the crucifix, breathing the "central, sticky, stale, indigestible and fruity smell of the flowered coverlet,"[38] staring at the floral wallpaper.

After washing the children with the very hot water that Ernestine had poured into the wash bowl to get rid of the grime from the trip, Jeanne handed them their night shirts, which had been warmed in front of the roaring fire in the hearth. Robert had gotten into bed first and was already asleep. She kissed his chubby cheek. Marcel, sensitive to the cold, had just finished undressing when there was a knock at the door: it was Ernestine bringing his hot water bottle—in Illiers they called it a "monk"—and she slipped it into the copper bed with its white curtains. "Pull your nightshirt down so you don't feel the cold on your legs, little wolf," Jeanne advised before bending to kiss him. She pulled the quilt over him. "I'm right next door, sleep well my wolf," she said one last time, taking the candle before closing the door behind her quietly. You could hear Jules downstairs, chatting loudly with his brother-in-law, and Adrien's laughter. Jeanne went to the dressing room and slipped on her bathrobe, shivering. Tomorrow was Good Friday. Her candle in hand, she got into bed, under the crucifix.

It was usually for Easter that the Prousts went to Illiers. They had probably sometimes gone in July, before the children were of school age (since at that time the school vacation began on August 1), and even in September, since classes didn't resume until October 1. As for the famous hawthorns, it's unlikely that Marcel ever saw them bloom in Illiers. Yet scholars and fans of Proust love to make pilgrimages to Illiers during the month of May—proof of the triumph of his fiction over his biography. We know very little for sure about the period and length of his visits. With one exception—during the settlement of his aunt's estate in August 1886—Marcel stopped going to Illiers when he was about twelve or thirteen according to Céleste Albaret, or about nine according to some of his biographers. This imprecision, along with the unforgettable pages of *Swann's Way*, has contributed to making Illiers into the mythical place called Combray. Today, people go to Combray to visit Aunt Léonie's house—which never existed.

Illiers was Adrien Proust's domain. His family was originally from Perche; they'd only settled in Illiers two generations earlier.[19] Most of his ancestors were farmers; others were merchants like Adrien's father, François Valentin Proust, who owned a grocery store on the Place du Marché, across from the church. He sold spices, thread, sugar, clogs, paper, and candles: all the necessities of a small country town. François Proust also supplied the parish with candles, which he made himself. Adrien grew up in an atmosphere where exotic, familiar, and religious aromas were intermingled. Who knows if, in that narrow storefront, his childhood dreams hadn't helped lead him down the roads on which supplies arrived from far away in their jute sacks. His first vocation was not foreign to the family activity: it seems he was planning to become a priest. Was it a vocation or merely the logical path to social mobility for a talented boy brought up in a modest Catholic family? He was a boarder and a scholarship student at the lycée in Chartres and only returned home for vacation. His childhood was anchored in that provincial environment, in the tangible reality of daily life.

Nowhere did Jeanne experience the difference in their backgrounds as much as in Illiers. This was the world that separated her mother-in-law, Virginie Proust, née Torcheux, from her own mother. Markers of social class were loud and clear in the nineteenth century and were intensified by the distinction between Paris and the provinces. The two women had nothing in common. One was a Jewish intellectual who had come of age in the most progressive circles of her society, who had frequented artists and thinkers and had lived with her family at the center of her clan; the other was a widow who, at her husband's death in 1855, bravely took over his business and raised her two children, Adrien and Elisabeth, on her own. She was a village woman, whose only view was the church steeple, directly across from her store; her only distractions were Mass and confession. A photograph shows her standing between Robert and Marcel in their Scottish costumes. Seventy years old in that picture, she still has brown hair. She stares at the camera, looking stubborn and probably ill at ease, her stomach thrust forward, a bonnet on her head, in strange contrast to the little princes whose hands she is holding; she looks more like their maid than their grandmother.

What kind of mother was she? Between her perennially ill daughter and her doctor son, did she feel isolated? For Jeanne, who was so close to her own mother and wrote to her every day when they were separated, Adrien's relationship to his mother was incomprehensible. In the Weil family, even the men, starting with Jeanne's brother Georges, practically worshiped their mother. In the Jewish tradition, filial love was raised to the level of a sacrament. Adrien, on the other hand, acted merely like a son doing his duty. Nothing more. Certainly Virginie could have closed up her shop as soon as her son could afford to provide for her, yet she lived alone in a two-room apartment. Perhaps she held onto this modest lodging in order to be near the Place du Marché, that unrivaled lookout that must have been the envy of her daughter Elisabeth. She had a view onto the side entrance to the church. In just a few steps she could get to Mass, a priceless advantage. This was her world, and she didn't want to change it. Adrien did what was necessary for his mother—strictly necessary. Between the former seminarian and the storekeeper, between the freethinking doctor and the pious widow, communication probably wasn't easy, and affection was far less visible than between Jeanne and her sons. Adrien saw his mother only rarely; she came neither to his wedding nor to his children's baptisms. We know no more about the relationship she eventually had with her son and her daughter-in-law than we do about her initial reaction, as a practicing Catholic, to the news that her son was marrying a Jewish woman. Like Madame Sureau, Madame Santeuil's mother-in-law, Virginie may never have recovered from the election of a radical mayor who refused to raise his hat to the priest: "In times like these, one should be surprised by nothing," Madame Sureau would say. If business was bad or the season wet, she regarded the secular schools as somehow responsible.[40]

Adrien spent his life traveling. But he saw his mother scarcely more than once a year, although Illiers is only 125 kilometers from Paris. How did this celebrated doctor, whose ambitions led him to the highest posts and who enjoyed the company of prominent men and women and heads of state, view his hometown? He probably felt a mix of tenderness and alienation. When his former schoolmates passed him on the street, did they see the son of a former grocer's wife or a wealthy Parisian bourgeois? While Jeanne, despite her marriage, stayed faithful to the world she was born into, Adrien created a gulf from his past. He felt legitimate pride in the distance he had come, thanks to his work. And he remembered with satisfaction that his name appeared on the honor roll at the school at Chartres. Happy to see the landscapes and streets of his childhood, he was conscious that his life was transformed, that he had become someone else. Every year he was delighted to return and relieved to leave again. Faithful to Illiers, to his family—the Amiots always remained in contact with the Prousts—he never renounced his background. But his studies and his marriage had allowed him to leave Illiers. Nothing in the world would make him go back.

"I must not forget that if I were not a professor at the medical school [. . .], you would never have thought of inviting me to preside over this prize ceremony," he once said in a speech at his former school.[41] Was there a slight trace of bitterness here? Perhaps, though it's likely that this positivist (a high-class version of Flaubert's Monsieur Homais)[42] felt less nostalgia than satisfaction—the satisfaction of a deserving former student at the pinnacle of a prestigious career.

We may wonder whether he was as sensitive as Jeanne to the bleakness of the houses built of grayish-black stones, "capped with gables that cast shadows down before them"?[43] Life in Illiers revolved around religion, matins, vespers, Sunday Mass, Corpus Christi processions. Time itself was marked by the ringing of the church bells every quarter hour. On a rainy Good Friday, Jeanne crossed the market to go to Mass. In Illiers, no one would understand if the Amiots' sister-in-law—"you know, the one who married the Proust boy"—didn't attend Mass. In this backwater of nineteenth-century France, anything else was unthinkable. Besides, she had also attended catechism with her sons, worried lest the priest be "a little too exacting," and intervening unapologetically: "I think that will do, Monsieur l'abbé. Don't forget he is only a child."[44]

Mass and catechism were part of her duties as a wife and mother, proof of her adaptation to social rituals and etiquette, signs of her desire to integrate. She was faithful to her commitment: the children would have a Catholic upbringing, if not a Catholic faith. Her indifference to religion allowed her to reconcile that attitude with fidelity to her origins, as though she kept her personal identity on one side and her social obligations on the other. At church, she shared with her mother-in-law the private pew that the priest rented yearly to the Amiot family. Aunt Elisabeth no longer left the house. Adrien didn't accompany his wife to Mass, taking advantage of the male privilege that allowed for abstention. Monsieur Santeuil not only got up late on Sunday morning and read quietly in the living room, but when he went out for a walk, he took a turn onto a path through a farm so as not to cross paths with the parishioners returning from Mass. And Madame was not to stand around talking when it was over because they had to sit down to luncheon at noon if they wanted to eat the leg of lamb medium rare. Jean accompanied his mother: "And, sheltered in the church from rain, where the light entered through windows of red and green and yellow, so that one could not tell at all whether there was rain outside or sunshine, [Marcel] would sit down next to his mother, though without saying 'good morning' since that would not have been good manners in such a place. [. . .] Once in church and seated motionless upon his bench, he could brood at leisure on the joint he had seen delivered to the tamed, industrious flames."[45]

On Good Friday, there was no leg of lamb. They would eat fish. In the Church of Saint-Jacques, immortalized by her son, Jeanne followed the Mass, gazing at her missal. No doubt she knelt along with the other churchgoers and made the sign of the cross, perhaps glancing over at her neighbors to make sure she was doing it right. Did she move her lips to sing Psalm 22 in Latin: "Deus, Deus meus, respice in me: quare me dereliquisti. My God, my God, why hast thou forsaken me?" Who is to say if she hadn't already heard it in Hebrew, "Eli, eli, lama sabacthani . . ."? As for Marcel, far from imagining the sublime descriptions he would later write, he was bored, like all children in church, sitting "motionless on his bench with nothing to think about."[46] No sign yet of Madame de Guermantes, no tapestries of Esther, just the *pater noster*, recited in a low voice, the Latin anthems and interminable readings, which he listened to with half an ear, dreaming perhaps about luncheon (brill and cardoons with marrow, or gudgeon—caught that day by his cousins—with spinach?). Without knowing it, the little boy was soaking up the atmosphere of the provinces and stocking the material for his future work of art. The church at Illiers, being the only church he went to, once or twice a year, was all the more imprinted in his mind.

What was Jeanne thinking about this Good Friday, as she listened to the sonorous voice of the priest, speaking in French, according to the missal, from his high pulpit?

— *You are familiar with this assembly of wicked men, the Jews. And this crowd of those who do evil. What kind of evil? They wanted to kill our Lord Jesus Christ.*

The congregation responded in unison, menacingly:

— *When the Jews had crucified Jesus, shadows covered the entire earth. And near the third hour, Jesus cried out loudly: "My God, why hast thou forsaken me?" His head fell forward and he rendered up his soul . . .*

And the priest started up again:

— *They sharpened their tongues like a sword. Let not the Jews come and say, "We are not the ones who killed Christ" [. . .] You Jews caused his death. How did you cause his death? With the sword of your tongue. Indeed, you sharpened your tongue like a sword. And when did you strike? When you cried out: "Crucify him! Crucify him!"* [47]

You could hear the rain against the stained-glass windows. Jeanne shivered in her spring coat. "Put on your coat or you'll catch cold," she whispered to Marcel, as the organ thundered and they made their way out.[48]

If Adrien and his children were excited about going to Illiers, Jeanne may not have been. For Adrien there was his brother-in-law Jules, with whom he'd always had a good relationship. Jules, a former cloth merchant (like Jeanne's own uncle, Samuel Mayer) owned several houses in Illiers. He also owned a beautiful park, known as the Pré Catelan,[49] on the other side of the Loir, at the end of town, which he generously made accessible to his fellow citizens. From a trip to Algeria to visit his daughter and son-in-law, who were in the wine business, he brought back all kinds of bric-a-brac—photographs of mosques and palm trees, mats, cushions, and rugs; he kept these memorabilia in an office into which he habitually withdrew, ostensibly to accomplish important work but from which he would emerge rubbing his eyes, as if sleep "had overtaken him in his wicker chaise longue, with a hookah within easy reach, just as he was about to start working, or rearranging his photographs."[50] He even had a small steam room, decorated with oriental tiles made in France.[51] Sharing a taste for exotic lands, both Adrien and Jules were freethinkers and anticlerical. Jules was among those to whom Adrien had dedicated his medical school thesis. For his brother-in-law, Jules represented a link to the past. They shared memories. Jules kept Adrien informed about properties for sale, urban renewal projects, changes in the local political scene—Jules later became a deputy mayor—and Adrien thoroughly enjoyed their conversations.

Unfortunately for Jeanne, Jules's spouse was not good company. Always ill, Aunt Elisabeth was confined to her room and lived reclusively. Nothing interested her other than gossip and religion. Her nephew Marcel, who became a recluse himself at the end of his life, portrayed her with relish through the character of Aunt Léonie. We don't know whether Adrien ever gave advice about how to treat his sister's mysterious ailment, or whether he simply gave up, as he was obliged to do in the case of his own son. He probably decided that they were hypochondriacs and that Elisabeth was no sicker than anyone else. Yet she died of an intestinal lesion that was operated on too late, surrounded by her Vichy water, her antacids, and her herbal tea. Jeanne, whom Marcel portrays as being very gracious to the cook, asking after her daughter and so forth, would go upstairs to Aunt Elisabeth's room and visit her briefly. I doubt that the pious old lady allowed her sister-in-law to stay with her for long. What would they have had to say to each other?

Jeanne must have been quite isolated. She may have spent time with one or two neighbors, a few country friends, like Madame Savinien in *Jean Santeuil*, with whom Madame Santeuil chats as they leave Mass. With Adrien she also visited Madame Larcher, on the rue de l'Oiseau fléché: the elite of Illiers gathered in her living room with its solemn tapestries. Madame Goupil, Dr. Galopin's daughter, was known for her regal demeanor and her impassiveness. "Her waxen and hieratic face" is supposed to have inspired the image of Saint Lucy on the stained glass window in the church. It's a good bet that Madame Goupil, who walked by "without an umbrella, in that silk dress she had made for her at Châteaudun" and could well get "properly drenched [. . .] if she has far to go before Vespers,"[52] owed a great deal to Jeanne's sardonic accounts of those visits to Illiers.

The children had their own diversions. Marcel enjoyed reading, day-dreaming in the garden, or fishing with his uncle. The Amiot cousins, much older than Marcel and Robert, were by now too old to play with them. In the morning, Jeanne "attended to her bit of correspondence,"[53] then read in the living room, sitting by the fireplace, while waiting for lunch. Meals were a central activity at Illiers. Ernestine was a magician, whether it was her roast leg of lamb on Easter Sunday, her pot roast, her roast veal on Saturday, the first green peas, round like little green marbles, "chicken smothered in boiling butter,"[54] or the asparagus that the poor scullery maid had to peel at breakneck speed, despite her allergies. Rice *impératrice*, cookies, brioches, apple pie, and chocolate cream concluded these ample meals, and they left the table sleepy, despite the coffee that Uncle Jules prepared himself in a glass contraption he set up on the table, "extremely complicated, because very primitive."[55]

In the afternoon, when the weather was good, the family would go for a long walk, armed with a snack of bread, chocolate, and fruit. Jeanne lent Marcel her umbrella if it was too hot. Sometimes they took along folding chairs, and she set up behind him with a book, while he fished. More often, they went walking right after lunch and came home in time for an afternoon snack. If it was cold, as it was during their vacation in 1880, when Easter fell on March 28, they simply sat in front of the fire and read. There was the year of *Captain Fracasse* and, later, the year of Augustin Thierry's *Norman Conquest of England*. When the moon was shining (there were no street lights in those days), Adrien, for "love of glory," would take his wife and sons for a walk by the Calvary cross, the viaduct, and the station boulevard. Returning, tired out, to the back garden gate, they rang the bell "with its ferruginous, icy, inexhaustible noise," so different from the "oval, golden double tinkling of the little visitors' bell."[56] Jeanne, who had no sense of direction, was amazed each time by her husband's strategic genius. For him, obviously, the streets of Illiers had long ceased to harbor any secrets.

> Suddenly my father would stop us and ask my mother: "Where are we?" Exhausted from walking but proud of him, she would admit tenderly that she had absolutely no idea. [. . .] Then, as if he had taken it out of his jacket pocket along with his key, he would show us the little back gate of our own garden.[57]

But on most evenings they stayed in the house, the adults chatting, the children playing cards. Jeanne, sitting in an armchair, did needlework, her face illuminated by the lamp. Sometimes she suggested a game of checkers to Marcel. And once in a while, to the children's great joy, they set up the magic lantern in Marcel's room before dinner. They would push the desk against the door, bring in chairs from Jeanne's room, draw the curtains, and replace the lampshade with a magic lantern. Bluebeard, Geneviève de Brabant, and Golo the traitor retained for Marcel the inimitable flavor of a part of his life that only writing could restore. Was Jeanne aware of what a profound impression these visits made on her son?

Conversation centered on the weather—Adrien tapped on the barometer every morning and announced his predictions with oracular solemnity—the dinner menu, and neighborhood gossip. For Jeanne, time passed very slowly at Illiers. While glad to see family members come together, she missed her parents and her brother, their discussions, their arguments, their conversations about books and painting, the sound of her mother playing the piano. Illiers was a sweet but slightly boring exile.

Sometimes, then, she went home a little early, taking the younger child with her and leaving Marcel with his father at Illiers. At least we infer as much from a story Proust wrote entitled "Robert and the Goat," one of only two texts in which he gives a role to his brother.[58] On that day, according to the story, Jeanne has planned to visit a friend, Madame Z, by train, taking five-and-a-half-year-old Robert along with her. Marcel and Adrien are to join them later, and they will all return to Paris together. When he wakes up that morning, Marcel, never lacking in sensitivity, figures out from his mother's first words to him that she's about to leave him: "Leonidas always put on a good face even in the greatest catastrophes . . . I hope my little canary will be worthy of Leonidas," which admittedly is enough to alarm any child (if he knows who Leonidas is: let's not forget that Marcel is only seven and a half). "You're leaving," he responds in a despairing tone. But he holds himself together, and the essence of his despair is transferred onto the character of Robert. At this age, Robert too is experiencing the drama of separation, but in his case it is separation from a baby goat that had become his companion. Of course it is impossible to take the little goat to Paris. The parents therefore arrange to leave it with some neighboring farmers. Little Robert is described throughout the text in rather derisive terms: his hair is "curled like the concierge's children when they're about to be photographed, his chubby face framed by a helmet of thick black hair decorated with big bows like the butterflies in one of Velasquez's infantas"; later, in his little holiday dress and lace skirt, he is likened to "a princess in some pompous melancholy tragedy," and then to Phaedra, sagging under the weight of her vain ornaments. Although Proust claims that he looked at Robert "with the smile of an older child for a brother he loves, a smile in which one does not really know whether there is more admiration, ironic superiority or affection," his smile seems tainted with a certain smugness.[59]

But Robert can't be found. Has he hidden, in revenge, hoping to make Mama miss the train? They look for him everywhere and eventually find him confiding in his little goat, expressing his sorrow in a speech worthy of a tragic heroine. Between sobs, he even manages to sing a song he's heard from his mother: "Adieu, strange voices call me far from you, peaceful sister of the angels." High culture for a five-year-old. Then, losing his temper and shrieking, he starts to break his toys, untie his bows, and tear "his beautiful oriental dress." Jeanne moves toward him, but he escapes and ends up sitting on the train track to defy her. A train could come by at any moment. "Mama, crazed with fear, leaped toward him, but as hard as she pulled, with an unbelievable force on his behind, on which he was accustomed, in better days, to sliding and running about the garden singing, he adhered to the tracks." Fortunately, at that very moment, the father arrives, and with two slaps, removes Robert from the train tracks. So much for efficiency! "I'll never let you use my goat cart again," declares Robert before retreating into silence— which suggests, incidentally, that Adrien did occasionally play with his sons.

Marcel, as the older brother, takes advantage of the situation to look good with Mama, showing himself worthy of her confidence: "Since you're older, be reasonable, please, don't look too sad when I go, your father is already annoyed about it, let's not let him be annoyed with both of us." Jeanne, as always, is caught between the demands of the men in her life.

They sit down to eat, "a full lunch with hors d'oeuvres, chicken, salad, and dessert." Robert, still not saying a word, is perched on his high chair, "alone with his sorrow." The others talk about this and that until interrupted by a piercing cry: "Marcel got more chocolate cream than I did!" Those words ring true. They describe a common relationship among brothers: the endless quest for justice. Marcel, in general, may well have received larger portions of chocolate cream, despite Jeanne's attempt at equity. But on that day, after all, Robert has the peerless privilege of accompanying their mother while Marcel has to stay on the platform. For a brief moment, Marcel imagines he will set fire to the house to put off her departure. He kisses his mother as much as he can, that is, less than he wants to. Finally they leave for the train station at Chartres. Jeanne watches her son's face fall apart as they approach. She squeezes his hand, her way of telling him to be strong. Such tests are part of her schooling him in willpower.

She boards the train. Calling on the ancients, once again, for assistance, she quotes—not without a little smile—Regulus, who remained astonishingly "steadfast in the most painful circumstances." Again, we wonder if this was the best way of reassuring Marcel. But Jeanne knew there was nothing Roman about her son (and certainly nothing Spartan). When Adrien walks away, she takes the opportunity to call out to Marcel a second time and whisper to him: "We understand one another, my wolf, don't we? Tomorrow, my little boy will get a letter from his Mama, if he's good. *Sursum corda*—lift up your heart!"—she adds in a last attempt as the train pulls away, leaving her little man at a loss, as though a part of him has departed also.

A long time later, Marcel confided in Jeanne his despair that day. She asked him:

> "What would you have done if your Mama had been traveling?"
> "Time would have passed slowly."
> "What if I had been gone for months, for years, for . . ."

"We both fell silent," Marcel Proust adds:

> "For us it was never about proving that one of us loved the other more than anyone else in the world: we never doubted that. It was about allow-

ing ourselves to believe that we loved each other less than it seemed and that life would be tolerable to the one of us who would be left alone."[60]

That is probably why the story of the goat associates the theme of separation with the little brother. To be loved more than anything in the world—this is what the older son asked of Jeanne. A tyranny of love that the passing years only amplified.

———•••••———

Eventually, the Proust family stopped going to Illiers. Adrien would return by himself to his childhood home. They said it was because of Marcel's asthma, even though in cold weather, as his mother would remind him, Illiers was always beneficial.[61] Years later, Céleste Albaret reported these remarks of Marcel's, proof of the kind of conjugal arrangements that make for a stable couple, if not a happy one:

> Father adored Illiers, and Mother was not the sort of woman to stand in the way. She went because she loved him too much to let him think for a moment that it bored her, still less that she disliked going at all. But he loved her too much not to suspect the truth, though he didn't let on. So one year the air at Illiers suddenly became very bad for my asthma. Father said so, and we didn't go there again.[62]

Mistress of the House

In the twenty-first century, the noise on the boulevard Malesherbes is end-less. Only red lights slow the delivery trucks, the taxis, the buses, the motor-cycles, and the cars as they move along the two-lane thoroughfare that goes all the way from the Porte d'Asnières, on the northwest edge of the city, to the Place de la Madeleine. An engraving shows this same boulevard at the beginning of the Third Republic. What a contrast! The entire lane is open, pedestrians stroll peacefully; a few carriages, equestrians, nurses accompa-nying children, couples. With its plane trees and its Morris Column,[63] the boulevard was both an urban space and a green space. It's easy to understand why Dr. Proust wanted his family to live there. The apartment building it-self, typical of Haussman-style construction, corresponded to the criteria for top-class dwellings according to the architects of the period:[64] double expo-sure, with windows looking over both the courtyard and the street, a luxurious facade, a generous portico leading to an interior courtyard, a vestibule with gold trim, a main staircase in stone, and a back staircase for servants. Another feature: the presence of a concierge, once reserved only for hotels. Gleaming copper, thick red carpets, the smell of fresh wax. The Prousts' apartment was at the back of the courtyard, on the first floor to the left. Eppler's glassed-in tailor's shop was located in the interior of the building; Marcel and Robert could see it from their rooms. Proust metamorphosed it into Jupien's workshop. But the building, unlike the one described by the narrator of *In Search of Lost Time* ("It was one of those old houses, some of which may still exist"),[65] was new: the public health doctor was insistent that his family benefit from modern conveniences and comforts: running water, gaslight, and gas stoves. Of course, there was no electricity nor central heating, and there was but a single, rather primitive WC with a toilet that didn't flush but was equipped with a board for writing, and two narrow wash-rooms without windows. It wasn't until the beginning of the twentieth century that modern hygiene made its appearance in French homes.

The Prousts lived in this huge apartment from 1873 until 1900. One entered through a fairly large vestibule (though smaller than the one at 45, rue de Courcelles, the luxurious apartment that the Proust family occupied subsequently, of which the entryway, wood-paneled and hung with tapestries, was Jeanne's pride and joy). The children's rooms were at the opposite end of the apartment from the parents, and a long corridor separated the kitchen from the dining room. As in most bourgeois dwellings, the kitchen and pantry were placed as far as possible from the living and sleeping rooms to avoid the odors and the smoke from the stove and to reduce contact between domestics and their employers. Between the dining room and the anteroom, a hatch had been installed that also served as a hot plate, thanks to a small stove, so the butler could serve food and keep the dishes warm without leaving the room. From details such as this, we get a sense of the quality of life enjoyed by the Prousts. On days when they had company and were not using gas heat, rather than lighting a wood fire they burned nuggets of coal in one of the salamanders that hung in the large fireplaces. Radiators and hot-air vents were installed at the rue de Courcelles. Lighting came from torches or candelabras, kerosene lamps or gas jets.[66] The quiet rhythm of the street outside and the soft lighting inside made for a subdued atmosphere.

Those who visited the apartment agreed that the decor lacked elegance. "The impression I had [. . .] was of a rather dark interior, packed with heavy furniture and thick curtains, smothered in rugs, everything black and red, the typical apartment for those days, not as distant as we thought from the dark bric-à-brac you see in Balzac novels," wrote Fernand Gregh.[67]

His memory didn't fail him, for in the period he mentions, Jeanne had inherited some red plush armchairs, a mirrored armoire of Brazilian rosewood with bronze streaks, and an old desk that had been at her Berncastel grandparents' place. The decor was luxurious but unrefined—Second Empire furniture, papered walls, velvet armchairs, huge ornate mirrors above the fireplaces, pedestal tables, Chinese screens, a pink marble slab perched on gilded hoofs, a Far Eastern piece with metal appliqué, along with green houseplants, Barbedienne bronzes, clocks, Chinese vases, and crystal bowls. In the living room, on the large Persian rug that Adrien had acquired on his travels, a round table, draped in heavy fabric, and a couch stood next to Jeanne's grand piano. Portraits of the heads of the household adorned the walls. Dr. Proust's study, its walls hung with tapestries, was adjacent to the living room and the master bedroom. Those three rooms looked out onto the rue de Surène, perpendicular to the boulevard Malesherbes. The center of family life, however, was the dining room. There the children did their homework on the large table covered in red felt, and recited their lessons to their mother. There, too, his back to the hearth, Marcel worked on his notebooks, enjoying the light from the Carcel lamp.

Through inheritance, Adrien's travels, various acquisitions and gifts, the furnishings increased, but nothing matched; there was no attempt at harmony or attention to taste. Roger-Henri Guerrand has remarked: "As the century progressed, bourgeois apartments became more and more like antique shops. Accumulation seems to have been the only guiding principle of interior design."[68]

Wallpaper, tapestries, rugs, and cushions covered every available bare space, making a safe, cozy nest, which, according to the historian Adeline Daumard, gave people a sense of protection from the outside world, perceived as dangerous since the insurrections of 1848 and 1871. There was no plan or general theme, but rather an approach based on sentiment rather than on aesthetics. While characteristic of the era and of a social milieu, this approach was dominant in the Proust family. They loved objects because they had belonged to or had been presented by those who were dear to them. Marcel spoke of his maternal great-grandparents' desk as a "very ugly old friend but one who has known everything I've loved most."[69] When she received her inheritance from Louis Weil, Jeanne put up the blue satin curtains from Auteuil in her room on the rue de Courcelles, as well as a large chandelier in the form of a blue bowl, and furniture and globe-shaped candelabras in the same color. In the armoires, sachets of Houbigant perfume left their scent. After Jeanne's death, those same objects moved to Marcel's room on the boulevard Haussmann, along with her needlework table, her dresser, and the rosewood armoire, which Marcel kept locked. Later, when Céleste Albaret unlocked it, she found a box of Valencienne lace handkerchiefs, monogrammed "J.P."

In the presence of Jeanne and Adrien Proust, Oscar Wilde is supposed to have sneered, "How ugly your house is!" before turning his back to them. Marcel gave the line to Charlus, "with a mixture of wit, insolence, and taste."[70] The first time Emile Straus paid the Prousts a visit, Marcel tells us, the lawyer looked in vain for an object he could admire in "our parlor whose ugliness was completely medical but which I find, in retrospect, more touching than many things of beauty, where bronzes, ferns, plush upholstery and mahogany had their respective roles."[71] Straus finally uncovered a little drawing by Henry Monnier, a gift from Caran d'Ache to Adrien, his doctor. How nice, how nice, he kept saying, relieved to have finally found something pleasant to say! But those were judgments from aesthetes and socialites, showing their disdain for bourgeois taste. Taste, after all, is eminently cultural and social. Perhaps the Prousts' interior decoration reflected Jeanne and Adrien's origins, which in both cases lacked an inherited tradition of "good taste" or refinement. It corresponded to the stereotype of bourgeois decor as conceived at the start of the Third Republic, modified by a certain austerity and habits of thrift that came as much from "40 bis" as from the grocery at Illiers. "Nothing flashy. A great deal of modesty. A very puritanical style," confirmed Emmanuel Berl, who was related to the Weil family on his mother's side.[72] That simplicity evolved with Dr. Proust's career.

In the Third Republic, the mistress of the house reached the high point of her reign. Dozens of guidebooks advised and celebrated her: "Like the mechanic at the opera, she controls everything that happens yet no one sees her doing it."[73] The ambiguity of this role, both secondary and primordial, essential and invisible, is perfectly illustrated by Jeanne Proust. She ran her household with the ardor and desire for perfection that many women today direct toward a successful career. Never did she question the role, finding in it an outlet that her intellectual, moral and artistic attributes, her culture and energy, might have sought elsewhere.

"Her name never figured among those women who were presidents, vice-presidents, or patronesses of charitable organizations. Never once had she signed any public appeal, nor even tended the sick in any hospital."[74] Rather, it was in the service of "the obscure field of family life," of her husband's career, of her sons' future, that she applied her skills, taking from her love for them the justification of her own existence. She betrayed not the least trace of bitterness, of regret for another possible life.

> Nor later had Madame Santeuil made any attempt to rouse Monsieur Santeuil to the level of her own ideals, but had confirmed her efforts to being as useful and as sweet to him as possible—giving dinners when he wanted her to, seeing that the strawberry *mousse* was made exactly as his friend Dester liked it, so that he should beg to be invited again, and later, when Monsieur Santeuil got easily tired, sitting by him of an evening reading aloud the books he found amusing, and writing letters for him.[75]

We have to admit that this supremely intelligent woman had no other ambition than the happiness of her loved ones. She wouldn't have conceived of her role as sacrificial, but let's hope there were some secondary benefits. To understand Jeanne, we must put aside our twenty-first-century feminist values.

The day started early. Jeanne was the first to rise, and the servants knew that breakfast did not escape her vigilance. The coffee was prepared according to draconian rules, a ritual that, for her son, verged on an obsession. It may have been a family tradition, for Jeanne's brother Georges followed the same rules. Might the complicated coffee machine described in *Jean Santeuil* have been taken from Louis Weil rather than Jules Amiot? It's possible. Coffee beans and filters came from Corcellet, but were purchased on the rue de Lévis from a shop where the coffee was freshly ground. Milk was delivered every morning from the creamery. It was accompanied by fresh bread or rusks, and jams from Tanrade's on the rue de Sèze, where syrups were also purchased. After waking the children and supervising their dressing—when they were little, they had a maid, Louise, who said of Marcel: "I don't know where that child can have picked it all up"—and making sure her husband had everything he needed before leaving for the hospital,[76] Jeanne instructed the servants, going over the menus and tasks for the day. With time, running the household grew more complex. But from the beginning, there was a cook, a chambermaid, a valet, and occasionally a coachman. This was the basic staff for a bourgeois household. For parties, they hired additional servants. Félicie Fitau, who worked many years for Jeanne, was one of the models (with Ernestine Gallou and Céline Cottin) for the character of Françoise, the cook in *In Search of Lost Time*. Tall and thin, she sometimes dressed in her regional costume when she went out: "Like Michelangelo spending eight months in the mountains of Carrara, selecting the most perfect blocks of marble for the tomb of Pope Julius II, Françoise [. . .] had been down to Les Halles in person more than once to choose the finest slabs of rump steak, the best shin of beef and calf's foot."[77]

Félicie's beef in aspic has entered literary history thanks to the little boy whose eyes were bigger than his stomach and whose pen was more delicate than his palate.[78] Like all children, he loved a *croque-monsieur* (a grilled-cheese-and-ham sandwich) and French fries, but later he could peerlessly describe a pineapple salad with truffles. The very model of the devoted servant, Félicie stayed to work for Marcel after his parents' death, and didn't leave him until the arrival of Nicolas and Céline Cottin, who would be succeeded by Céleste. The cook was the key servant in a household. It was she who fed the family, she on whom the reputation of the mistress of the house depended, in an era where meals played such a major role in social life. The cook had assistants who obeyed her, and her temper was often as hot as her oven.

Félicie, "like Vulcan at his forge, would be stoking up the fire raking the glowing coals with an iron tringle, in an atmosphere of flame, and heat, and crackling which sounded like the mutterings of Hell,"[79] wrote Marcel in *Jean Santeuil*, comparing her thick hands to those of certain sculptors, from which masterpieces emerged. With Félicie, the Michelangelo of cooking, Jeanne's own authority—she was the mistress—as well as her diplomacy were put to the test. Nothing escaped Madame Proust, and though she was "sweetness itself, when she said something she meant it."[80] She could be very strict and even demanding. Everything had to be perfect. She personally supervised both the cleanliness of the house and the work going on in the kitchen, including whatever was simmering on the stove. An anecdote recounted by Céleste Albaret demonstrates the necessarily ambivalent relations between servant and mistress. One day, a burning hot casserole was on the stove. Félicie took the pot holder off the lid and said to Nicolas, the valet, "When Madame comes—we know her—she won't be able to resist taking the lid off." Madame Proust arrived, "gave one look, then said to Félicie: 'Would you mind taking the lid off that casserole for me, please?'"[81]

In contrast to the stability of the cook was the ballet of the chambermaids—younger women, likely to marry, return to their provinces, or be dismissed. Eugénie, Catherine, Gabrielle, and Marie were just a few of them. Jeanne brought one of Félicie's nieces to work for her at the hotel in Trouville, adding a cook and a helper if she rented a house. A charmer called Marie who gave Monsieur Marcel a red quilt was given leave, suspected of being a bit too pleasing (to Marcel alone?). Another chambermaid, more elegant than Jeanne but smelling of wine, attacked her mistress when threatened with dismissal, and turned out to be a dangerous fugitive murderer. And you needed to trust them because they came into the most intimate contact with the family, like Catherine, "to whom," Jeanne wrote to Marcel, "nothing that belongs to us is unknown" and who "led me straight to the drawer of your little table, with which she seemed to me to be on the most familiar terms."[82] As for the valets, Jean Blanc, Arthur, and Nicolas Cottin, their role amounted to opening the door for patients and guests, running certain errands, serving at meals, and helping Monsieur.

The brighter side of Jeanne's close watch over her servants was her concern for them. Proust has his narrator's mother making inquiries about the cook's family problems, and Jeanne's letters show her running out at dawn to buy a blouse for Eugénie, who was succumbing to the heat, or for Philomèle, her parents' chambermaid. On July 14, dinner was served at a quarter to seven "so that the people are free in good time for their festivities," she wrote, with a touch of condescension.[83]

Madame gave her instructions to the people, and the people—in this case, the cook—did the shopping. They only used vendors with the best reputations—Marcel would remain faithful to them after Jeanne's death. Ice cream and petits fours could come only from Rebattet, on the rue du Faubourg-Saint-Honoré; Jeanne insisted they were the best in Paris. "One day when my friend Reynaldo Hahn, the composer, had called to see me," Marcel told Céleste Albaret, "and we were having tea with Mother, Reynaldo began teasing her about her petits fours and said, 'I bet that if I were to bring you some from Potin's instead of from Rebattet's you wouldn't know the difference!' You should have heard Mother! 'All right, my boy. Just try, and then you'll see.'"[84] Snobbishness? Or a social ritual that allowed a group to identify itself through these signs of distinction?

The Prousts' brioches came from the Bourbonneux bakery on the rue de Rome; their chocolate desserts, when they weren't homemade, were from Latinville's on the rue La Boétie; fruit was from Auger's on the boulevard Haussmann. Every week, a man from the laundry, La Maison Bleue, came to pick up the dirty linens and brought back the clean ones, which Jeanne inspected carefully. The rugs were cleaned at La Place Clichy, a department store patronized by Madame Zola. For her own shopping, Jeanne preferred

"Les Trois Quartiers," a more elegant department store and much closer besides. Flowers were purchased at the florist Lemaître, also on the Boulevard Haussmann. All these luxury stores were nearby. Nineteenth-century Paris still had a neighborhood life, which was strengthened by Baron Haussman's horizontal plans for urban renewal (the rich at the center, the poor at the periphery). Favorite shopkeepers and friends were within easy reach. Moving to another neighborhood was practically the equivalent of changing towns.

A well-bred woman did not go out into the street in the morning, the how-to manuals advised. Anyone who might recognize her should pretend not to, for she was probably engaged in some discreet charitable act. Jeanne, with some exceptions (exceptionally hot days, in particular), stayed home. A very light lunch was served precisely at noon.

The afternoon was spent taking walks, making calls, reading. There was a daily outing in the Bois de Boulogne with Madame Félix Faure, the wife of the future president of the French Republic, to whose social niceties we shall return. In the image of women of her milieu, Jeanne had her "at homes," as we see from the postscript of a 1899 letter from Marcel to his mother: "I gave your message to Madame Richtenberger, who left today I think. She didn't ask for anything in Paris, so I didn't have to tell her anything about your at homes, etc."[85] This social institution lasted until 1914, assigning women of high society to their own residence at least one afternoon in the week. The degree of sociability was quite variable, as the work of Marcel Proust shows— and what better example is there? Generally, visitors were received from 3:00 P.M. to about 6:30 P.M.; the visitors stayed for between fifteen minutes and a half hour, both by custom and convenience, since they could visit several houses in the same afternoon. Hostesses and guests talked about books and theater or just gossiped. Jeanne received her guests in the living room. Sometimes she had little Marcel come in, bringing with him "like some scientist without understanding of his science, or a magician, all his picture books about the moon to show how many he had."[86] Jeanne was visibly proud of his precocity and his depth. The passage just quoted from *Jean Santeuil*, backed up by correspondence, is one of the first demonstrations of her maternal pride. It also shows that family life was always a priority for a woman who joked that she had never appreciated gossip until the day that Lucie Faure, daughter of the future French president, told her about Anatole France's esteem for Marcel, while her friend Madame Catusse reported having heard laudatory remarks about Robert.

That Jeanne may have frequented the Deligny swimming pool, near the

Pont de la Concorde, may be surmised from a passage in *Jean Santeuil* in which the child, fascinated, contemplates "seeing his mother splashing and laughing there, blowing him kisses and climbing out again, looking so lovely in her dripping rubber helmet," like a goddess emerging from the waters.[87]

Art being part of a society woman's general culture, Jeanne was a frequent visitor to the Louvre.[88] To Marcel, she wrote:

> At the Louvre?? I saw the Watteau on your behalf and Hahn's, then went to throw myself at the feet of da Vinci and Titian (and all the rest of them!!!). At this time of year the galleries are almost empty in the morning. The only occupants are a few poor old spectacled women, who, despite having perched atop their ladder to see their model closer, don't manage to steal any of her celestial fire.
>
> Then a few Englishwomen, concerned mostly with keeping up with their catalog.[89]

But Jeanne's favorite pastime, to which she devoted long hours, was reading, a passion she shared with the entire Weil family. In Paris, she was a member of Monsieur Delorme's lending library at 80, rue Saint-Lazare. Georges also was a great reader, and never came over without a book. We know, for example, that he lent his sister Théophile Gautier's *Journey to Russia*. And *The Debacle*, Zola's novel about the war of 1870, published in 1892, was passed around from one family member to another, all the way to Uncle Louis. The Weils not only exchanged books but also read passages from journals and newspapers aloud to one another, such as the article by historian Lavisse on the youth of Frederick the Great, or Brunetière's and Fauget's columns in *La Revue des deux mondes*. *Le Figaro*, *Le Journal des Débats*, and *Le Temps* were the starting points for heated conversations. They discussed articles, criticized them, read books that had been recommended to them. Often further along in her reading than her women friends, Jeanne was asked to give her opinion on novels they hadn't read yet. She had to tell Madame Catusse about Loti (whom she loved); she advised her *not* to read him, she reported to Marcel with a touch of irony, because her friend "has nothing but admiration for Bourget's *Le Coeur* and doesn't care for Maupassant."[90] The critics at the time were contrasting Paul Bourget's *Un Coeur de femme*, the archetypical psychological novel, which had appeared in serial form in *Le Figaro*, with *Notre Coeur*, rumored to have been inspired by Maupassant's love for Madame Edouard Kann.

Jeanne's tastes were eclectic, as we can tell from this passage in a letter to her son: "My reading (according to the time of day) varies among Loti, Sévigné, and Musset (*Fantasio, Caprices de Marianne*, etc.). What do you think about that? After Loti I'll start on *Mauprat*."[91]

Her knowledge of English allowed her to quote from Shakespeare's *Richard III* in the original. Unlike Marcel, she also loved the eighteenth century, whether it was Madame du Deffand's *Memoirs*, Goethe's *Wilhelm Meister*, Marivaux's play *The Surprise of Love*, or the works of Voltaire and d'Alembert. One of her favorite books for bedtime reading was the *Memoirs* of Madame de Rémusat, with whom she felt "a cordial intimacy." "I see no reason to treat women less seriously than men," wrote Rémusat, an aristocrat whose father was guillotined in 1794 and who recommended that education be based on reason and enlightened religion.

The similarities between Claire de Rémusat and Jeanne Proust are striking. A voluptuous brunette like Jeanne, Claire was married young to a man seventeen years older than she, Napoleon's right-hand man, whose title was "first chamberlain to the court of Napoleon" and then prefect. "Happy daughter, happy wife, happy mother," she wrote, arguing that when you confront life's sorrows, "there is always a tight spot to be got through, and after that you feel better than expected."[92] Her own fragile health and an ailing son didn't prevent her from maintaining her serenity and demonstrating an optimistic philosophy that was surprising in a woman whose disposition tended toward melancholy and whose great passion was her son Charles. He "derived from her his qualities alike of heart and mind; he was bound to her by the tie of close similarity of ideas, as we; as by that of filial affection."[93] As she advanced in years, her daughter, Claire, came to resemble her mother more and more, just as Jeanne came to resemble Adèle; but it was with her son that Madame de Rémusat formed an ever-strengthening bond. There's no passion without suffering. Madame de Rémusat never stopped feeling anxious about Charles, never stopped fearing that something bad might happen to him: "What is between us is like nothing else."[94] Jeanne might have said the same thing.

Books were part of Jeanne's mental universe, reflecting a vibrant cultural life that was not just a form of distraction for a socialite. She was typical of a Jewish milieu for which intellectual life was primary and considered superior to any other activity. As Emmanuel Berl would say: "It was a milieu where the mind was developed first and foremost," where "the prestige of the University, of intellectual life, dominated the prestige of money, even among people involved in business and commerce."[95] The transmission of those values was essential. Thus, we see Madame Santeuil attempting to get her son to like Lamartine's *Meditations,* Corneille's *Horace,* and Hugo's *Contemplations.* But he preferred Verlaine.

Culture, appropriate behavior, and cuisine were all elements of the same art: the art of the perfect mistress of the house.

> On things whose rules and principles had been taught to her by her mother, on the way to prepare certain dishes, to play the Beethoven sonatas, and to entertain graciously, she was sure to have a precise idea of perfection and to discern whether others approximated it more or less. For those three things, moreover, perfection was almost the same: it was a kind of simplicity in the means, a kind of sobriety and charm. She rejected with horror the idea that one would put spices in dishes that did not absolutely require them, that one would play the pedals with affectation and excess, that "when receiving" one would depart from perfect naturalness and speak of oneself with exaggeration. At the first mouthful, at the first notes, on receiving a simple message, she would claim to know whether she was dealing with a good cook, a true musician, a well-bred woman [. . .] "It may be that she is a very learned cook, but she cannot fix a beefsteak with potatoes."[96]

These qualities were at one with her caustic wit, her taste for euphemisms, and her refusal to talk about herself.

Jeanne spent the end of each day working on her correspondence and writing her diary. Like all women of her era and milieu, she wrote a great deal. Unfortunately, only an infinitesimal part of those letters has come down to us. And the notebook where she jotted down her favorite quotations and personal thoughts—especially following the deaths of her mother and her husband—is lost.[97]

Dinner was followed by quiet evenings, unless Jeanne and Adrien went out. *Jean Santeuil* gives a somewhat idealized image of these hours en famille. Jeanne would play the piano for her husband (Mozart's *Don Juan; Fidelio,* for which there still exists a copy of her sheet music, and other works by Beethoven, her favorite composer), or sing. She would enliven the evening by vividly recounting her day. She also read aloud, and used to put her husband to sleep by reading him Vigny's poetry. Adrien dozed off, his slippers against the andirons. After all, he had a long workday behind him, and his wife's literary conversation must not have interested him much.

Adrien and Jeanne sometimes went to the theater, and Marcel retained the memory of his young, beautiful mother dressed in a black velvet coat trimmed with braid and lined with cherry-colored satin and ermine.[98] One evening in the fall of 1883, the Prousts attended Meilhac's play, *My Comrade*. As the years advanced, Professor Proust's career meant more and more involvement in high society—dinners, parties, official receptions. Jeanne, in turn, would entertain frequently, fulfilling with grace her role as the model spouse of a leading Parisian doctor.

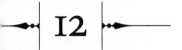

12

The Sickly Child

On a February day in 1880, a crowd had amassed along the route of the funeral cortège and was blocking the entrance to the Montparnasse cemetery.
The hearse, draped in black, was barely visible beneath the mound of bouquets and wreaths. On Adolphe Crémieux's coffin lay his senatorial insig-
nia, his lawyer's gown, and his Freemason's scarf—signs of a lifetime spent
serving justice and the Republic, and his belief in his fellowmen. But those
symbols could not possibly reflect his simplicity, his incredible generosity, or
the fact that his pocketbook and his heart had always been open to all those
in distress. "I have borne only feelings of moderation and fraternal tolerance. The day I'm carried to my grave, there's something I want said about
me as I'm placed in my final resting place. I want it said, 'He was good.'" [99]
It could indeed be said. *Le Journal des Débats* had recalled the previous day
that Senator Crémieux had offered 10,000 francs out of his own pocket—a

colossal sum—to help pay the war debt to Germany and had proposed to open a special bond issue for French Jews: "Let us tell our beloved France," he had urged the Alliance israélite universelle, "behold those you made into citizens; behold the sons of those you adopted in 1871, they are your most devoted children. They have proved it to you in times of combat, they will prove it to you in times of misfortune."[100] At the same time, little Thiers was complaining that the state was giving him only 1,500,000 francs to repair his house, which had been destroyed by the Commune.

The previous day, the Chamber of Deputies, on a motion by the minister of the interior, had decided without debate and almost unanimously that Crémieux's funeral would be funded by the state. Ten thousand francs was budgeted for that purpose. "The government of the Republic is paying back a debt of gratitude and fulfilling a duty of honor in asking you to grant to Adolphe Crémieux the recompense reserved for citizens who have rendered great services to their countries," declared the minister.

Jeanne had been sad to learn of her great-uncle's death. But in truth, everyone had expected it. Destiny had not been kind to him during his final years of life. Gustave, his son, who died in 1872, had been separated from his wife, the soprano Mademoiselle Monbelli (a pseudonym for Marie-Françoise Rabou), and had requested in his will that his only child, Louise, have as her guardian Gustave's own father, his mother, or by default, his sister Mathilde or his brother-in-law, the prefect Alfred Peigné. He had also requested that the courts pronounce the dissolution of his marriage so as not to "stigmatize Louise's future."[101] Four years later, Adolphe was shattered by another death, that of his granddaughter Valentine, stricken with fever two months after her marriage to the painter Lecomte de Nouy. She was twenty-one years old. Amélie, Adolphe's wife, remained his only and eternal source of comfort. Despite their differences regarding Judaism, their love had remained intact. When Amélie died, on January 31, 1880, the old man lay down, never to get up again. He died ten days later.[102]

"Crémieux died a martyr to his love, his conjugal passion. [. . .] The unhappy man would call loudly for his wife. He asked that the objects that had belonged to his dear departed wife be brought to him. He held them to his lips; he then yielded again to his terrible despair, invoking death," wrote one newspaper.[103] The entire press, even the very serious *Journal des Débats*, referred to his passion. It isn't every day that a man of state dies of love.

The pallbearers were Gambetta, Georges Cochery (minister of the post office and telegrams), Jules Ferry, Camille Pelletan, Théodore Cazot (minister of justice), Etienne Arago, and Alphonse de Rothschild. Military honors were rendered by a squadron of the Eighth Regiment of Dragoons, led by its colonel. Great-uncle Adolphe was anything but a warrior, Jeanne thought. But the old lion had been a proud fighter in his fashion, "a man of justice rather than a hero."[104] Walking behind the hearse were Commander Lichtenstein, representing the president of the Republic, then Alfred Peigné, leading the mourners, who included the entire family. Jeanne, pensive on Adrien's arm, followed Adèle and Nathé, dressed in black. Generals, politicians, deputies, senators, financiers: France's elite paid its respects to the first French Israelite to have accumulated so many official honors—three times a deputy, senator for life, twice a member of the government he had even led for a few days. A banner recalled the decree of October 24, 1870, that had granted citizenship to the Jews of Algiers. At the entry to the Jewish section of the cemetery, the chief rabbi of Paris, Zadoc Kahn, halted the cortège and recalled the role of Adolphe Crémieux in the community over the past fifty years.

The hearse, preceded by cantors from every synagogue in Paris, then entered into the cemetery. In front of the house of purification, next to the tomb, the cortège paused once again. Speech followed speech in the dry cold of that February morning. Adrien couldn't help but glance at his watch a couple of times. Crémieux's political life, his career as a lawyer, his Freemasonry (mentioned by his friend Arago), the Alliance israélite universelle, Algeria . . . The chief rabbi movingly evoked his friend's humanity. A Romanian student had the final word, telling how, several days earlier, Crémieux had once again taken up the defense of his people. Jeanne, shivering in her furs, realized with melancholy that a page was turning. The generation of the first Jews born with citizenship was disappearing: Moïse and Godechaux Weil, Merline and Benoît Cohen, her uncles and her aunt, her grandparents Nathan and Rose Berncastel—instinctively, she squeezed her mother's hand and glanced at her. Thank God, Adèle was alive and well! Nathé, too. Georges was looking into space. His uncle Alphonse, in full uniform, stood at attention. Louis responded to the oration with a wink and a feigned sigh. The ceremony was getting long.

"I can imagine only one figure to whom he might be compared," wrote the columnist for the *L'Univers israélite* the day after Purim, "and that is Mordechai, whose name has just resounded in our temples. Yes, my brothers of Israel, when yesterday you heard the glorious testimony in the Bible to the Vizier of Ahasuerus, didn't it seem to you that you were listening to the

funeral oration of the man we have just lost?"[105] Jeanne would not have dis-
avowed this comparison, for she had always seen her uncle Adolphe as the
same kind of person as Esther's uncle.

I can't help but think of Esther when I look at Anaïs Beauvais's portrait of
Jeanne painted that same year.[106] Jeanne was then thirty and at the pinnacle
of her beauty. Her very dark head of hair merges into the background of
the painting, in contrast to her golden face. Black, dreamy eyes with heavy
lids, a sensual mouth, a rounded chin, a generous bust under a gauzy blouse
decorated with wildflowers—everything suggests nobility and a rich inner
life. The strong woman of the Bible? Yes, if you take into account the studied simplicity of her dress, the depth of her gaze, and the natural authority
she exudes. The portrait treats her in the style of the Dutch masters; the
pendant earrings caressing her neck emphasize Jeanne's oriental beauty: a
daughter of Israel, both austere and fulfilled, her charm is timeless. Her elder son would never part with that painting.

Those were happy times for Jeanne. Her husband, named medical director at the Lariboisière hospital, had been elected to the Academy of
Medicine two years earlier. He is immortalized in a portrait by Lecomte
de Nouy, clad in a Greek toga, pen in hand. The children were growing up,
going to school. According to Robert Dreyfus, Marcel was sent to the Pape-
Carpantier primary school. Should we see in this decision a desire to make
him a little more independent, to detach him from a mother whose absence
he still couldn't bear, even at his age? The least separation overwhelmed him.
At sixteen, he still had to choke back tears when she went away. Nothing really tells us where his hypersensitivity, his vulnerability, came from. But they
were echoed in Jeanne, who experienced her communion with her son both
as a burden and as a joy. We might compare this intensely bonded relationship with the one Jeanne had with her own mother. The two women saw
each other almost every day, and always had difficulty separating. Marcel
recalls:

When Grandmother got up to go, my mother would go with her. There'd
be a first halt at the door, where they'd go on with their conversation.
Then, still talking, they set off down the stairs. At the bottom they sat
down on a sofa and continued sometimes for another half-hour. Then suddenly Grandmother would cry, "Goodness, the time! I shall just see you
back to the door, and then I must fly!" And they went upstairs and started
all over again. They couldn't tear themselves away from each other.[107]

They shared the same passion for Madame de Sévigné, from whom Adèle would quote entire passages in the course of their conversations. And what was Madame de Sévigné's correspondence if not that of a mother passionate about her daughter—a daughter who had the salutary instinct to go and live with her husband at the other end of France? The extraordinary lover's monologue that so delighted Adèle and Jeanne was a portrait in miniature of their own maternal feelings. Adèle, Jeanne, and Marcel: variations on mother-child dependency. If Marcel used some of Jeanne's characteristics in describing Adèle, if he made it difficult to distinguish between them, if the character of the mother and the grandmother in *In Search of Lost Time* are two sides of the same maternal love, a love on two levels but also with two faces, it is because he felt the extent to which the two women, though not alike, were virtually one person. Two faces: the grandmother's, indulgent; the mother's, more severe. So the child perceived them, as they must have been.

Jeanne's love for her son did not exclude strictness and authority, and sometimes mockery. Determined to reason with her own anxiety, she was sometimes unable to understand her child's needs. She would impose reasoning on him that wasn't right for his age, that he couldn't yet put into practice. Then he got angry with himself and suffered still more, as the bedtime scene shows. Thus Jean Santeuil's mother tries to show him the difference between his unhealthy hypersensitivity and love:

> "Loving one's parents is more than just liking to hug them, than crying when one is separated from them. *That* is not loving, but something one does in spite of oneself, because one is sensitive and a victim of one's nerves. It has nothing to do with true goodness of heart." "Nothing?" asked Jean. "No, nothing," replied Madame Santeuil; "even Nero could suffer from nerves."
>
> "[. . .] Loving one's parents means controlling oneself, exerting one's will, so as to give them pleasure."[108]

To exert his will was at the heart of the education Jeanne tried to give her son. But how could one promise the impossible? Jeanne was perplexed.

Marcel was said to be a nervous child. "Nervosity" was considered a genuine disease in those days, and of course its proper treatment was uncertain. Some recommended cold water, others hot water. Jeanne's anxiety had been lodged within her since her pregnancy and Marcel's difficult birth. That anxiety, transfused from mother to son, became an existential bond. Only his life's work—but at what great cost—would allow Marcel to sublimate it. His intense emotions, his sometimes tyrannical dependence, and his fragility all nourished Jeanne's anxiety in the course of the childhood illnesses that afflicted him and other children of his time.

This child who devoured her, whom nothing could reassure or appease, whose weight fell entirely on her shoulders—the eminent doctor merely shrugged his shoulders at Marcel's everyday little hurts—this child for whom she trembled even when she wasn't thinking of him, whose capriciousness, tears, and sorrowful looks often weighed on her: how could she not subconsciously resent him, despite all her love? She would occasionally get irritated, refuse to give in, scold him. Then she would feel guilty and smother her guilt by overprotecting him. Jeanne was a loving, captivating, all-powerful mother, whom no detail could escape, who wanted to know everything about the smallest acts and desires of her son. Here is an example from a letter Jeanne wrote to Marcel when he was eighteen and on vacation with his friend Horace Finaly:

> Somewhere I read a touching story about a mother who was paralyzed and blind, yet still realized that her daughter was in love, followed her progress, warned her when need be, etc.—I, who am paralyzed by distance and receiving far too little clarity from your letters, which neglect too many of the essentials, can feel your pulse beating too quickly, and I absolutely demand *calm,* a sensible routine, periods of solitude, refusal to participate in excursions, etc.—and if need be I will solicit Monsieur Horace to watch over the execution of the present decrees, having total confidence in his thinking—(don't conclude, my wolf, that I have none in yours).
>
> Could you not also, my darling, date each of your letters; I'd follow things more easily. Then tell me:
>
> Woke at
> Went to bed at
> Hours of fresh air—
> Hours of rest—
> Etc.
>
> For me the statistics would be most eloquent and in a few lines you would have successfully fulfilled your duty.[109]

Solicitude, anxiety, authority, humor, closeness, and the art of a medium who could feel her eighteen-year-old baby's heart beating at a distance—it's all here. At a distance? Without the other, each became incapable of autonomy, incapable of living, as if both of them had lost their point of reference. Here is a letter written a few days earlier than the one just quoted:

> My dear little wolf,
> We will write to you everyday now that we've been alerted—but notice, my boy, that having received only the few lines that were returned to me from Auteuil (to which I responded instantly)—I in no way guessed how lonely and demoralized you were. Now in possession of your second letter I am so sorry to see your *sense* turned upside down and also that you spelled it *sanse* upside down etc. . . .
> Poor wolf who has lost his senses *sans* Maman . . .

In light of this exchange between the grown boy with a mustache and his mother, we can imagine both the distress in which the son often lived and the protection in which Jeanne enveloped him. Marcel's vivid imagination, his sensitivity, the difficulty he had differentiating between fantasy and reality, his inability to *exist* outside of his mother, to assert himself, to be simply someone other than the person she wanted him to be, are balanced by Jeanne's worried tenderness, her demands, her intelligence, her possessive nature.

Her anxiety was to be nourished and amplified by an event that disrupted all their lives. One day in 1881, the Prousts were walking in the Bois de Boulogne with their friends the Duplays. Professor Duplay, a well-known surgeon, was a colleague of Adrien's; their wives got along well and their children too, despite differences in age. On this Sunday in springtime, the chestnut trees were in bloom, the temperature was mild. Other visitors to the Bois were dawdling, greeting acquaintances; the ladies opened their parasols, children played. Suddenly, as his brother Robert later told it, "Marcel was overcome by a terrible attack of asthma that nearly killed him right in front of my terrified father, and ever afterwards the constant threat of similar crises hovered over our lives."[110]

We can imagine the spasms of coughing, the wheezing, the difficulty breathing and the near impossibility of exhaling, the child's pallor, the growing asphyxia, the dread feeling of suffocation, the breath becoming rarer and rarer, the child's eyes filling with tears, his mouth searching for air: a drowning on dry land witnessed in horror by family and passersby. The agony of seeing one's own child suffocating without being able to do anything, the panic—"he's going to die, he's going to die, he's not getting any air"—his face was turning blue, his heart was racing, the wheezing was becoming a rattle, the child's frail body stiffened with convulsions and chest pains.

Around him, everyone was agitated: "We need to lay him flat"—"No, no, sit him up"—"Go get water, quick!"—"My wolf, my little wolf . . . let the doctor attend to him." Jeanne stepped back. She too was suffocating, her head frozen. She was soaking in sweat.

And then, after an eternity, the coughing returned, the wheezing grew fainter, and the white-faced child, exhausted, in pain, gradually got his breath and returned to his normal heartbeat.

Two professors of medicine had watched the crisis, powerless. In the mind of seven-year-old Robert, this paternal impotence was doubtless the most striking. We can imagine that Jeanne's terror was at its peak. As for Marcel, he lived from then on with the memory of this journey to the edge and with the apprehension of death. The only evocation of his illness in his work is tied to this first experience:

> A child who from birth breathes without ever having paid attention to it does not know just how essential to his life is the breath that, unnoticed, so gently swells in his chest. Suppose, however, that during an attack of fever or a convulsion he happens to choke. In his deepest, most desperate efforts it is almost his life he is fighting for—and for his lost tranquility, which he will have again only at the return of the breath he didn't know could be withdrawn from him.[111]

Today, asthma is still an incurable disease. It can reappear at any moment, precipitated by some factor that can't be predicted with certainty. Its unpredictability adds to the anguish of both the sufferer and the sufferer's family. The bronchial lesions never heal, and in chronic asthma the episodes become more and more severe.

A few years after his son's first attack, Adrien Proust wrote a preface for Dr. Brissaud's study of hygiene for asthmatics, published in a collection of short treatises on practical hygiene of which Adrien was general editor.[112] "True asthma is a pure neurosis," claimed Professor Brissaud, painting a discouraging portrait of the disease:

> When asthma attacks repeat themselves one after the next, without remission, without rest, for days, weeks, months, resistance of the nervous system breaks down, the effort is too great and especially too lengthy for the patient's energy, already limited, to be equal to it. [. . .] Life, constantly

threatened because it is at the mercy of the least pathogenic influences, is only possible if it is reduced to the minimum of vegetative acts. [. . .] The base of the lungs becomes congested, the extremities turn blue, grow cold, and even the most robust patients die.

Considering that Professor Proust endorsed this ghoulish vision, and that Marcel and the whole family used Brissaud's treatise as their bible, we realize that the anxiety that came with the disease itself was exacerbated by the absence of hope.

Treatments were those designed for the condition known as "nervosity": cold showers (hydrotherapy was the great resource of mental pathology, as demonstrated by Dr. Blanche at his famous clinic in Auteuil), a calm and steady way of life, pure air, and, in extreme cases, mercury baths. The good Professor Brissaud concluded sensibly: "The patient, in many respects, knows what is good for him, what is bad for him. His experience is as good as ours, and we would be wise to pay attention to it."

The "terrified father" also was conscious of the limits of his science. He was increasingly absent or preoccupied by his writing—no less than thirty volumes, ranging from *On Basic Pneumothorax or Pneumothorax without Perforation* to *Lead Poisoning among Workers Involved in the Manufacture of the Electrical Capacitor* and including *The Defense of Europe against Cholera; The Defense of Europe against the Plague* (which Albert Camus consulted for his novel *The Plague*); *Elements of Hygiene, Intended for the Secondary Education of Girls; Treatise on Hygiene* (nearly 1000 pages); and *Nutritional Problems Following Nervous Disorders*. Every aspect of medicine seems to have interested him.[113] "Papa told everyone that there was nothing wrong with me and my asthma was purely imaginary," Marcel wrote to his mother in 1899.[114] Dr. Proust left to his wife the responsibility of caring for him. She was the one in charge of transmitting parental advice to her son.

The inconsistent father in *Jean Santeuil* is not a total invention. The character reveals the way Marcel experienced his father's lack of involvement in family life, attributing it to weakness or selfishness. Jeanne's omnipresence was a result of her husband's absence. The authority of Jeanne's own father, and often of Adrien himself as reflected in his wife's letters, was that of a man to whom one often *pretended* to defer. But Adrien's scholarship in the eyes of his adult son was derisive: neither meteorology nor medicine are exact sciences. The territory he abandoned was invaded by the mother. God spoke through his mouth, but she was the oracle. A child as sensitive as Marcel must have understood this very early on. "Nothing is more likely to foment or maintain in these patients moral depression and hypochondriacal preoccupations than assiduous caretaking, constantly repeated questions about the state of their health, and suggestions made by people in their entourage," wrote Professor Proust on the subject of neurasthenics.[115] He spoke from experience.

> Maman, do you remember how you read *La Petite Fadette* and *François le Champi* to me when I was ill? You had sent for the doctor. He prescribed medicines to bring down my temperature, and a light diet. [. . .] It was the same story when Robert was ill, you allowed him to lay down the law, and as soon as he had gone away—"My dears, he may be a great deal more learned than I am, but your Mama knows what is right."[116]

Jeanne effectively never stopped giving "assiduous care" and "recommendations" to this child, in whom she feared the slightest sign of illness. What else could a mother do whose son was in danger of suffocation and lived with a terrible illness lurking in his chest? She took the initiative and didn't hesitate to disobey the doctor's prescriptions.

"I have the feeling that because of my poor health I was the bane and the torment of her life," Proust would write after his mother's death.[117] Marcel was a child "not like the others"; unable to run or jump, he moved at his own pace.[118] His sickliness, his asthma, contributed to tightening the bond between child and mother, a complex network of love, resentment, guilt, and dependency that united them permanently. Their emotions were in unison. For both, their love was haunted by the threat of separation.

"My poor wolf, I am even less tempted to criticize you since I was as upset as you and haven't stopped thinking about you," wrote Jeanne to her son in 1888 from the spa where she had gone for treatment.[119] How not to lose oneself in the other without losing the other? A Berber proverb says that the mother is fondest of her little one as long as he hasn't grown up, of her ailing child as long as he hasn't been cured, and of her traveling child as long as he hasn't come home. Marcel never grew up and was never cured. Nor could he ever distance himself. "For her I was always a four-year-old," he noted after her death.

In winter, Jeanne stuffed his pockets with hot potatoes and roasted chestnuts so he wouldn't get cold; he acquired the habit of layering sweater over sweater. He needed air, but not too much; heat, but not too much; nature was an enemy always likely to set off an asthma attack. Illiers was replaced by vacations on the seashore, with Adèle, in Dieppe and Cabourg. His absences from school for health reasons multiplied: in his fourth term (the equivalent of freshman year at high school), he missed the second trimester and the rest of the year from May on; the third term (sophomore year) was reduced to a few weeks of classes. In second term (junior year), he missed so much school that he had to repeat the whole year. His illness then subsided somewhat until he was twenty-three, when the asthma attacks reappeared. They became more and more violent, especially after Jeanne's death, until they were a part of his daily life and profoundly marked his existence. His chronic asthma led to his death; he succumbed to pneumonia at the age of fifty-one. For a long time, Mama hadn't been there to look after her little Marcel.

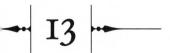

Taking the Waters

Since the Second Empire, taking the waters was all the rage. None other than the emperor Napoleon III and the empress Eugénie set the tone by going together to Saint-Sauveur, a small spa town near the Pyrenees. The development of railroads, travel guides, and the mineral water companies did the rest. From then on, there was no natural spring whose powers of healing weren't vaunted. After the war of 1870, a fever took hold of investors, and hotels multiplied, transforming reclusive villages into fashionable spas.

The medicinal properties of the salty waters at Salies-de-Béarn had long been recognized. The first spa was opened by Dr. Nogaret in 1858—a dozen cabins with wooden bathtubs—but it was Dr. Coustalé de Larroque, one of Napoleon III's physicians, who was responsible for attracting a wealthy clientele from Paris by publishing an article praising the spring's therapeutic qualities. More than 800 kilometers from Paris, twelve hours by train, it was quite an expedition—but that didn't discourage Jeanne Proust, who embarked with children and luggage for the little town in the Béarn. Her trunks were full—the *Hachette Almanac* for 1896 recommended twenty different toiletries; thirty-four other items including a pocket inkwell, a portfolio with photographs of one's husband and children, and an account book; and thirty-five items of linen, shoes, and clothing.[120] Jeanne was not the only one to benefit from the new railroad: in thirty years, the number of visitors taking baths at Salies increased tenfold. The biggest expansion occurred between 1886 and 1889, the years in which Jeanne took the cure.

The choice of Salies was not accidental. Dr. Proust knew the field: a few years later, in his capacity as inspector-general of sanitary services, he would represent the minister of the interior at the Hydrology Congress in Clermont-Ferrand, proclaiming "the need to create local resources solely designed to improve thermal establishments and the hygiene of spas."[121] Very often, it must be said, the spas were not prepared to accommodate the seasonal influx of visitors. Thus, at Salies, the irrigation canal from the Trotecâ mill had become a veritable cesspool, and the need for a sewage system was obvious. Dr. Proust, for his part, like Napoleon III before him, preferred Vichy. Did he enjoy his stays there as much as the emperor, who went for assignations with his mistresses? I have no idea; in any case, Jeanne, accompanied first by both of her sons and later, during the last two years, only by the younger one, had a legitimate reason for her trips to Salies: treatment by chlorinated water, ten times saltier than seawater, rich in minerals and "oligo-elements" that were reputed "to fortify and heal the procreative parts of the female, to heal genital deformities in boys and to make men of them." The spa was especially known for its gynecological treatments, whether the problem be infections or uterine fibroids. If Dr. Durand-Fardel, president of the hydrological society of Paris, had doubts about the effects of the treatment for ovarian cysts, he judged it effective for "fibroid tumors of the womb, on the condition that they be treated at onset."[122]

Jeanne's symptoms, presumably, were bleeding and pain. After Salies, she went to Kreuznach, in Prussia, where similar ailments were treated. She also tried seawater baths in Trouville, Dieppe, and Tréport. Women's diseases were considered secret, shameful conditions. There's no indication that she was simply tired, or confined to bed. Jeanne was not the type of woman to complain; the role of patient belonged solely to her older son. Marcel's letters amount to health bulletins, with a surfeit of details, leaving nothing to the imagination. We should add that he found in his mother an exceptional correspondent: "Keep a close watch on Monsieur's bowels so that we don't have the 90,000th copy of *La Débâcle!*[123] she wrote to her twenty-one-year-old son, combining medical suggestions with literary allusions to the latest Zola novel, which was creating a sensation in 1892. As for her own condition, was it a fibroid? A cyst? A tumor? Until the end of her life, her major concern was not to worry her family, and especially not Marcel. But according to his friend Maurice Duplay, Marcel was overwhelmingly preoccupied by his mother's health as well as his own. So each was secretly tormented about the other.

"Every time I saw her looking poorly," he confided later to Duplay, for Jeanne suffered from frequent illnesses, "I had complex feelings towards Mama. I resented her for tormenting me. Toward her, I'm in the situation of a supplicant toward his henchman. But in my case the supplicant cherishes the henchman and hates him precisely because he cherishes him."[124]

In those days, the Béarn region seemed to be at the end of the earth. The people spoke a patois. "It adds a lot of local color and is rather annoying, which comes to the same thing," Marcel explained to his grandmother.[125] As late as 1908, a guide to the Cauterets sternly condemned the use of any local dialect by staff during their service. During high season, all of Salies lived according to the rhythms of the spa-goers: families crowded into a single room so as to rent the rest of their house; camped in a lean-to in their garden; looked for work as porters, doormen, bath attendants, washerwomen, launderers, ironing maids, or masseurs; they sold postcards and trinkets; they set up stands along the avenues or in the public gardens to offer their services to the spa clients.

The treatment lasted twenty-one days. Jeanne and the children arrived August 26, 1886, at 12:15 P.M., in stifling heat. In those days, you didn't reserve a hotel room in advance. Special greeters were on hand to orient the tourists. When changing trains at Royan, Jeanne and the boys had boarded a train car with some people who were familiar with the hotels in Salies. She had made the acquaintance of the manager of the Hôtel de Paris, where she lunched with the children upon arrival, before inquiring about lodging. That same day, everything was arranged: they were to stay at the Hôtel de la Paix. If Marcel thought the heat a "sufficiently meridional" trait,[126] Jeanne suffered from it. They passed their time on the hotel terrace, "full of chitchat and tobacco smoke."[127] Built by Madame Laborde in 1883, it was one of the best-known establishments, along with the Hôtel Bellevue and the Hôtel de France et d'Angleterre. The food was delicious. The Hôtel du Parc, the fanciest hotel in town, which housed the casino, wouldn't be built for another decade, nor would the bandstand in the public gardens, facing the spa. Jeanne had chosen a small spa at the dawn of its expansion, which may explain her boredom. "Truly Salies is not as bad as Mama must be telling you, if I am to believe her reactions day by day," Marcel protested in a letter to his grandmother.[128] Like Robert, he was enthralled at first by the cattle, whose heads struck him as Christlike. But he was quickly disenchanted. There wasn't much to do for an adolescent as unathletic as he. Robert, at least, could indulge his passion for riding.

"Robert arrived dreaming of horses—and didn't find any sufficiently thoroughbred. But we also had to find someone to keep him company, rather than a guide (which he wouldn't have tolerated),"[129] wrote Jeanne, who, two years later, had plenty to do between her elder son, inconsolable in Paris, and his breakneck younger brother in Salies. She hoped Robert would make friends with a boy whose father was the famous engineer Gustave Eiffel and whose aunt, Madame Hénocque, was a friend of Jeanne's. But to Jeanne's disappointment, Monsieur Hénocque forbade his nephew to ride. The following year, however, at age sixteen, Robert rode with such energy, despite the heat wave, that he had "intolerable nose bleeds" and muscle pains, sweated profusely, and then caught cold. "I will no longer let him ride in this intense heat," Jeanne concluded firmly.[130]

Riding horses and mules was one of the principal activities for ladies in the mountain spas. Social life was another. The regular rhythm of the treatments, the meals taken collectively, a heat so fierce that "one [could] not venture outside before five in the afternoon," all contributed to the formation of social bonds. Life at the spa was a comedy of manners:

We met up again (as we were bound to!) with the decadent Belgian from last summer, who has sunk still lower and only has eyes for Joséphine Péladan.

There's also a Brazilian who pounds the piano from eight o'clock in the morning until midnight and only stops to give way to a young lady from Libourne who sings arias. With all the energy left in her throat the poor little creature launches into: "Yes—ssssss/sorrow-ow-ow-ow/will cut shoort-ort-ort my life!" Her mother accompanies her with her lorgnette—then her chin drops to her chest, so jolting is the beat of the rhythm she is trying to obtain. The poor girl's twenty-four mawkish double-crochets have to keep to the tempo. Afterwards, the mother gets to her feet, barely suppressing her triumph, and arranges the music, etc.[131]

After this piece of bravura worthy of her son, Jeanne is careful to add: "These are the limited distractions—and we are not here to amuse ourselves." She had a sharp eye and was as quick as Marcel to capture the ridiculous, whether in the hotel manager, Madame Biraben, "as happy for her rivals as for herself to lodge a governor and who will point out his presence to one and all by a firework (of dishes—and rockets)," or in Robert, glued to his preparations for the baccalaureate exam and "still persuaded that Gazier has branded the word 'failed' on his forehead."[132]

Marcel's favorite target was the dentist, Dr. Maitot, whom he dismissed, in a letter to his grandfather, as an "odontologist." Now fifteen, and full of satiric verve, he referred approvingly to critical ideas about odontology and religious beliefs, confirming the hypothesis that Nathé Weil was an atheist.

Jeanne and her sons made other, more pleasant acquaintances. It was in Salies that Jeanne got to know her great friend Marguerite Catusse. An excellent musician, Marguerite sang Massenet and Gounod in the hotel parlor, to Marcel's great delight. Sacrificing a game of croquet with his friends, Marcel strained to describe the lady in a letter to his grandmother: Madame Catusse had promised to sing an aria for him in exchange for this verbal portrait! "A charming face, two bright, gentle eyes, a face worthy of figuring in the dreams of a painter enamored of perfect beauty, framed in lovely black hair"; the clichés abounded, to the despair of the budding writer.[133] Too bad, he would save the celebration of her physical charms for a letter she wouldn't see. To his grandfather, he vaunted "her very great, very remarkable intelligence [. . .], an extraordinary friendliness that wasn't lacking in the liveliest candor—all in all, much originality and charm."[134] In other words, he had fallen in love with his mother's friend.

Marguerite and Jeanne remained very close, and one can only regret that their correspondence has not survived, for it would surely have revealed many of Jeanne's intimate thoughts. Marguerite's husband, Anatole Catusse, was a prefect, general director of indirect contributions, then became Conseiller d'Etat and finally plenitentiary in Sweden; he died in 1901 at the age of fifty-one. After Jeanne's death, Marguerite was a precious source of support for Marcel. Her son Charles became a journalist and married Meg Villars, the second wife of Willy, Colette's former husband.

Another friendship made at the spa was with Louis Tirman and his wife. Louis was president of the PLM Company, a former deputy, a future senator from the Ardennes, and, at the time, governor of Algeria. Jeanne appreciated the Tirmans' company so much that she read less than usual when they were at Salies. They got together in the evening in the parlor with its piano and potted plants. Jeanne wasn't shy of showing her talents as a pianist, making what she called "her little Binder effect" (an allusion to a German composer known for light opera).[135] But finding the "hotel full but socially empty," she spent most of her time reading, including works by Madame de Deffand, "the only relationship I don't disdain but cultivate,"[136] and Brunetière's articles in *La Revue des deux mondes*. She also devoted herself to corresponding with Marcel and others:

> I received a letter from Madame Rayet that I'm passing along, or rather I'm changing my mind and sending you Nuna's letter to your grandmother and will send you the other tomorrow after having responded, since I have to respond to you!
>
> This morning I received a letter from your father, from his trip, things going "admirably" etc. A very funny letter from your uncle G[eorges].
>
> Well, my big boy, everyone is inspired except your poor Mama, who is suffering from the most complete intellectual impoverishment.[137]

Correspondence circulated. Letters were written to be read and appreciated by the whole family, except where indicated to the contrary, as in Jeanne Proust's postscript to a letter in which Marcel described Dr. Magitot:

> My darling Grandpa,
> I don't want to deprive you of a letter from your grandson, but for special reasons that I'll explain when I see you, I don't want anyone other than you and Mama and Georges to read this letter and would like you to destroy it right away. J.P.[138]

The family was never far, even at a physical distance. They wrote to one another often, and when Marcel stayed in Paris for a year, he was in charge of keeping his "exquisite little Mama" up to date on the latest gossip. He let her know about a fight in Auteuil between Louis Weil and Jeanne's cousin Nuna (whose real name was Hélène Bessières), whom Louis declared "*incompetent in painting*" because she didn't like Ingres. The previous week, Nuna had made fun of Uncle Louis because he confused Raphael and Dürer:

It was in the garden, in the evening after dinner. Suddenly a shadow flitted by. My uncle had just gone out to pee and was hurrying back for fear of catching cold. Nuna, in a stricken voice: "Wasn't that your uncle who just passed?" "Yes." Horrified: "Then he heard it all." "No. Not a thing."[139]

Mother and son shared the same desire to entertain, spinning anecdotes like so many conspiratorial winks. They would reread one another's letters, just for the pleasure. Imagine a Madame de Grignon with the letter-writing talents of her mother, Madame de Sévigné. For Jeanne, Marcel, and certainly Adèle, a letter was not only a message of love, it was an art. Furthermore, as for many other children in their milieu, letter writing was an apprenticeship and sometimes, during vacations, a duty for the Proust boys. Neither mother nor grandmother spared their sons this training. Marcel's letters, despite their infelicities, already revealed the care he took to "write well." Maternal encouragement played a significant role.

The meals at the spa, always abundant to the physicians' despair, allowed those taking the cure to get together with their families at their boarding-house or hotel. They lunched early, around ten-thirty. Jeanne and her two sons had their special table; the two boys, in navy blue sailor suits, sat on either side of their mother, dressed in white. Their manners were perfect, and their appetites made Madame Birabel proud:

> We have at least five courses at every meal, dessert in the morning, dessert in the evening, divine food, gargantuan in gigantic quantities, deliciously refined, to which the skinny squires of Auteuil give themselves whole-heartedly.
>
> This morning (I'm taking this example at random, when I gobbled less than usual) I ate:
> One boiled egg
> Two slices of beefsteak
> Five (whole) potatoes
> One cold chicken drumstick
> Three helpings of baked apples in a special sauce
> (At 8:30 café au lait and bread)[140]

In September 1888, when Jeanne was at Salies with only her younger son, the quiet existence there was disrupted by a fire that broke out in the bath-house. The alarm was sounded in the middle of the night by an employee on his way home from work. According to *Le Mémorial des Pyrénées*, the Hôtel de la Paix barely escaped the flames. Arrangements were made the next day to supply the hotels with the salty waters: those taking the cure could have their baths right in their lodgings.

Jeanne held back from providing these details. She merely noted that "after the night's alarm, we have only to recover from general discomfort and from the exhausting heat."[141] She needed to spare her little wolf, who still didn't deal well with her absences. The rest of the family was less understanding of his yearning for his mother. After getting a sermon from Uncle Louis, who called his sadness "egotistical," Marcel wrote to Jeanne:

> Grandfather was much gentler and only called me an idiot very calmly. Grandma just laughed and shook her head, saying it didn't prove at all that I loved "my mother." I don't believe anyone but Auguste, Marguerita and Madame Gaillard realizes how unhappy I am.

And he continued with a note of pride:

> I behaved very well at table, I didn't catch a single furious look from Grandfather. Just a bit of a remark because I was rubbing my eyes with a handkerchief. A vestige of grief.[142]

Nathé, we might add, had given up tea and taken to orange flower infusions. And Marcel was seventeen years old. And how can we not be touched when he ends with these words:

> The least annoyance I may have caused you fills me with remorse. Forgive me. Many many kisses.[143]

Yet when we read these letters, written at the very same time that he was writing to his friends Daniel Halévy and Jacques Bizet, we have to wonder whether Marcel wasn't *acting* like a baby with Jeanne. He was responding in the same tone as that of the mother, who treated him like a baby and tried to conceal from him the fact that he was becoming a man. But that was the year in which he had been denied the trip to the spa, perhaps to toughen him up. Robert played the gallant escort instead.

From Jeanne's point of view, one of the major virtues of taking the waters may well have been to get Marcel used to separating from Mama.

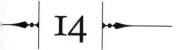

14

A Model Couple

"We raise our daughters like saints and we hand them over like fillies":
George Sand's famous line applies to many young ladies in the nineteenth
century.[144] Jeanne was no exception.

There was doubtless a considerable gap in experience between the
twenty-one-year-old virgin and the thirty-six-year-old man. Adrien Proust
was a physician, he had traveled, he'd been with women. What did Jeanne
know about life? Daughters were raised in total ignorance of the reality of
marriage. Like all young girls of her generation, she had read Alfred de Musset and George Sand, had played Chopin, and had sung, nourishing her romantic dreams and a certain idea of love. Her piano and her diary were
her confidants. She admired her brother Georges, two years her elder. He
shared her taste in books, he made her laugh, they conspired together. As
Alain Corbin has noted: "A brother was the only male with whom a young

girl was allowed to behave familiarly. Similarly, a sister was the only decent girl of whom a boy possessed an intimate knowledge."[145] We find in Romantic literature examples of these brother-sister couples—Chateaubriand and his ambiguous attachment to his sister Lucile, Stendhal and Pauline, Balzac and Laure. Jeanne and Georges remained inseparable, united by strong feelings that didn't preclude mutual teasing. Georges stopped in at his sister's for morning conversation, provided companionship when her husband was away, and joked with his nephew, who enjoyed making him miss his omnibus by chatting with him. Jeanne watched over her brother, deploring, for example, the fact that he took no advice from her husband before taking a cure. She wrote to Marcel:

> Since your uncle is not the kind of man to put off even for an hour what he has quietly resolved to do, he will clearly leave tomorrow according to his random concept for the North, the West, the South, the East, or the Center.
>
> Before leaving, he helped himself to a stack of my books, including Théophile Gautier's *Voyage en Russie.*[146]

A sense of reality, an understanding of social conventions, and a desire to start a family tempered Jeanne's romantic aspirations. She married, like her mother and her aunts, without giving it much thought. Marriage was a brutal initiation for young women in an era where virility was associated with speed and an energetic assault. A first son ten months after their marriage, a second two years later, and the door to the conjugal bedroom closed. The wife's pleasure was not written into the marriage contract. That was terra incognita; it was never discussed. Her duty was to produce children and manage the household. Jeanne was equal to the task: two sons and a perfect household. The image conveyed by the Proust couple and piously transmitted was that of perfect harmony. If, according to *Jean Santeuil*, this couple was "united not as a matter of free choice, but as a result of middle-class conventions and respectable notions," yet would "remain together until death breaks the bond," we can trace the pattern of a marriage typical for its era.[147]

There's no denying that Jeanne loved her husband. And as with many women of her day, her love would be put to the test. But Jeanne Proust was no more a Romantic heroine than an Emma Bovary or a Flora Tristan. She was neither a dreamer nor a rebel. Not given to fantasies. Totally unsentimental, she had nonetheless a warm heart and deep feelings. Her aspirations were rooted in reality and in her love for others: she wanted the success and the happiness of her family. Her realism and her pragmatism allowed her to tolerate the difficulties of her conjugal life. The advantages of the doctor's status more than compensated for the few inconveniences. Jeanne's ability to invent, to play for time, and a sense of duty gleaned from her education made her a model spouse, docile in appearance, willful in reality. She kept her dignity. If there were scenes and reproaches, we know nothing about them. Only her humor indicated the distance she was able to take on occasion toward her husband. But her penchant for mockery—the Weil temperament—spared no one, not Adrien or Nathé or Robert or Marcel. The one exception was her own mother, Adèle—as if Jeanne was counterbalancing the somewhat cruel attitude of the rest of the family, described by Proust in *In Search of Lost Time.*

Adrien and Jeanne had little in common. Indifferent to literature and art, Dr. Proust shared none of his wife's interests. Flat conversation, dogmatism: he was, as André Germain remembered him, "really dull and insignificant."[148] Jeanne and he simply weren't kindred spirits. George Sand (Aurore Dudevant) had a similar problem; as she wrote to her husband Casimir in 1825, before she had assumed her pen name,

> I saw that you didn't like music and I stopped playing because you fled from the sound of the piano. You read out of complacency, and after a few lines the book fell from your hands, from boredom and sleepiness [. . .] I started to feel genuine sorrow, thinking that there could never exist the least connection between our tastes.[149]

And even if Adrien was of a somewhat superior caliber to Sand's husband, Jeanne still hadn't married an artist or a hero whose ideas she could share, but rather a doctor bent on advancing in his career. In August 1890, he returned from a mission to the Spanish border. "Travel is a charming thing, since one is delighted to leave and delighted to come home," he wrote triumphantly to his wife, who was repelled (perhaps fortunately) at the very idea of his trips: tours of sanitary facilities; missions in Spain, Egypt, or Algeria; taking the cure in Vichy or Carlsbad; international conferences in Vienna, Venice, Rome, Dresden . . .

He would write to her, and she would wait for his return, often uncertain. "Last evening at nine, letters from your father—who's slaving away—spent four hours on horseback—and gives no sign of when he's coming home." Three days later, Thursday, she was still on the lookout for a dispatch announcing the return of her Ulysses but received only another letter, written "at the Cerberus train station (departure or arrival?)" and noting: "The people here are astonished by the speed with which I'm traveling."[150] "So let's be astonished by speed!" Jeanne commented philosophically, "and wait."[151]

At 1:00 P.M., a new missive, sent this time from Lamalou: Adrien was coming home on Sunday. Jeanne recounted their reunion in Auteuil in detail and with humor to Marcel, away doing his military service:

> At 9:10 A.M. Madame President descended incognito from the bateau-mouche—and at 9:15 the faithful Jean arrived in his carriage—and at 9:40 the President himself arrived: his first word: "And Marcel?"—we were obliged to answer, "My President, he has returned to active duty!"
>
> As for your father himself, delighted—tolerated the brutal heat admirably—rising at 4 and 5 A.M. each day and days where he hadn't three minutes of rest. All dusted off and new today—we breakfasted at 10 A.M.—left together at 11 for Paris—from where I'm writing you (Blvd. Malesherbes).

And she added, conspiratorially, "I sang your praises—loudly."[152]

Often, their letters crossed, and they were separated by their respective spa treatments—Jeanne in Dieppe, Adrien at Vichy. She would remain in Paris while he hurried from Carlsbad to Aix-les-Bains. "Since our letters can never match up with one another, they give me the feeling you get when you look in a gallery catalogue for the title of a portrait, mistake the catalogue number, and find: 'Still life,'"[153] she wrote wistfully. Still life?

Frequently away on business trips, absorbed by his professional activities, Adrien was not averse to certain extracurricular activities. As Jean-Yves Tadié notes, "In the model couple depicted by LeMasle, Adrien Proust's official biographer, who took his cue from Robert Proust (who himself . . .), one spouse was rather more 'model' than the other."[154] Adrien's exotic journeys involved a number of delightful stops. Shown gallantly escorting ladies in the photos of a trip to Luxor, Dr. Proust also liked to visit the backstage of the Opéra-comique, where he served as official physician. That task must have been highly enjoyable for a man in the prime of life. The demoiselles of the Opéra furnished an inextinguishable supply for respectable gentleman with an interest in the arts. A photo autographed to him on October 23, 1881, by the soprano Marie Van Zandt dressed as a man (like Odette de Crécy as Miss Sacripant) and another by Juliette Bilbault-Vauchelet leave little doubt as to the nature of his relations with these young women, who were also friends of Louis Weil, "the most aimiable of men," as one of Louis's conquests wrote. The photos help to explain this comment of Marcel's:

> On the way home [. . .] my parents used to laugh about Uncle Louis and his pretty girl friends. Sometimes, on the way there, Father would say, "I wonder which cocotte he has found this time." It was usually Father who joked. Mother, as always, gently played things down. And she knew well that Father didn't dislike it all as much as he would have people believe.[155]

Adrien must have been influenced by the Weil family's taste in women, since, like Uncle Louis, he had a special friendship with the demimondaine Laure Hayman, one of the models for Odette de Crécy (who also lived at 4, rue La Pérouse). Marcel, too, paid homage to the charms of this very pretty woman, loved by sovereigns, painted by artists, and celebrated by Paul Bourget, who made her his "Gladys Harvey," bragging to his schoolmates about their intimacy. "When Proust met her for the first time, in the fall of 1888, she was thirty-seven," wrote the painter Jacques-Emile Blanche:

> He was only seventeen; she was plump, but she had a wasp waist and wore very low-cut dresses, decorated with dangling pearls (three rows on each side) barely covering her bosom. Her hair was ash-blond, braided with a pink ribbon; her eyes were black, and when she was very excited, they tended to open extremely wide.[156]

Laure affectionately called Marcel "my psychological little Saxony porcelain"—not a bad nickname for the descendant of a porcelain manufacturer. The most surprising aspect of these liaisons was their familial nature—as if they resulted from a masculine complicity, an official filiation. Did Jeanne know she had this in common with her dear Madame de Sévigné, whose husband and son shared the favors of Ninon de Lenclos? Three generations of Weil-Prousts had fallen for Laure: Louis, Adrien, and Marcel, the latter shifting to a platonic level a liaison that the other men in family knew how to keep in its place. As usual, he went too far. After his father's death, he wrote to Laure:

"He spoke of you whenever he wanted to cite an example not only of youthful elegance and beauty, but also of intelligence, taste, kindness, tact and refinement of feeling."[157] Laure, as we shall see, like her young friend Marcel, specialized in condolences.

We thus learn that the "lady in pink" whom the narrator of *In Search of Lost Time* meets at his Uncle Adolph's had become "a subject of family conversation":

Every time Papa saw you and through you learned some little thing about me, what great and obvious pains he took to keep me from knowing who had told him. "You were seen . . ." "It seems that . . ." Etc. And I would guess instantly that you'd been to see him that day."[158]

The men had their rituals, and to walk openly with a courtesan on one's arm or to slip her a little present was no more compromising than smoking a good cigar while sipping cognac. Decorative, often witty and cultured like Laure Hayman, the demimondaines amounted to a display of wealth. In most cases, they were the indispensable complement to a married couple, the guarantee of its equilibrium.

For the bourgeoisie of the Third Republic, it was common and even considered legitimate for a man to take his pleasure outside marriage, while his wife closed her eyes to it. The "confident and malicious" young girl evoked in *Jean Santeuil* developed with the passing years into an understanding spouse. This image has been widely diffused in literature, from Maupassant to Zola, from Dumas fils to Colette, not to mention vaudeville, which has played it to the hilt. Better a frigid wife than a hot-blooded one who threatens the social order, as illustrated by the disastrous example of Madame Bovary. Once she'd accomplished her role as childbearer, the wife made room for the mistress. Alain Corbin suggests some of the reasons:

Many things drove [frustrated] husbands to the brothels: unyielding wives, often retiring women forced into unsuitable marriages; the chilling influence of the confessor; castrating mother images; the frequent interruption of sexual relations owing to menstruation, pregnancy, and breast-feeding; cessation of sexual relations after menopause; the prevalence of gynecological diseases; and the need for contraception.[159]

Lovemaking took place backstage at the theater, not in the marriage bed.

In Jeanne's case, gynecological troubles appear to have started early. Should we, like Christian Péchenard, entertain the hypothesis of a venereal disease passed on to her by the good doctor?[160] We have no proof, even though there were plenty of cases of wives being infected by their husbands. Such diseases were very frequent at a time when there was no adequate treatment: one doctor in 1865 estimated that 80 percent of women were infected by leukorrhea.[161] The first chair in venereal disease was established in 1880 for Alfred Fournier. In any case, it is surprising that Adrien Proust, professor of medicine who held a chair in hygiene, should spend time with demimondaines and send his adolescent son to a brothel to cure him of his habit of masturbation. Was this behavior contradictory? The ambiguity is interesting in the light of Marcel's own obsession with germs. In the family of the professor of hygiene, the great master of the cordon sanitaire, there was a profound struggle between cleanliness and dirt. As far as Marcel's experience at the brothel was concerned, it was a disaster. Frustrated at having flunked his virility test, the young boy broke a chamber pot; then, on his mother's advice, he wrote to his grandfather to ask for money to try again, still hoping to satisfy a father who sought a guarantee of his son's manliness. The whole family battled Marcel's "bad tendencies."

> Thursday evening [May 17, 1888]
>
> My dear grandpa,
> I'm appealing to your kindness for the sum of 13 francs that I would like to ask Monsieur Nathan for, but that Mama prefers I ask you for. Here is why. I so needed to see a woman to cure my bad habit of masturbating that papa gave me 10 francs to go to the brothel. But (1) In my addled state I broke a chamber pot, 3 francs, (2) in this same state I wasn't able to fuck.[162]

Nothing allows us to cast doubt on Jeanne's love for her husband, whether that love followed the wedding, as her son indicated, or whether it was the basis for the marriage itself. The image given in *Jean Santeuil* is quite close to reality, despite its idealization of the maternal figure. Jeanne combined an independence of spirit and tenderness, caustic humor and devotion. Despite "a fear, each time she began to say anything, that her humble, eager tenderness might bore her husband, might distract his thoughts, his digestion and his rest," she wasn't inhibited from "incessant teasing about everything."[163] "Much cleverer than her husband," Madame Santeuil, endowed with tact, artistic taste, and charm, demonstrates "docile subjection" and unfailing self-denial. She kisses her husband, plays the piano and sings for him. "The smallest kindness, coming from one whom she deeply loved, who had been so little used to showing her consideration, sufficed to stir her feelings," the narrator acknowledges.[164] That love goes as far as self-sacrifice: if he had cheated on her, "she would have sacrificed her own feelings to the need of ensuring her husband's happiness."[165] Nonetheless, Robert Soupault tells us:

> The gossip was that he flirted around with ladies of easy virtue, and that one day, joking with one of his colleagues, he protested: "They're getting

dreadful. Soon, we'll be expected to pay them." He was also supposed to have had some success with society ladies. This did not go far. There is no report of any conjugal incident. Madame Proust, a very sensible wife, did not notice, or did not wish to notice anything. Much later, Marcel said privately: "Maman never knew anything." But he was very much aware.[166]

Which amounts to saying that his mother did know, whether about her husband's escapades or her son's. We don't know whether she ever spoke of it. Did she exchange confidences with some of her closest friends, like Madame Félix Faure, whose husband, the future president of the Republic, continually cheated on her, even at the very moment of his death? Or did Jeanne, with her reserve and pride, refer to the subject only obliquely? I can't imagine Jeanne's complaining about her husband's infidelity or his absences, even to her best friends. But here and there she may have dropped a biting remark, cracked a bitter-sweet joke.

We learn from a rough draft of *Time Regained* that Professor Cottard's wife discovers her husband's infidelity only after his death, when she finds his correspondence. He has been carrying on an affair with Odette since he was a young man. Proust imagines a burlesque dialogue between the doctor, worried about not having all his wits about him for a speech to a learned society, and his mistress: "The sacrifice has been consummated. I, who did not want to consummate the sacrifice, good God, I'm expected at the subcommittee for contagious diseases, it's late." "It's never too late to do good," the future Madame Swann replies sweetly.[167] These interchanges often take place in "Madame Cottard's apartment, while the patients [wait] in the large parlor." Madame Cottard suffers even more from that posthumous betrayal than from the death of her companion. The narrator regrets that he can't console her:

> From the moment he cheated on you, if he took so much care that you shouldn't find out, it was because he was afraid to hurt you, because he respected you and loved you best. You're the only one who didn't know how much he loved you. To his mistresses he said that you were an angel, that he never could have had the career he had without you. In heaven, you're the only one he'll wish to see again.[168]

Meager consolation, but one that rings true and mirrors well the classic veneration of the husband for the wife he is cheating on. Jeanne, in a sense, wasn't merely the mother of his sons.

Nonetheless, we should not conceive of Madame Proust as an embittered or melancholy wife. "Sexuality, a central part of every modern marriage," Alain Corbin reminds us, was then "merely a backdrop to married life."[169] We see Jeanne accompanying her husband in his carriage to visit his patients or to go to the hospital, writing letters, reading him letters from Marcel. She helped to manage their large fortune, as certain documents from the time of Robert's marriage show. According to Robert Soupault, she was "her husband's secretary, his collaborator, she cheered him on." She took walks with him on summer nights; they took "their official tour by way of Passy" on foot. That most bourgeois couples were united by genuine affection is evidenced by the language of wills. Adrien Proust's handwritten will, which named his wife as his sole beneficiary, was no exception.

The humorous edge that often appears in Jeanne's letters to her son where her husband is concerned seems to me to be a form of prudery as much as a personal or familial characteristic. We can only measure the husband-wife relationship in Jeanne's correspondence with Marcel, where what is most obvious is the close bond between mother and son. Yet there is no trace there of any tension in the marriage; rather, a complementarity that is said to make for solid unions. Each spouse had his or her realms of excellence; for Adrien it was science, honors, the circles of power, endless work; for Jeanne it was family, culture, and the attributes of the high bourgeoisie. She knew how to deal with him and, if necessary, how to admire the small talents of which he was so proud, such as his taste for meteorology: "Yesterday your father made me read him eight columns by Parville, which taught me that every time the weather is bad, it's for some reason!" she wrote with gentle irony.[170] How did they really talk to each other? What little nicknames did they have? How did they sign their letters to each other? We don't know, for their entire correspondence is missing. Probably Jeanne saw Adrien as he was: always busy ("the Hôtel Dieu hospital, and all the rest of it," she wrote); happy and sure of himself; hungry for recognition; evolving energetically in the superior realm of great minds; a little disdainful of those overly sensitive intellectuals, his wife and elder son; and often absent.

Adrien's good sense, his precise mind, his taste for observation (which his son considered vulgar), his authoritarian nature, his annoying penchant for naming everything he saw, his "proud irrational positivism," all "those self-confident and arid illusions which at one time had filled his life"—did Jeanne know how to decipher them, carried along as she was by her love, "that gentle, submissive creature, devoted to others and self-sacrificing"?[171]

She brought him her finesse, her sensitivity, her liveliness of spirit, her love of art, her sense of human relationships, her rich family circle. She brought him what centuries of Judaism had wrought, the sense of the Law, a way of considering oneself different while wanting to be like others. Her critical sense and her generosity, her anxiety and sense of humor. Though he considered himself naturally superior, Professor Proust respected his wife. She was ballast to his career, a mother for his sons, a companion for his old age. He never regretted having married her. This dissimilar couple appears, upon reflection, behind its conformist facade, "united unto death," as the ending of *Jean Santeuil* indicates. "When her husband dies, it is most unlikely that she will kill herself," writes the young novelist; "still she will die of sorrow." Then he adds, "But no, she will not let herself die if she still has her son," correcting himself with the obvious truth.[172]

————•••••————

Adrien and Jeanne were also of one mind, according to the correspondence and *Jean Santeuil*, in wanting to correct the "bad tendencies" of their elder son. Did they speak of it in private? Along with nervousness, lack of appetite, hypersensitivity, asthma, and insomnia came a new worry for the parents: onanism. The symptoms added up to a total clinical picture in an era when, as Michel Foucault has shown, parents, doctors, and educators paid close attention to childhood sexuality, questioning it, tracking it, forcing confessions. The second half of the nineteenth century consolidated medical discourse on sexuality—encompassing in its general "will to knowledge" diseases of the nerves, perversions, and homosexuality.

The onanistic child was one of the great medical and hygienic obsessions of the bourgeoisie in the nineteenth century. The doctor took the place of the confessor to extricate confessions and threaten the worst punishments. Dr. Tissot's work *Onania* was republished regularly between 1760 and 1905. Doctors were unanimous: masturbation exhausted the vital essence of anyone who gave in to it; as a threat to healthy procreation, it was a vice and a danger both for the individual and for the species. Tuberculosis, premature senility, and death were the stages of an enfeeblement that nothing could hinder. In boarding-school dormitories, means of surveillance were established; latrines were designed with doors that allowed for watching the occupants; specialists even proposed, as late as 1914, custom-made bandages. And as a last resort, there was surgery and cauterization of the urethra.[173]

At the stage of puberty, the subjects predisposed by hereditary defects to morbid impulses of all kinds will be placed under particularly attentive surveillance.

Awakening instincts and sexual desires are profoundly disturbing to the equilibrium of the adolescent's nervous system. Most of them give in to the practice of onanism in an abusive manner, and this we have often found, as has been seen in the study of the causes of neurasthenia, to be a powerful factor in nervous exhaustion.[174]

These words of Dr. Proust's leave no doubt as to the "attentive surveillance" exercised over his son. It would be difficult to find a better subject of observation: several times, both in *Jean Santeuil* and in *In Search of Lost Time*, Marcel claims his propensity to acquire this "first pleasure," "for at the age when love is not yet known one is only concerned with oneself."[175] Associated with lilacs and the iris, the phallic flower par excellence, solitary pleasure was a source of enjoyment and terror. One tends to think that Marcel was satisfied all his life by this "first pleasure," varying only his partners and changes of scene. Papa's lessons were in vain. Not for lack of effort: he would go as far as to beg his son to "stop masturbating for at least four days," and offer him, as we've seen, a session at the brothel to put an end to the habit and to "empty himself."

Masturbation was an issue dealt with by men (the father, the grandfather). Although it was Jeanne who advised him to write to Nathé to borrow money, rather than to their cousin Charles Nathan, she was not supposed to know what the money was for.[176] It's possible that the sexuality of Marcel, age seventeen, was something so ordinary it could be debated at the dinner table. In any case, considerable liberty of speech seemed to reign in this doctor's family. But that liberty was at the service of a form of control and an absence of intimacy that today appears humiliating and infantilizing. Children in the nineteenth century were in a state of subjection, even in liberal families like the Prousts, where they addressed their parents with the familiar *tu* and entered into conversations with them. Did his father interrogate Marcel in the morning? Did the boy have to give reports as faithful as those demanded by his mother about his sleep? How did Dr. Proust *know*, unless the guilty adolescent confided in his father about his irrepressible need to pleasure himself? "But I have so much to say, it comes pouring out of me," he apologizes to one of his comrades at the end of a long letter.[177] In a draft of *Swann's Way*, Marcel wrote that in the little room smelling of iris and lilacs where he had hidden, "an opal stream spurted out, in successive bursts, like the moment the fountain painted by Hubert Robert at Saint-Cloud gushes out."[178]

Marcel's parents were clearly involved in every aspect of his health, both interior and exterior: temperature; intestines; secretions; the flow of the humors; the taste in his mouth; his flatulence; his coughing fits; the nature, length, and quality of his sleep; his stomach acidity—the list is endless, as if this adolescent body could have no secrets from his progenitors. Scrutinizing his every nook and cranny, he furnished them with the smallest variations on the functioning of his organs, exhausting their curiosity and sometimes, one senses, even their interest. These verbal revelations were the very opposite of the extreme physical prudery he was to demonstrate all his life, as his housekeeper Céleste Albaret would testify. The more he unveiled his body in words, the more he covered it in clothing, layered sweaters, overcoats, protective gauze.

The bourgeois family kept its children under close watch. When the father was a leading authority on hygiene, in charge of public health, his word had even greater weight. The pressure he exerted on his son to confess was imbued with so much prestige that Marcel saw no other solution than to hide, lie, or blackmail. Those tactics worked. Adrien was reduced to pleading with his son to stop masturbating. Check and checkmate. Marcel never gave up his "bad habit."

15

From Treble to Bass

Was this really her son, her little wolf, this boy acting so unnaturally, as if he'd slipped into someone else's skin? Everything about him had changed, everything was still changing: his limbs were too long for his body, his oval face had become pointed, facial hair was appearing on his upper lip, even his voice switched without warning from treble to bass. He slouched, he struck poses, he rested his head on one shoulder, his fingers clasped, and—something new—he locked himself in his room to write messages to mysterious correspondents. Since he'd started rhetoric class, he was unrecognizable. Just a few months before, he'd been writing charming letters to little Antoinette Faure in which he'd mix analysis of General Boulanger with comments about their mutual friends at the Champs-Elysées, where he went to play almost daily. He would read these letters to his mother before sending them. Jeanne had torn one of them up, the writing was so bad. He had had to start over again. In Antoinette's notebook, her son had responded to the series of questions that would one day become known as the "Proust Questionnaire."[179] Madame Faure had shown it, laughing, to Jeanne: Marcel's answer to one of the questions was that his greatest unhappiness would be to be separated from Mama. As if she didn't know!

The affectionate child was replaced by a sneaky, stubborn adolescent, who veered from crazy laughter to tears and from confessing secrets to stubborn silence. He would still come to his mother, wanting to be cuddled like a baby, and it took all of Jeanne's reason to prevent him from sitting on her lap or snuggling against her as if he were four years old; at other times, he would barely glance at her. She was losing him. Not long before, he had had a huge crush on one of his playmates, Marie Benardaky. Jeanne had been forced to calm him down. As usual, Marcel had gone too far, bursting into tears when he couldn't meet her at the Champs-Elysées, spending hours at the window waiting for a ray of sunshine, or going outdoors despite his poor health. All this just for a friend, a child, who was certainly pretty but boisterous and quarrelsome, and whose family, of Russian origin, was known for its fortune and its eccentricities.

But now Jeanne would have given anything to get Marcel to display affection once again for little Marie. Because of his asthma, he had to repeat second term and skipped school for almost the entire trimester of his rhetoric class. He was so pale that Jeanne frequently asked him to walk up to the window so she could find a little color in his cheeks. He worked with indifference on subjects that didn't interest him. Like all young people, he was headstrong: he loved his French teacher, Maxime Gaucher, but couldn't get along with his Latin teacher. Monsieur Gaucher, aware of his talent, had him read his compositions aloud, provoking sneers and boos on the part of his fellow students. Marcel loved Verlaine, Mallarmé, and Leconte de Lisle, and, like many boys his age, he wrote poetry.

Jeanne knew Marcel's friends at the Lycée Condorcet: Robert Dreyfus, a serious boy; Jacques Bizet, who had already attended the Pape-Carpantier class with Marcel; and Jacques's cousin, Daniel Halévy. Intelligent boys, a little younger than Marcel. Boys from good families: they belonged to the same world, the grande bourgeoisie. They lived in the same neighborhood. Daniel's father, Ludovic Halévy, was a famous writer, a witty member of the Académie française, and author, with Meilhac, of the librettos for Jacques Offenbach's La Belle Hélène and Georges Bizet's Carmen, the opera whose failure hastened the death of its composer, Jacques's father. Inconsolable for many years, Jacques's mother, Geneviève Halévy (who was also Ludovic Halévy's sister), remarried; her new husband was a lawyer, Emile Straus. She held a popular salon, where she reigned with style. Jeanne knew the family well. Generations of Weils and Halévys were part of the same Jewish consistorial circles; Godechaux, Jeanne's uncle, had given the funeral oration for Elie, Daniel's great-grandfather. They had many mutual friends. And through Dr. Blanche, whose clinic in Passy was not far from the rue La Fontaine in Auteuil, the Prousts were well aware of the nervous ailment that seemed to be eating away at the Halévy family, hanging over them like a malediction: Geneviève's mother had been hospitalized repeatedly, and her sister had died under mysterious circumstances.

To his mother's deep concern, Marcel seemed totally taken with little Jacques, Madame Straus's son. Jeanne didn't know what she should fear more: this unnatural attraction, or the object of Marcel's affection. Probably a combination of the two. For how could she not worry about a relationship for a boy as fragile, as emotional, as sensitive as Marcel? This Jacques Bizet was having a bad influence on Marcel, she was sure of it. She forbade her son to spend time with him.

How did she realize what was happening? "Perhaps from your face," wrote Marcel, shattered, to Jacques in June 1888,

> perhaps from hearing my brother speak about you, or Monsieur Rodrigues, or did she walk in while my brother was talking about you with Baignères, or did my brother say something bad about you, because we're often bad together, but mainly I think because of me, my excessive affection for you.[180]

We note that in Marcel's eyes, the primary suspect was Robert, his fifteen-year-old brother, whose interests were so far from his own. Robert was in second term, like his older brother's friends. He was a good student, interested in mathematics, with a passion for sports and only a moderate interest in reading, despite his mother's efforts. Did the little brother play the snitch with Mama? Did Mama ask indiscreet questions, which he answered in good faith? There was distance and typical quarrels between brothers only two years apart, but also a probable touch of rivalry for maternal affection. One crisis had followed the other since the previous winter. The parents were already threatening to send their elder son to boarding school, perhaps as blackmail to force him to study, or a way of distancing him. "I have a lot of troubles, my family is very bad for me. I think I'm going to be sent to a boarding school in the provinces," Marcel complained to Jacques, ending "I kiss you and I love you."[181]

So he was told he must not see Jacques. But Marcel, far from a docile child, resisted strenuously. Jeanne made a strategic retreat: all right, but they must not see each other either at Marcel's or at Jacques's home (which shows that what she feared most was their intimacy). Rage, despair, threats, poor health—any weapon was viable, including blackmail by way of illness, Marcel's specialty. But Jeanne didn't give in. There was nothing to be done. And while they were at it, his father brought up the burning question of masturbation. That may not have been very politic, but it's obvious what connection the parents were making.

From this moment on, Jeanne knew. And her son knew that she knew, as the beginning of a letter he wrote to Jacques makes clear:

> My dearest,
>
> I've no idea why. And for how long? Perhaps forever, perhaps for a few days. Why? . . . Perhaps she worries for my sake about this affection, which is a bit excessive, don't you think? And which could degenerate (she may think this) into . . . *sensual* affection . . .[182]

So not only did his mother know everything, but she very soon suspected and tried to put a brake on a condition that could "degenerate," as her son wrote. The "perhaps" that punctuates his letter shouldn't distract us. Certainly, Jeanne wasn't sure of anything. But she *felt* something. Marcel's sensitivity, his tendency to become attached, his need for love—she knew all about that. First Marie, now Jacques. Marcel was young; he couldn't tell the difference between a passionate friendship and forbidden feelings. It was up to her to protect him by separating him forcibly from this boy. The rest would take care of itself in due course.

From then on, she was always on the alert. Once she was absolutely certain, she began to worry about his suffering, his bad relationships, the gossip, his being ridiculed for his pose in a photograph—all the talk. For a long time she hoped he might marry. With each new friend—for Marcel loved women or said he loved them—she hoped. Introduce him, she would say to his friend Maurice Duplay, who was a connoisseur of beautiful women. But Marcel wasn't lacking in young women—he was lacking in desire.

Finally, she accepted it all. For he was her son. Nothing would ever be said about it between them. But she knew. According to Maurice Duplay, "Madame Proust knew about her son's ways and his bad reputation."[183] "Go on as if I didn't know" would be their secret password,[184] a tacit release from an interdiction that weighed less on things than on words. The shameful secret would be both hidden and obvious between them. "Sons without a mother, to whom they are obliged to lie even in the hour when they close her eyes," Proust would write of the "accursed race" of inverts in *Sodom and Gomorrah*.[185] A lie that was also the ultimate protection from maternal intrusion.[186]

So, she knew. Or suspected. But there were some things she didn't know. First, Jacques in no way shared Marcel's tastes. Even if he wasn't shocked by his friend's love and seemed to receive it with some amusement, he kept his distance and made it clear that he did not reciprocate, to which Marcel responded: "I admire your wisdom while at the same time deploring it. [. . .] Maybe you are right. Still, I always find it sad not to pluck the delicious flower that we shall soon be unable to pluck. For then it would be fruit. . . . and forbidden."[187] And second, Jacques wasted no time in showing Marcel's passionate letter to his best friend, Daniel Halévy, who copied it into his diary and started to play a rather perverse game. Suddenly Daniel and Jacques stopped speaking to Marcel. Marcel was confused. Had he done something wrong? Did they find him too "clingy"? "What do they want?" he wondered. "I used to think they were so nice."[188] Poor Marcel, full of psychological finesse but never very clever when it came to his own affairs of the heart. Robert Dreyfus, younger and less involved in that "sentimental education," served as his confidant. The four boys all wrote poetry and started a literary magazine, then another. But the literary facade hid complex affective relations among those talented adolescents. Daniel Halévy pulled the strings. And it was he who gathered, or provoked, the most explicit confessions and professions of faith. For the ensuing months, from spring to summer 1888, from rhetoric class to philosophy, Marcel would explain his "pederasty," conjugating literary references and personal experiences, justifications and poems, declarations and strategic retreats: "As for your pederasty, virtual or not, " he wrote to Daniel Halévy,

> you might well be mistaken. I know [. . .] there are young people (and if you are interested and you promise to keep it *absolutely secret,* even from Bizet, I'll give you some very interesting evidence on this point of view, addressed to me), young people and especially guys between eight and seventeen who love other guys, always want to see them (like me with Bizet), cry and suffer when away from them, and only want to kiss them and sit on their laps, who love them for their flesh, who gaze longingly at

them, who call them dearest, my angel, very seriously, who write them passionate letters and who wouldn't commit pederasty for anything. However, love usually triumphs and they masturbate together. But don't make fun of them or of the one you're talking about, if that's the case. After all, they are in love with each other. And I don't know why their love is any more inappropriate than regular love.[189]

He also confided to Robert Dreyfus, "I would like to tell J.B. [Jacques Bizet] that I adore him, and X and Y that I am decadent,"[190] admittedly because he wanted to indulge in a little play-acting. He was—he insisted—"a man of declarations" and "while pretending to love a comrade like a father, he loves him like a woman."[191] How playful were these declarations? How much sincerity or self-persuasion was involved?

Jeanne was in Salies-de-Béarn with Robert at the time. She consoled her "little wolf," who had a heavy heart from being left alone. "What issues from my mouth will be the purest truth," he lied to her confidently in a letter whose last words, already quoted, now take on new meaning: "The least annoyance I may have caused you fills me with remorse. Forgive me. Many many kisses."[192]

The short stories "Before the Night" and "The Confessions of a Young Woman," as well as the character of Mademoiselle Vinteuil in *In Search of Lost Time,*[193] are already present in embryonic form in these letters that reveal feelings contradictory on the surface yet profoundly coherent . How to leave one's childhood while prolonging it, how to tear oneself away from Mama while holding onto her? Desire and guilt were closely intertwined. Of Mademoiselle Vinteuil, Marcel wrote: "It was not evil that gave her the idea of pleasure, that seemed to her attractive; it was pleasure, rather, that seemed evil."[194]

"Oh! My sweetheart, why am I not on your lap, my head against your neck, that you can't love me?" exclaimed the seventeen-year-old boy in a text dedicated to Jacques Bizet and written for the *Revue Lilas* with instructions that the original be destroyed.[195] Like Mademoiselle Vinteuil, who "jumped on her friend's knees, and chastely presented her forehead for a kiss, as a daughter might have done,"[196] Marcel could only imagine love in the form that was, to his mind, the ideal: the love between a son and his mother.

Verlaine, Rimbaud, Montaigne, and Socrates: he called all of these "decadents" to his aid, undoubtedly both to understand himself and to justify himself in his own eyes and in the eyes of his comrades.

One letter, written to a schoolmate, Raoul Versini, and signed "Marcel" is supposed to have contained a troubling confession: a first homosexual experience connected with a rape. But it seems certain that this letter was attributed erroneously to Marcel Proust. He was never intimate enough with another boy to reveal such confidences.[197]

"My parents learnt of it and didn't do anything too hasty, in case they upset me too much," he wrote at the beginning of "The Confessions of a Young Woman": "At first I was filled with agonized remorse, I made confessions that were not understood. My comrades put me off the idea of persisting in trying to tell my father. They slowly persuaded me that [. . .] my parents merely pretended not to know."[198]

Marcel Proust came of age during a transitional period, 1870–90, when views of homosexuality were changing. The word itself was first used by the Hungarian writer Karoly Maria Kertbeny in 1896; the condition was analyzed systematically for the first time in 1870 by a Dr. Westphal. From sodomy, "a criminal act before God," there was a subtle shift to the notion of perversion on the part of an ailing individual whose illness came under the purview of the physician. While French law, influenced by Cambacérès, no longer considered sodomy a crime, and while the neoclassical aesthetic and the rediscovery of antiquity might have justified a culture of pederasty, the last third of the nineteenth century was marked by the birth of new stereotypes, validated by the fields of psychiatry and public health. The homosexual joined the hysteric and neurotic patient under the rubric of perversions and mental illnesses. Jean-Martin Charcot, Richard von Krafft-Ebing, and Havelock Ellis—pioneers in conceiving of homosexuality outside of a medical context—devoted books to the subject.[199] On the one hand, there was a fear of contamination, of seduction that might corrupt the innocent; on the other hand, there was suspicion that the condition of homosexuality was biologically predetermined—an innate disposition, a degenerative condition that locked a woman's soul inside a man's body. Like masturbation, homosexuality was antisocial and constituted a threat to the family. "In transforming the criminal into a patient, psychiatry displaced social condemnation without suppressing it," Florence Tamagne has noted.[200]

Through the correspondence of young Marcel and the reactions of those around him we can trace the emergence of this new discourse on homosexuality. The link to friendship, the subtle shift from platonic tenderness to desire is obvious. Wasn't that what alerted his mother in the first place? "The reason [homosexuality] appears as a problem, a social issue, at this

143

time is that friendship had disappeared," explains Michel Foucault. "As long as friendship was something important, was socially accepted, no one realized men had sex together."[201] The family was established as a defense to protect the intimacy of its members. Basic socialization and upbringing was in its hands. Every relationship had to be lived out in the midst of the family and in its interests.

Marcel's excessive fondness for Jacques was thus experienced by his parents as a danger, both for his health and for the social future of the family. As long as Jacques Bizet was the only concrete threat, they may have thought that separating the two adolescents would be enough. As soon as they realized that the problem was *within* Marcel, they changed their attitude. Adrien had followed Charcot's work; he was very interested in what is now known as neuropsychiatry, as several of his works indicate. Paternity, psychiatry, and hygiene: his son's homosexuality concerned him on several fronts. And almost certainly, like his colleagues, he conceived of it as a perversion that would leave Marcel as impotent as asthma would. His son was sick.

One reflection of this pathological concept of homosexuality appears very early on in Marcel Proust himself: "The cause of such love is a nervous impairment which is too exclusively nervous to have any moral content," he writes in "Before the Night," a short story published in 1893 in *La Revue blanche*.[202] Ailing, therefore not guilty. He was nonetheless distraught, if we are to believe these lines from *Jean Santeuil*, attributed, according to his usual technique of inversion, to a female character: "You will never know the full extent of my suffering. Some of my friends hit me, others wouldn't even say good morning to me. But nothing had any effect. My confessor could find nothing to say to me. The doctor said I was mad."[203] How could Jeanne not have realized her son's problem?

Robert Dreyfus realized that the (relative) ostracism experienced by Marcel in school was due in large part to his homosexuality, which made his schoolmates uncomfortable. He was pushed away, isolated, jeered at— the flip side of a genuine admiration for a boy so different from the others, whose extraordinary qualities they also recognized.

"There we were in the courtyard of the lycée," Daniel Halévy wrote later in *Pays parisiens,*

> three or four strapping boys, Jacques Bizet, Fernand Gregh, Robert de Flers, and suddenly we felt a presence, someone breathing down our necks, brushing against our shoulders. It was Marcel Proust, who had

come up quietly, like a ghost; it was he, with his huge oriental eyes, his big white collar, his cravat flapping. There was something about him that we didn't like, and we responded with a hurried word; we thought about hitting him. We never followed through: it was impossible to hit Proust, but at least we showed that we wanted to, and that was enough to hurt him. He was clearly not boy enough for us, and we considered his kindness, his thoughtfulness, his caresses [. . .] mannered, a pose, and we even told him so to his face: then his eyes grew even sadder. Nothing, however, could discourage him from being nice.[204]

The following passage from Halévy's diary, written after the letter Marcel wrote to Jacques, casts him in a cruder light:

> Take Proust. More talented than anyone. Watch him overexert himself. Weak, young, he fucks, he masturbates, he pederasts, perhaps! Perhaps in the course of his life he will reveal hidden pockets of genius. And we will deplore his bohemian ways, we'll cry over what he *might have been*. Idiocy! If he hadn't done all that, he would no longer be himself. [. . .] Imagine a Proust with an exemplary life. He couldn't possibly amount to anything. Given his character, he must enact his genius.[205]

Life, friendship, passion, desire, sex: all the problematic issues of adolescence are present in the few letters that have survived from this period, incredibly explicit in their sentiments, voiced with a freedom that indicates the atmosphere that reigned in his family and reflects the confidence of the boy who always thought one could *say anything*. He would learn otherwise. He wouldn't forget the lesson.

In response to a doctor's survey, one homosexual wrote: "We all had a crazy desire to confess, to cry out our love; at certain times, we would tell it to passersby, if our mouths weren't sealed by the double anxiety of coming up against disdainful indifference or exposing ourselves to all sorts of social obstacles."[206] Marcel, to the contrary, didn't hesitate. In a sonnet entitled "Pederasty," returning to the subject dear to him, he wrote to Daniel Halévy:

> I would love forever to sleep, love, or live
> With a warm child, Jacques, Pierre, or Firmin.[207]

The response he got was "a small correction to the rules," to which he responded at length, during philosophy class:

You think me jaded and effete. You are mistaken. If you are delicious, if you have lovely eyes which reflect the grace and refinement of your mind with such purity that I feel I cannot fully love your mind without kissing your eyes, if your body and mind, like your thoughts, are so little and slender that I feel I could mingle more intimately with your thoughts by sitting on your lap, if, finally, I feel that the charm of your person, in which I cannot separate your keen mind from your agile body, would refine and enhance "the sweet joy of love" for me, there's nothing in all that to deserve your contemptuous words, which would have been more fittingly addressed to someone surfeited with women and seeking new pleasures in pedestry.[208]

These "sensual and intellectual friendships" were transitory, however. Thus Marcel concludes:

Don't call me a pederast, it hurts my feelings. If only for the sake of elegance, I try to remain morally pure.[209]

Above all, he was learning prudence and critical distance, dissimulation and lying. Already, Monsieur Straus was applauding the excellent intellectual influence Marcel was having on his stepson Jacques. Jeanne, finally persuaded that Jacques didn't share Marcel's tastes, could only encourage their association. Better yet: in the same period, Marcel started to visit Laure Hayman, the woman admired by his great-uncle Louis and his own father. A few months later, Marcel wrote a poem for her; its last strophe is enough to give us an idea of the whole poem:

My glorious mind will never see the sunrise
But a god sent you: you slay me, I adore you!
I braided that laurel wreath for you,
Laure![210]

At the same time, he distanced himself from Jacques Bizet. Soon his excessive admiration would go in the direction of Jacques's mother, Geneviève Straus.

"You can say anything," Marcel Proust would declare years later to André Gide, "as long as you don't say 'I.'"

He would no longer say "I." Jeanne could breathe easy.

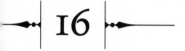

A Woman of Forty

On April 21, 1889, Jeanne turned forty. Her figure was fuller, but there wasn't a strand of gray in her thick black hair, still gathered in a chignon; she had the same dark velvety eyes, the same tender yet sardonic tone of voice. "When you saw her, leaning slightly backward, as if pulled by the weight of her hair, she seemed to posses the most adorable face on earth," wrote Fernand Gregh, invited to dinner at the Prousts' a few years later.[211]

"Her beautiful Jewish features" hadn't changed.[212] Though not vain or flirtatious, she took care of her appearance, in keeping with her milieu: with her high collars, she had the austere look of Right Bank society ladies. She wore silk in winter, light muslin in summer, with the pinched waist and padded flounce that fashion inflicted upon women; a little hat with a veil, a fox stole, jade or black pearl necklaces when in mourning, a velvet or fur muff in which she could slip her gloved hands when it was very cold. Her milliner, Lebel, specialized in round shapes. His shop on the rue Saint-Honoré was more than competition, Madame Proust claimed, for Pepita and Clarinda. The touchstone of chic, a hat was essential in an era when a woman wouldn't think of leaving her house bare-headed. Yet photographs of Jeanne Proust don't reflect the image of an elegant woman. She bore no resemblance to the great beauties of the Faubourg Saint-Germain, the ravishing Countess Greffulhe, or Laure de Chevigné, whom her son would admire greatly. Jeanne was as far from them as the mother of the narrator in *In Search of Lost Time* was from the Duchess of Guermantes or from Odette, who showed off her mauve outfits on the avenue du Bois. When Jeanne walked down the avenue du Bois, it was to visit her Aunt Ernestine who had just had surgery. Her femininity seemed entirely devoted to motherhood and to her sense of family. No attempts at seduction; she was a dignified bourgeois woman, with something of the bluestocking about her. And there was her incomparable gaze "with the intelligence shining forth from her lovely eyes," the same "splendid eyes" as her son, according to Fernand Gregh, who was clearly smitten with her.[213]

Jeanne was no prude. In the stifling summer of 1892, "flattened by the heat," she undressed "in the most audacious manner," as she remarked to her son, who may have preferred not to know this.[214] Meticulously clean, she did her "little ablutions" each morning and dressed in a white peignoir before having her chambermaid carefully brush her long brown hair. She was proud of her perfect teeth; the dentist she went to regularly could find nothing wrong with them. His successor had to make do with working on her gums, claiming "to give them new vigor in the course of three appointments, without causing me any pain whatsoever."[215] She was beginning to feel a touch of rheumatism when she had remained too long inactive. But she exercised. She walked a great deal, and in summer she swam. A passage in *Jean Santeuil* shows the hero's mother emerging from the waves of the Deligny swimming pool on the Seine.

Forty was a ripe age for a lady of her time. Marcel was preparing to take his baccalaureate exam and would get his results in July; Robert was a junior in rhetoric class. On March 19, 1889, Jeanne's mother-in-law died. Although there is no written record, it is likely that the family, or at least Adrien and Jeanne, went to Illiers for Virginie's funeral. An announcement was printed in Paris, doubtless worded by Jeanne, who "forgot" to include the standard cross, unless she was purposely following the anticlerical leanings of her husband and brother-in-law Jules Amiot.[216] She had never felt very close to

Virginie, but her death must have set her thinking about her own mother. Still, Virginie, born in 1808, was much older than Adèle, who had just celebrated her sixty-fifth birthday.

In September, Jeanne returned to Salies-de-Béarn to take the waters. The results were unimpressive, to say the least, and the heat was stifling. She would never go back. As we have seen, she took Robert with her and wrote long letters to Marcel, also on vacation. For the first time, after his ritual visit to Auteuil, Marcel actually went away on his own. He stayed in Ostend with the family of Horace Finaly, a schoolmate from the Lycée Condorcet. Horace's father, Hugo Finaly, ran the Banque de Paris et des Pays-Bas. The Finalys were a Jewish dynasty of high finance, inspiring Proust's portrait of the Bloch family. Horace's maternal great-uncle, Horace de Landau, would become the model for Bloch's uncle, Nissim Bernard. Ostend, on the North Sea, was considered a very fashionable resort, suitable for families, but Jeanne, always concerned about her little boy's health, still worried. Was he eating enough? Was he sleeping well? Was he going out too often? Did the sea overstimulate him? Other people's worries were of less importance to Jeanne, who reacted characteristically to Marcel's excessive sensitivity when he seemed overwhelmed by Madame Finaly's concern about her own mother's health: "I understand how upset you are about poor Madame Finaly's sorrow, but how old is her mother anyway?" she asked.[217]

She watched over him from afar, had books sent to him from her Paris bookstore, Delorme, but nonetheless hoped he would stay in Ostend until Adrien's return. Was she afraid of his being alone in Paris? From her exile in the Béarn, she made a chart of their various vacations, like a good family manager. It wasn't easy, with all of her husband's comings and goings. By the end of that year, the familial universe on which her happiness was based would be shattered.

First came Marcel's departure for the army. Perhaps this was his attempt at autonomy, although he had to volunteer if he wanted the advantage, in that hundredth anniversary of the Revolution, of having to serve for only one year rather than the normal five, before a change in the law took effect that would require every man to serve for three years. Enlisting on November 11, 1889, he joined the seventy-sixth Infantry Regiment as a soldier (second class), at Orléans. From this period, seventeen letters have survived from Jeanne to her son, and only one from Marcel to his father, written at the very end of his tour of duty. The rest of the correspondence, including all of Marcel's letters, is lost. But Jeanne's letters, covering a period of ten months (December 14, 1889, to September 23, 1890), are essential for understanding the relationship between mother and son at the crucial moment when he was trying to achieve some independence. He could have sought an exemption (his health and his father's connections would have made it possible), or put off the obligation. He didn't. His departure for the army was very much in line with the events of the previous two years. He was eighteen, the age at which escape from the familial cocoon becomes a goal. Contrary to all expectations, army life agreed with him. Although he coughed so much at night that his commanding officer suggested he look for lodgings in town, he suffered no melancholy or black moods, he reported to his father. He adapted, and if his performance at sports was quite poor—unlike Robert, he was incapable of mounting a horse—he succeeded very well in this initiation into manhood and always had excellent memories of it. Only the first month must have seemed tough, and Jeanne tried to comfort him with images better suited to a ten-year-old than to a young man in uniform:

> Oh well, my dearest, a month has passed, only eleven pieces of the cake remain to be eaten, and one or two slices will be consumed on leave.
>   I've thought of a way of making the time seem shorter to you. Take eleven bars of the chocolate you are so fond of, make up your mind to eat one and no more at the end of each month—you'll be amazed how quickly they go—and your exile with them.[218]

So much for orality as separation therapy . . .

But those childish consolations were also part of a game between mother and son, a coded language that Jeanne only used when Marcel was unhappy. So she instinctively used words and images that consoled the child in him and reassured him. She responded to her son's anguish with the soothing words that used to calm him when he was little. A maternal tenderness designed to work wonders.

It was their first true separation. And we might ask for whom it was more difficult: "For a single Sunday without you, how many Sundays *with* you are to come . . . Given all the military operations in the world, there remain an infinite number of hours in which to occupy myself in your absence," she wrote to him, playing on the mathematical metaphor.[219] But of her own worries she wrote nothing, or she let them be understood between the lines. How could she not be worried about this fragile boy who just a few months earlier could barely refrain from crying whenever she left? She feared for his health, she worried about his lack of physical aptitude and his terrible "lack of will." Wouldn't his rougher, coarser comrades be bound to make fun of him? And what if he fell in with the wrong crowd? She had a thousand reasons to be apprehensive about his experience, and a thousand reasons to hope for its success. "Keep well and win the battle, the reward will be your happiness and ours," she encouraged him.[220] We find a mixed message throughout these letters: be a man but remain my little boy. *Sursum corda,* little wolf!

In these missives we also sense the void left by her son's absence. Jeanne watched for the mailman, anticipated Marcel's leaves. When a leave was canceled (or Marcel spent it elsewhere, for example on the rue de Miromesnil at the home of Jeanne Pouquet, his friend Gaston de Caillevet's fiancée), what a disappointment! "Ah, how long is the time of my impatience!" she sighed, quoting her beloved *Esther.*[221] Sometimes she was the one who took the train to see him in Orléans:

> If next Sunday you don't plan to come, then I'll come to you—but if you were free the next week, I'd be even happier.
>
> Think about whether we'll see each other in Orléans next week on whatever day you suggest.[222]

She must have scolded him rather severely, hoping that there would be no more "nebula in our firmament."[223] Marcel, like a child, no doubt promised to made amends, and Jeanne waited for those promises to be kept:

> First act of contrition, says your merciless mother, please, I beseech you, purchase ten notebooks of squared letter paper (which comes to sixty double sheets).
>
> Two packs of white envelopes perfectly formatted (a total of fifty envelopes).
>
> And you will use them specifically for writing me sixty letters; I'll find that most agreeable.[224]

"I'll find that most agreeable": what a queen! We can understand why military discipline seemed like nothing to Marcel. Since he had only two more months of service, he now had to produce a daily letter for his mother. And the size of the envelopes would allow the sheets to fit in properly without being torn.

Demanding, authoritarian, tender, funny: the combination is typical of their relationship. Most of the time, however, there was nothing excessive or infantilizing in her terms of endearment: no "little cretin" or "ninny," or "your Mama thinks that," as in Marcel's version in *Against Sainte-Beuve*. Jeanne's hold on him was much more subtle. She now signed her letters "J.P." and not "your mother" or "Mama." "Dear little one" is the greeting she used most often; only once or twice did she call him "wolf" (a name she used for Robert too, Marcel would note) or "my darling." "A thousand and a thousand kisses," "I kiss you a thousand times," are natural expressions for a loving mother to use when her son is gone. On one Thursday, filled with disappointment after not having received a letter from him, she wrote, "I leave you tenderly, kiss you tenderly, love you tenderly and plan to hold you tenderly, Saturday?" A lover's language.

Most of her letters are devoted to what she called "the quick report on my day" and to family news. A large part is spent on Robert, onto whom she had transferred some of her maternal solicitousness:

> Robert is going to Boutrou's class today and will not miss another.
> 'philo sum et nihil philo mihi etc.'
> My pet, this morning, since your father wasn't coming home, I had lunch at half past 10 with Robert, then I saw to wiping the keyboard of my son's piano, the candle was stalactizing the dust on it, then—conscientiously practiced exercises for an hour—while Robert read his physics book beside me.
> Then—stiff and rheumatic—I stopped and dictated algebra problems to Robert, which he wrote on the blackboard.[225]

We note that she supervised her younger son's homework with as much care as that of her older boy, just as she supervised his friendships. For good reason, since Robert would pass two baccalaureate exams that year, in science and in literature. That didn't prevent Jeanne from making fun of Robert, whom everyone called Proustowitch or Dick or Robichon. She made fun of his grouchy, sometimes intolerable disposition; she mocked, somewhat cruelly, his ignorance of poetry:

> This morning I made him recite: Oh, how chic! from Casimir Delavigne whom I'd labeled as Lamartine (I must admit there were only two lines). Extraordinary—he took it as he was meant to—with laughter.[226]

A subtle way of dividing in order to conquer? To retain her special bond with her elder son ("my son") by making fun of the younger? In the absence of any surviving correspondence with Robert, we may assume that she played a similar game with him. Her remarks concerning Robert, nearly always caustic or critical, had nothing to do with her love for him. She described her own brother Georges, her father, and her grandfather as having "bad dispositions." Perhaps she was reproducing her own mother's attitude toward Georges, reserving for Marcel the privileged relationship she had with her mother. A studious boy, Robert was also elegant and athletic, a bon vivant, independent, everything his elder brother wasn't. At eight in the morning, "meticulously dressed," he met a friend to go boating in the Bois de Boulogne. "Home at noon, snacked on a half pound of meat, bread, vegetables, cheese and prunes—dressed to a tee, and left again with Clément—who's reappeared out of nowhere—for unknown destinations," Jeanne reported to Marcel.[227]

It's difficult not to see the resemblance to the active, indefatigable Adrien, who too was "always off somewhere!" Clearly, Robert was a man's man. He was escaping from his mother. Meanwhile, Marcel was the poor exile, close to his Mama's heart, the needier of her two children.

Jeanne's only consolation was the photos. The ones they sent back and forth to each other were the subject of long commentaries between mother and son. A picture of Marcel in his military coat, bowl cut, one hand in his lap, and a book in the other, made him look—as Ghislain de Diesbach put it—"like a clown disguised as a municipal security guard and a sultan's page trying out a dance step," but it still warmed Jeanne's heart. Marcel is smiling, cheerful. He looks healthy. But Marcel seemed disappointed in a photo of his mother. It was the photographer's fault, Jeanne argued. She had to pose for too long. Another was taken by Robert from above, hence her inspired look. Clearly she was not photogenic. The candid shot was better than the pose. Here we see the germs of a theme that would play an important role in both the life and the work of Marcel Proust. Substitute, fetish, symbolic possession, the photograph sometimes reveals secrets to the observant that too great a proximity blinds us to. Were Jeanne's "pursed lips" a sign of a "moral preoccupation" as Marcel thought, or a simple matter of "focus"? To each, his or her own version.

Jeanne's letters to Marcel also served as a family chronicle, from which anything tragic was eliminated. Georges was taking the cure or having supper with her and Nuna in Auteuil; Nathé was taking part in the prize ceremony for the deaf and dumb; Louis, characteristically, was proving himself both generous and boastful. Jeanne couldn't resist the pleasure of recounting the following anecdote to her son:

Your uncle, wanting to reciprocate for a pair of curtains that Marie embroidered for him this winter, is giving her on August 15, for her saint's
day, a gold chain, purchased at Dupont's [Dupont was Mayer Dupont-
Mouillot's grandfather]. And since Jupiter never leaves Olympia, he's been
busy at the table for eight days making proclamations about Dupont intended for Octave's ears:

"Is it not, Nathé, the very best store in Paris?"

"So those princely baskets, all those great purchases, that's where they
came from?

"Ah, it's the most expensive store of all, but for good reason, they have
every right to be. A store like that that stocks the very finest goods," etc.

Every evening the same theme, with variations.

Sooner or later we'll be hearing, "that's the store that furnished the
'queen's necklace' that was stolen from Marie-Antoinette."[228]

Jeanne's sharp tongue and spirit of rebellion spared no one. It was part of the
gaiety that animated her letters, her amused look at the world, a powerful
way of eliminating or masking any negative feelings: no rancor, no anger,
no suffering.

But even beyond the absence of her son, Jeanne had every reason to be
profoundly unhappy: her mother had just died.

Jeanne Proust with her two sons, circa 1895.
© Bibliothèque nationale de France.

Rose Berncastel, née Silny, Jeanne's maternal grandmother.
© Archives nationales.

Two plates signed by Baruch Weil. © Catalogue Sotheby's Monaco 1977.

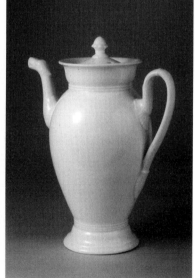

Porcelain plate and coffeepot from Baruch Weil's Fontainebleau factory.
Musée de Sèvres. © R.M.N.

Nathé Weil, Jeanne's father.
© Nadar, Centre des
monuments nationaux, Paris.

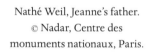

Adèle Weil, née Berncastel,
Jeanne's mother.
© Nadar, Centre des
monuments nationaux, Paris.

Georges-Denis Weil,
Jeanne's brother.
© Nadar, Centre des
monuments nationaux, Paris.

Amélie Weil, née Oulman,
Georges-Denis's wife.
© Nadar, Centre des
monuments nationaux, Paris.

Jeanne Weil, photographed by Otto.

Adèle Weil, Jeanne's mother.
© Bibliothèque nationale de France.

Jeanne as a child.
© Bibliothèque nationale de France.

Dr. Adrien Proust.
© Bibliothèque nationale
de France.

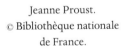

Jeanne Proust.
© Bibliothèque nationale
de France.

Robert and Marcel, 1876.
© Bibliothèque nationale
de France.

Virginie Proust, née
Torcheux, with her grandsons.
© Bibliothèque nationale
de France.

Marcel and Robert, circa 1882.

Marcel Proust, 1902, photographed by Otto.
© Bibliothèque nationale de France.

Robert de Flers, Lucien Daudet, and Marcel Proust.
© Bibliothèque nationale de France.

A manuscript page from Ruskin's *The Bible of Amiens*,
translated into French by Jeanne Proust, with Marcel's corrections.
© Bibliothèque nationale de France.

Madame Proust
on vacation.
© Bibliothèque nationale
de France.

———◆———

Jeanne's notebook.
© Bibliothèque nationale
de France.

Above left and opposite,
Jeanne Proust, December 5, 1904,
photographed by Nadar. © Nadar, Centre
des monuments nationaux, Paris.

The pleasures of reading. © Bibliothèque nationale de France.

Facsimile of a letter from Marcel to his mother, from Proust, *Correspondance avec sa mère* (Plon, 1953). The fragment reads: "Went to bed at one [underlined]. My dear little Mama, Each minute of these past two days has brought new things to tell you (nothing disagreeable of course! . . .)."

17

Vergiss mein nicht

Vergiss mein nicht, in gothic lettering, signaled a past emerging from the depths of time, something that was and yet was not a part of Jeanne, something almost inexpressible. A woman so French, so enamored with the French language—her son would become one of its masters, though some people still criticize him for the length of his sentences and their complex syntax, for being unfaithful to the elegant ways of French—Jeanne perceived in that angular, medieval calligraphy traces of the ghetto, of sordid alleys, dark shops, beards and side curls, women in wigs, pale children. A gothic hand that only a few Germans still use today, a link to generations of Berncastels born and raised in Trèves—shopkeepers, watchmakers, dealers in secondhand goods or in porcelain, lamps, or knickknacks, whose descendants would try their luck in France, in England, later in the United States, and still later in Australia.

Six words that Jeanne wrote with a kind of tenderness—a farewell—give us a glimpse into her enduring affection for the language of her foreign ancestors. Everyone whose ancestors have come from somewhere else understands how it happens: the words become rarer and rarer with successive generations, until there is no one left who speaks the old language. The foreign element, once dominant, diminishes and finally disappears. Jeanne has blended into French society; she is married to a professor of medicine, the son of a grocer from the Beauce (no Jewish shopkeeper, thank you!). The children are baptized; they've taken their First Communion. They're French Catholics, like everyone else. And a few words slip into a letter, an unconscious homage to her mother and to her maternal grandfather, Nathan Berncastel, who arrived in the thick of the emperor's war, speaking scarcely a word of French. French citizenship, for him, was a gift rather than his due.

German words were unusual coming from Jeanne. As Proust would show, using a few modest objects that had belonged to his mother, Jeanne slipped a few words from her family's language into letters written just before and just after her mother's death. The first occurrence was at the end of a letter written to Marcel while he was staying at the Finalys' in Ostend: "Farewell my darling. Tausend Küsse, as they say in your new language."[229]

His new language, or his former, ancestral one? Like the Berncastels, the Finalys came from Germany. Madame Finaly's mother still lived in Austria. In a way, Marcel was going to language camp. It was one of those educational opportunities Jeanne never let slip. And it was a wink at their common ancestry with the Finalys, who would be so ferociously caricatured—or so it's said—in Proust's portrait of the Bloch tribe.

The second time Jeanne used a German term was also connected to Horace Finaly: "I shall try to see Finaly and get some news of you. But from what I know of his character, I fear he will have stopped at the Gebäude and not tried to penetrate your life and state of mind."[230] The *Gebäude* is the main building, the construction, that which has been built on the foundations. The *Gebäude* allows the facade to be seen but not the true self. The *Gebäude* can lie about what's essential, what can't escape a mother's eye. There's the *Gebäude* of success in society, not to mention the pressure to produce descendants. But there's also the facade of her letters, which reveal almost nothing about Jeanne's profound anguish: the absence of her son, her mother's illness:

I'm counting on a good long letter tomorrow, which will have to substitute a little for your company.

Your grandmother is on milk today—still in homeopathic doses—she only consents to take it if it has no taste of milk.[231]

Proust would explain in *The Guermantes Way* how Dr. Cottard's treatment for albumin would fail, because salt was added to the milk to mask its taste.

It was now September 1889. It's likely that the first signs of Adèle's illness had already appeared. Dizziness, extreme fatigue, pallor, nausea, low-grade fever, swollen limbs, temporary blindness, deafness—Proust gave a very precise, clinical picture of his grandmother's condition leading up to the final illness, the stroke and the death throes. He wasn't present at the various stages of the renal failure that led to her death, because he was at Orléans. But in the absence of surviving letters, we can safely assume that Jeanne kept him informed about the health of the grandmother he adored. Perhaps she didn't give every detail, but she tried to reassure him. We know that in the devastating pages in *The Guermantes Way* about his grandmother's death, Proust also drew on his memory of his own mother's death throes, since Jeanne, like her brother Georges, succumbed to the same illness as her mother.[232]

Jeanne's third and last German phrase says it all: *Vergiss mein nicht*, forget me not. Adèle was dead. In one April letter to Marcel, Jeanne had combined the lilac and the forget-me-not, her son's fetish flower and the flower of memory, just as earlier in the same letter she had connected Loti's *Novel of a Child*, which her son had given her to read, with Madame de Sévigné: "Adieu, my darling, I kiss you tenderly with a pedal point to be sustained until the next kiss. Your white lilac is drooping, but the Vergissmeinnicht is quite fresh."[233]

Reading Loti "did her good," and she found in Madame de Sévigné words that evoked her absent mother and gave her pleasure.[234] We will never learn anything about Jeanne's profound suffering, the pain she didn't want weighing on her son. He showed her the same decency—he wanted to avoid showing her his sorrow. Mother and son mirrored one another, like mother and daughter before them. In a moving letter, Jeanne guided Marcel in the ways of mourning, doubtless thinking that one day it would be her own death he would have to confront:

Dearest,

Why didn't you write: "because you were crying all the time, and I am feeling sad as well"? I would not have been any sadder at that moment, my dearest, because you had written to me. Your letter would have been the reflection of what you were feeling and for that reason alone it would have given me pleasure. First of all, I am never saddened by the idea that you think about your grandmother; on the contrary, that is extremely comforting. And it is comforting, too, to stay close to you through our letters—as I would be close to you here—and for you to reveal yourself in them, all of you. So, my darling, do not devise a system of not writing to me in order not to make me sad, for it's the opposite that will occur. And then my darling, think of her—cherish her with me—but don't let yourself give in to days of crying that enervate you, which she wouldn't want. On the contrary, the more you think of her, the more you must be the way she loved and must act according to what she would want.[235]

Much later, Marcel would be able to generate the memory of maternal sorrow, the gathering around the sickbed that day, and the inconsolable wound to Jeanne's heart. She had scarcely informed him about his grandmother's mild stroke than he wrote: "No sooner had I started to speak than my mother's face was stricken with a paroxysm of despair, yet a despair already so resigned that I realized she had been holding it in readiness for years against an uncertain but decisive day."[236]

Jeanne asked no questions, she was "weeping with a tearless face."[237] She rushed to her mother's side and helped her get up, but didn't look at her twisted face out of a sense of propriety, out of respect, out of pain, and, Proust adds, "perhaps better to be able to preserve intact in her memory the true face of her mother, beaming with intelligence and kindness."[238] Mother and daughter competed to minimize the illness and to spare each the spectacle of suffering and decline. "I am not suffering," the mother claimed; "I'm crying because I have to stay in bed on a beautiful sunny day." "Maman, you'll soon be well again, your daughter will make sure of that," the daughter replied:[239]

And, stooping over the bed, with her knees bent, almost kneeling, as if the humility of her posture would facilitate the acceptability of this passionate gift of herself, she bent her face down toward my grandmother with the whole of her life contained in it, like a ciborium she was holding out to her, decorated with folds and dimples so enamored, so sorrowful, and so sweet that there was no way of telling whether they had been engraved on it by a kiss, a sob or a smile.[240]

The daughter's kissing her dying mother reminds us of the goodnight kiss, long awaited by the child Marcel—a believer waiting to receive the host.

Jeanne watched over her mother day and night. Morphine was powerless to lessen her mother's pain. Adèle lost consciousness, and intermittently returned to life; after the last heartbreaking rally, she was reduced to a ravaged old woman they had to force back into bed. Medicine was of no use. Proust would describe the absurd procession of notable doctors called to the bedside, ending with the famous Dr. Dieulafoy, Adrien's colleague, whose duly remunerated visits were habitually followed by funerals. The grandmother was surrounded by her immediate family, as well as a cousin, a veritable harbinger of misfortune, referred to by everyone as "No flowers by request."[241] This cousin, with his beard and his nickname based on Jewish funerals, seems to have come straight from the Weil family. As for Adèle's brother-in-law, a priest whose order, strangely, was located in Austria, he seemed less like a priest (he used no Christian liturgy) than some pious Jew "reading prayers and meditations yet never once shifting his penetrating gaze from the invalid."[242] The dying woman's two sisters didn't come.

> "You heard about the telegram her sisters sent? My grandfather asked my cousin."
>
> "Yes, that Beethoven business. I was told about it. It ought to be framed. But I'm not surprised."
>
> "And my poor wife was so fond of them," said my grandfather, wiping away a tear. "We mustn't hold it against them, though. They are stark raving mad, the pair of them. I've always said so."[243]

This passage from *The Guermantes Way* may be based on a memory of the two Berncastel sisters, Amélie and Ernestine, music lovers like Adèle.

Dignity, an extreme sense of propriety: among Jews from Alsace-Lorraine or Germany, emotion was always contained. If people showed emotion, they did so despite themselves and noiselessly.

> At the foot of the bed, convulsed by every gasp of the dying woman, not weeping but at moments drowned in tears, my mother stood with the heedless desolation of leaves lashed by the rain and torn back by the wind.[244]

The only sobs that could be heard came from the maid.

Adèle Weil, born Adèle Berncastel, died on Friday, January 3, 1890, the eve of the Sabbath. She was buried the following Monday in a religious ceremony in the Weil family plot, in the Jewish section of the Père-Lachaise cemetery.

Jeanne said nothing to her family about her grief. They knew. Marcel returned from Orléans. His mother's letters were gay, full of her worries about others. Each day she went to her father's apartment to relieve Georges, who still lived on the rue du Faubourg Poissonnière. There she looked after Nathé, tended to him when he was sick, read to him. Reality is a great tutor. In a notebook with a gray cover, she confided her grief, her scattered thoughts, quotations, secrets. Based on her notebook, Marcel Proust composed the scenes in *The Guermantes Way* devoted to his grandmother's death, scenes also marked by his mother's death. There were bonds of ink between mother and daughter, mother and son.

Part Three

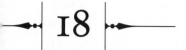

18

A Woman in Black at the Beach

Low tide, a gray and brown monochrome beach. The changing sky that I contemplate from my window at Les Roches noires is the sky that Jeanne and Marcel Proust would have seen during their September visits to Trouville. Les Roches noires was the most luxurious hotel there, with its banners waving in the breeze; its huge terrace; its white canvas tent; the dandies with canes, in their white pants, tailored jackets, and floppy neckties; the airy muslin of dresses, mother-of-pearl in hue like the clouds; the parasols; the wrought-iron balconies; the stone façade: all these, against a misty sky and oyster-colored sea, were painted by Claude Monet near Honfleur in 1870. You breathe the vibrant salty air. You hear the cry of the seagulls (absent from Monet's painting) and the muffled sound of voices on the beach, the murmur of waves and idle conversations.

While the fashion for ocean bathing dates back to the July Monarchy,

Trouville's reputation as Queen of the Beaches (it was nicknamed "Queen of Pebbles" by devotees of her rival, Dieppe) was established only at the end of the nineteenth century. First brought to the public eye in 1825 by the painter Charles Mozin, this fishing village with a few hundred inhabitants attracted Dumas, Musset, Flaubert, Boudin, Monet, and Courbet, gradually transforming itself into an elegant seaside resort. Alongside the artists was the cream of Parisian society: aristocrats, financiers, members of the grande bourgeoisie who erected opulent, colorful villas in an architectural mix of stone, brick, and wood. Oriental, Norman, or Neogothic in style, these buildings continue to endow Trouville with its special charm.

As with mineral spas, the rise of the seaside spas was tied to the expansion of the railroads. After a station was built at Trouville in 1863, visitors from Paris could get there in barely five hours. In that year, Adolphe Crémieux purchased a 105,000-franc "chalet," built by Celinski, just behind Les Roches noires. A year later, Madame Aubernon, who reigned supreme over her Parisian salon near the Prousts' apartment, built her Manoir de la Cour brûlée. In 1869, Les Frémonts, "a splendid new L-shaped villa," was built for Arthur Baignères "on the crest of the cliff," with a panoramic view of ocean and countryside.[1] Marcel Proust used it as a model for La Raspalière, the Verdurins' property. The house was rented to the Finalys, the wealthy financiers whom Marcel had visited in Ostend two years earlier. Horace de Landu, Madame Finaly's uncle, had purchased Les Frémonts as a present for his niece. Marcel stayed at the house in October 1891 and August 1892; while there, he met not only Arthur Baignères and his wife but also the Strauses—the parents of his friend Jacques Bizet—who would build their own villa at Trouville.

The Parisian salons moved their venue to the seaside during the summer season, which lasted until October, when the hunting season began. Organdy dresses and panama hats far outnumbered the red caps of the fishermen, dragging their shrimp nets as they waded in the cold water. There was theater, music, horse racing at the Hippodrome de la Touques in Deauville, parties, promenades on the boardwalk, outings to country inns in the vicinity of Trouville and Honfleur, and, of course, for those who desired or needed it, bathing in the sea.

Bathing was less for pleasure than for therapeutic reasons. Salt water with iodine content was thought to have the same healing virtues as at Salies-de-Béarn, here with the addition of wind, never absent for long from the Normandy beaches. The Weils preferred Cabourg and Dieppe, where

Marcel and Robert had been taken as children by their grandmother. Writing to his mother from Cabourg, Marcel recalled "those years at the seaside where grandmother and I, melted together, walked against the wind as we conversed." Jeanne solemnly copied the "Letter from my little Marcel at Cabourg September 1891" in her notebook. Nathé enjoyed the Paris-Dieppe train line, which allowed him to buy a first-class round-trip ticket, so that he could visit his family and still sleep at home.

But Marcel's friends were in Trouville. And Robert de Montesquiou, whom he had just met, stayed at Les Roches noires. It was Marcel who urged Jeanne to change her habits. "I agree with you completely," she wrote her son, who handled the reservations. "I only want you to be sure to get a reply from the Hôtel des Roches noires as soon as possible."[2] She suggested he take the liberty of choosing his own room, since she was bringing a chambermaid and would add a cook and a servant if they decided to rent a house once they were there.

Three years had passed since Adèle's death. Jeanne's grief had lost its edge, but the loss, though sometimes diluted by everyday concerns, deepened. Jeanne had to learn to live again, not *without* her mother, but with the illusion that her mother was still there, that she was guiding her in her decisions, her reading, her talking. Her mother lived in her, through her. Jeanne expressed her sorrow only in her notebooks and diaries. Even her son had no idea what she was feeling. Going to Trouville instead of Dieppe may also have been a way of avoiding memories that were too painful. Marcel hadn't forgotten the few days he and his mother spent together at Cabourg during his army leave in September 1890, eight months after his grandmother's death. Jeanne was still in full mourning; Marcel was ill and stayed in bed most of the time. Later, in *In Search of Lost Time*, he wrote:

> Then, for the first time, and because I felt a sorrow that was nothing in comparison with her own, but which had opened my eyes, I realized with terror what she might be suffering. I understood for the first time that the fixed, tearless gaze [. . .] that she had had since my grandmother's death had been dwelling on this incomprehensible contradiction between memory and nothingness. [. . .] But above all, the moment I saw her enter in her black coat, I realized—what had eluded me in Paris—that it was no longer my mother I saw in front of me, but my grandmother.[3]

Jeanne, Marcel realized, had lost something of her own personality, "her common sense, and the mocking high spirits she took from her father"[4]—

having never hesitated to tease during Adèle's lifetime, even at her own mother's expense. She teased Adèle about endlessly quoting Sévigné; she quoted her in turn in her own letters to her son. By way of imitation, she swore to idolize everything Adèle had loved. Marcel recalled:

> Not only could my mother not be parted from my grandmother's bag, more precious to her now than if it had been of sapphires and diamonds, from her muff, from all the garments that brought out still more strongly how alike the two of them were in appearance, but even from the volumes of Mme de Sévigné that my grandmother was never without, copies that my mother would not have exchanged for the manuscript of the Letters itself. [. . .] Holding her mother's *en-tout-cas* in her hand, I saw her from the window, advancing all in black, with timid, pious steps, across the sand that cherished feet had trodden before her, and she seemed to be going in search of a dead body that the waves were to bring back to her.[5]

Each day at Cabourg, just as her mother had done before her, Jeanne went down to the beach to sit and read, taking her two favorite books, Madame de Rémusat's *Memoirs* and Madame de Sévigné's *Letters*. Steeped in sorrow, haunted by her mother, she only woke from her reverie to insist that her son take a little walk with her. The trip to Cabourg came too soon for her after Adèle's death.

Strict rules of mourning delineated grief, codified it, authorized it, and tracked its progressive diminution. After nine months in deep mourning, when only black wool clothing was allowed, came six months in black silk; this was followed by three months in half-mourning, when velvet or silk (either matte or glossy) could be worn in any shade from gray to violet. Jeanne never ceased wearing black. Her dark profile made quite a contrast with the light, elegant outfits of Trouville, where people didn't hesitate to change clothes five or six times a day. Trouville had become "the boulevard des Italiens of our Normandy beaches," crowded with "the best-born aristocracy of Parisian bathers."[6]

Jeanne and Marcel stayed at Les Roches noires from September 6 through September 28, 1893, returning the following year for the same period. The previous year, guests at the hotel included the marquis de Boyen, the baron de Gary, the Singers, Count Stanislas Kzewaski, the Randolphs, the Hausers, and Emile Zola. Removed from the center of town, at the far end of the beach, it looked directly onto the sea. The guidebooks praised the hotel's "magnificent view of the mouth of the Seine and the cliffs of Le Havre." Its elevated terrace dominated the shoreline, setting its guests apart from ordinary beach-goers. Built in 1865, Les Roches noires was designed by the architect Alphone Crépinet, who worked for the Pereire brothers and designed the Grand Hôtel on the boulevard des Capucines, near the Opéra, in Paris. The facade of Les Roches noires recalls the buildings in that Paris neighborhood, though the general layout, with its symmetrical wings, was inspired by a château. Around 1880, the building became the property of an English banker, Gustave Palmer Harding. With three hundred rooms, twenty parlors, bathrooms, a billiard room, a café, a restaurant, private dining rooms, and a stable, it became the first hotel, and for many years the only one, with an elevator for all four floors. The famous "lift" in *In the Shadow of Young Girls in Flower* is probably based as much on the one at Les Roches noires in Trouville as on the one at the Grand Hôtel in Cabourg. The vast main dining room was adorned "with a fireplace of Pyrenees marble carved in a sculptural manner." Oriental rugs, plants, an elegantly dressed staff, and shining silver made it the archetype of nineteenth-century grand hotels. Everything was conceived for the well-being of a demanding clientele, accustomed to the very best. The English were enthusiastic about its modern facilities. All the more surprising to find Marcel's description, two months after his stay:

> Last year I spent some time at the Grand Hôtel of T., located at the end of the beach. The stale odor of cooking and dirty water, the luxurious banality of the draperies—the only variation on the grayish blank walls that rounded out this décor of *exile*—had reduced my soul to a nearly morbid depression.[7]

Was this description necessary for his story, or was it a genuine impression? Sanitary conditions in the grand hotels did leave much to be desired. Trouville was a hotbed for infection, and the Touques river, which ran through the center of town, was a sewer. Sanitary facilities were inadequate for the seasonal influx of tourists. Only in 1897, under the guidance of one of Adrien Proust's disciples, was a sewage plant built. And only in 1903 would the hotel get electricity and telephone service, central heating and new bathrooms. At that time a glass-roofed extension was added to the central dining room.[8]

Mother and son stayed on the second floor, facing the beach. "The weather is delightful," and the guests appreciate "the sun shining on the sea," Marcel explained to his father, the family weather expert, who was taking the waters at Vichy, as he always did at that time of the year. The son added, somewhat caustically: "as Baudelaire says in a line of verse whose power I hope you will appreciate." Father and son were involved in a conflict that appeared unresolvable. Adrien wanted Marcel to take up a serious career: diplomacy or law, for example. Marcel swore only by literature and philosophy. If there was one thing that revolted him, it was the prospect of practicing law. Anything was preferable, even becoming a stockbroker like his grandfather—but never a lawyer. The conflict worried Jeanne. She knew that Marcel wasn't made for the kind of career his father had in mind. Socializing and writing took up the better part of his time. He had brought with him to Trouville the page proofs of articles forthcoming in *La Revue blanche*. A number of his friends, from Fernand Gregh to Daniel Halévy, also planned to devote themselves to literature, and in March 1893 he made the acquaintance of Robert de Montesquiou, in whom high aristocracy was combined with the prestige of an inspired poet.

That summer, Marcel gave a dinner party for his friends, in the presence of his parents and his brother. To Jeanne's right sat Count Charles de Grancey; to her left, her friend Willy Heath. Along with Jacques Baignères and Robert de Flers—fourteen people in all at the table—they were joined that evening by Abel Desjardins, the painter Paul Baignères, Pierre Lavallée, Léon Yeatman, and several others. Other dinners followed; Jeanne hosted them with wit and grace. She knew how important they were to her son, and she noticed how minutely he planned the seating and the menu, fussing over every detail.

But Jeanne also knew that her husband had a point. Marcel had turned twenty-one and had received his law degree. Chatting in salons, filling pages and pages of social correspondence, and writing a few short stories hardly constituted a future. She knew what dangers, what easy ways out lay in wait for Marcel; she feared his lack of willpower and his taking refuge in illness. Did she ever think about Madame de Sévigné's son, a lazy socialite and a bad sort? She knew Marcel's qualities, she knew there was something exceptional about him. She was sure she wasn't mistaken. But it would be so easy for him to waste his talent in useless charm. She had worked for so long to shape his character. "I have no desire to see my son become an artist of genius," says Madame Santeuil in *Jean Santeuil*.⁹ Did Jeanne already intuit his genius and fear for his unhappiness? All her maternal efforts were directed toward giving him that sense of work and discipline without which genius comes to nothing.

A profession could give him the structure he was missing. He would have to get up in the morning like other people, have a regular rhythm to his life, go out less often. The three weeks alone with him in Trouville might enable Jeanne to persuade Marcel that he must compromise with his father—agree to a career, if not as a lawyer. Determined not to be "a lawyer, a doctor, a preacher, or a —"[10] Marcel was clearly not yet ready to embrace a "practical career," but he was beginning to get used to the idea.

In Trouville, Jeanne shared her son's schedule of activities, met and spent time with his friends and acquaintances. They went on walks with the Strauses, spent the evenings in the company of the writer Porto-Riche, who lived next door with his wife, and with the historian Schlumberger, an avowed anti-Semite but nonetheless a guest of the Strauses and an attorney for the Rothschild family. The Princess of Sagan, whose villa overlooked the beach, and the Princess of Monaco both made appearances. Marcel's infatuated admiration for Geneviève Straus would evolve over the years into a deep friendship. How did Jeanne feel about the adoring looks her son gave a woman who was the same age as she,[11] and whose own son he had once pursued? It was obvious how much the two women had in common: Geneviève, like Jeanne, belonged to the assimilated Jewish grande bourgeoisie; she too had first married a non-Jew, the musician George Bizet, before her current husband, the lawyer Emile Straus. A nonbeliever and nonpracticing Jew like Jeanne, Madame Straus remained attached to her Jewish identity. She liked to joke, "I don't have enough religion to change religions." Her role during the Dreyfus affair was decisive. She was famous for her wit, and her ironic one-liners made the rounds of the best salons in Paris. Geneviève Straus was a society version of Jeanne.

Geneviève's son Jacques was as passionately attached to his mother as Marcel was to his. But this gifted boy—who wrote, like Marcel, and began medical school, like Robert—turned into a suicidal dilettante, then an alcoholic and a drug addict, depleting his mother's fortune and finishing his life tragically with a bullet to his mouth. Did Jeanne perceive in Jaccques Bizet a hint of the failure her son might become?

The similarities with Madame Straus stop there. Deprived of affection in her youth, heir to her father's family, the Halévys, who were prone to mental illness, daughter of an unstable mother who spent long periods in Dr. Blanche's clinic and with whom she had a very bad relationship, Geneviève had a vital need to be surrounded by admirers and to be adored. It was her safeguard against doubt and depression. "Her beautiful Tzigane face, her eyes burning, shaking with nervous twitches," betrayed an indelible melancholy, which she fought with veronal and other drugs.[12] The darling of a whole literary and social milieu, she was far from possessing the stable temperament and down-to-earth qualities of a Jeanne Proust, who drew on her mother's love and her father's authority to safeguard her own equilibrium.

When Jeanne and Geneviève met in Trouville in September 1893 (though they must have known each other earlier, since their sons had attended the same nursery school and lycée), the Strauses had just moved to the house they had had built on the cliffs, Le Clos des mûriers. It had taken three years to finish the house, the builders working from six in the morning to six at night. This three-story mansion, with its terraces, its bathrooms, its rooms of all colors perfumed by bouquets of roses, was set high above the sea and was surrounded by a magnificent twelve-acre park, so dense with vegetation, one visitor recalled, you could go out in your pajamas in complete privacy.[13]

Country walks along the upland paths of Normandy with their "combined scent of leafage, milk and sea salt,"[14] strolls along the boardwalks, concerts in the afternoon at the bandstand, the casino: there was no shortage of activities. When Jeanne didn't accompany her son on his social outings, she would sit on the terrace and read. Both of them spent time on their correspondence. Jeanne probably went bathing, for she loved the water. Well protected by her robe under one of the tents set up on the sand, she could then take a quick dip in the area reserved for ladies under the watchful eye of one of the lifeguards—easy to spot by their tanned muscles, their leather hats, and their red scarves with yellow fringes, and drawing admiring glances from Marcel, careful to stay clear of the spray.

In July 1894, Marcel got to know the musician Reynaldo Hahn. He ran into him again in August at Madeleine Lemaire's, after a bout with rheumatic fever. The Finalys were gone, Léon Yeatman was in Etretat; other than the Strauses, the only person Marcel knew in Trouville was the ravishing Madame Trousseau, whose husband owned the Villa Simonian, and the marquise de Gallifet, one of the "Belles of the Empire," who had just built her Manoir des Roches. More and more intimate with Reynaldo, Marcel tried in vain to convince his friend to join him after Jeanne's departure on Sunday, September 23. "There's no one I can talk to about you since Mama left," he complained, making it clear to us that he had confided in his mother.[15]

Jeanne was certainly under no illusion, any more than she had been about her other son, who had almost been killed in an accident a few days earlier (September 8, 1894). Riding a tandem bicycle with a girlfriend, the athletic Robert was hit by a coal wagon, which rolled over his thigh. He was admitted to a clinic in Rueil, where he spent "the 'most charming hours' he had ever spent," according to Jeanne. Withdrawing to a room at the back of the clinic to write her elder son, she waited for the crowd of "interns from Ivry and all sorts of brothers in arms" who had surrounded the twenty-one-year-old intern to disperse. Adrien arrived from Vichy, "very upset by the news of his son's fall."[16] *His* son? Robert was also Jeanne's son, but it's difficult to detect her worry beneath the banter of her letters. Certainly Robert was receiving excellent treatment and was out of danger; Dr. Proust confirmed it. As soon as he was better, they would move him to Auteuil, and Jeanne would rejoin Marcel at Trouville. Her retreat might also be explained by another feminine presence at Robert's side. Jeanne's maternal discretion was exceptionally tolerant for the times. As Marcel wrote Madame Catusse in 1915, "Mama fraternized at his bedside with the cocotte who was tending to him."[17] After all, Robert didn't really need his mother. Adrien returned to Vichy. Jeanne's brother Georges, who had been sick with cholera in August at Versailles, was out of danger. She might as well go back to Marcel.

A year later, we find Jeanne in Dieppe, this time in April, and alone. Georges, who was supposed to accompany her, had reneged:

> Little sister, I am very uncertain about Dieppe. I hate the wind and today's weather really bothers me. Aside from that, I'm lazy about going anywhere.
>
> I've been taking walks for two days. It seems to agree with me fairly well. Perhaps I'll keep up with this walking, but perhaps also if the temperature improves and you send satisfactory reports from out there, I'll send you a telegram announcing that I'm coming to join you.
>
> Much tenderness."[18]

Marcel had opted to stay with his friend Pierre Lavallée. Jeanne may have stayed at the Métropole, one of the few hotels that were open in that season. In September 1896 she was alone again at the Hôtel Royal, right by the beach and the casino and described in the guidebooks as having a "splendid view of the beach, the jetty and the pier. Vast dining room. Large parlors for reading and conversation. Small and large suites, elegantly furnished. Equipment for promenades and excursions. Special cars on all the trains. Superior dining. Exquisite wine cellar; a collection of fine and foreign wines." What memories were there? This solitary pilgrimage to the beach of her youth must have been quite melancholy. She was once again in deep mourning, afflicted with a double loss: her uncle Louis and his brother Nathé, her father, had died six weeks apart.[19]

Nathé, age eighty-two, "allowed himself to starve to death within the week, during which he insisted on being carried thrice daily to his bath, where Papa, terrified, never stopped taking his pulse," Marcel wrote a few months before his own death, worried at having reached the same level of starvation as his grandfather.[20] Nathé's terrible end must have affected Jeanne all the more in that she had showered him with affection, taking care of him on a daily basis since her mother's death. As for Louis, he was her beloved uncle, as much a part of her life as her parents. Whether at 102, boulevard Haussmann, where she so often went for lunch with her husband and children, or at Auteuil, their second residence, he was part of many memories. The family coped with these deaths in unison: Adrien, Marcel, and Robert surrounded Nathé just as they had surrounded Adèle in her final moments. The familial clan stayed together, and Adrien was clearly part of this seamless solidarity. The nearly simultaneous deaths of two brothers prefigured those of Jeanne and Georges, who also died within a short time of each other.

Deeply affected, Marcel attempted to console his mother. He himself had lost the confidant of his youth, his beloved grandpa, whom he could ask for money as easily as for political advice. Uncle Louis too had played an essential role in his education and had had long discussions with Marcel throughout his adolescence. According to his friend Robert de Billy,

> the conversations with his uncle, Monsieur Weil, witty and caustic, were very important for Marcel's intellectual development. There was an affection there; he never felt he needed to protect Marcel for facing reality head on, something for which Marcel was grateful. I believe it was through those conversations that he came to understand in detail the structure of Jewish society.[21]

Another friend, Maurice Duplay, recalled Louis's cloth skullcap (reminiscent of the yarmulke?), his vague demeanor and mysterious ways. Uncle Louis died an epicurean, without suffering, from an attack of pneumonia that lasted a single day.

Nathé was cremated, and his ashes were buried, with a graveside ceremony, on July 2 at ten in the morning in the eastern part of the Père Lachaise cemetery.[22] This was probably according to his last wishes. The cremation may well have been an expression of his freethinking, since it was contrary to Jewish law. In any case, it explains Marcel's remark in a letter to his mother: "I am very sad at not seeing you. Very sad for too many reasons. And yet to what purpose? When one sees, as we saw the other day, how everything ends, why grieve over sorrows or dedicate oneself to causes of which nothing will remain."[23] Among these "pains" for "too many reasons" was the ending of his love affair with Reynaldo Hahn. Still, he strove to help his mother, who once again was putting on a brave face. "Mama isn't doing too badly. She seems to be bearing up better under her great grief than I expected," he wrote to Reynaldo.[24] He showed the apartment on the rue du Faubourg-Poissonnière to a potential buyer and accompanied his mother in August to Mont-Dore, where her treatment didn't agree with her. On June 12, Proust published his first collection of short stories, *Pleasures and Days*, with a preface by Anatole France and illustrations by Madeleine Lemaire, and waited anxiously for the first reviews. Nonetheless, he shared Jeanne's sorrow, understanding that it did no good to hide it from her as he had after his grandmother's death. We can imagine his attachment to this grandfather, who may have been the true paternal figure for him. Thus he shared his mother's mourning, united with her, speaking for the two of them, experiencing the same feelings with no apparent generational difference:

> That photograph of grandfather is a very good one. I keep thinking what a real injustice it is, not that we are parted from him, but that he is parted from us, who belonged to him, as we still do, so closely, whom he loved so dearly, whom he had accepted as, and made, his own. We are like a house with no master.[25]

Having just returned from Mont-Dore, Jeanne left for Dieppe. Did her poor health make this necessary? Nothing of the sort comes through in her son's letters. He was preoccupied with his own health, providing Jeanne with copious details: the time he got up, the time he went to sleep, his medications, everything was there; his mother couldn't complain, she would know everything. Her son was doing well, she had to be reassured. She traveled alone on the train. After Dieppe, she went on to Tréport, savoring the journey. And this time, following the instructions of the bathing establishment, she went swimming. "Go for walks, bathe, don't *think* too much, don't tire yourself by making your letters to me too long, and let me thank you once more for the tranquility of these last few weeks, which you made me spend so happily," Marcel wrote her tenderly.[26] Each watched over the other at a distance. And even if Marcel gave her a few chores (present his credentials to Madame Lemaire, write on his behalf to Robert de Billy and Robert de Flers, and so forth), the chores themselves were proof of their bond. He gave her news of Robert, who'd been charming to him on the return trip—which was perhaps less common than one might think—and reported the most minute domestic matters on the boulevard Malesherbes. Jeanne wrote to Robert, too, and, more surprisingly, corresponded with Reynaldo Hahn, who revealed, to Marcel's great annoyance, that Marcel came to see him every day in Saint-Cloud.

Despite the wind and the rain, Jeanne was determined to continue her treatment. "I'm not hot before bathing," she explained from Tréport, her next port-of-call, where she was still alone, "Because I've been sitting for at least three-quarters of an hour. I'm not cold when I get out because I always drink something after leaving the water. What hurts a lot are the pebbles under my feet. Espadrilles really offer no protection."[27] Like everyone else, she was required to obey the instructions of the bathing establishment.[28] Sometimes she had to have a very early lunch, at 10:30 in the morning, in order to bathe in the afternoon. A three- or four-hour wait for digestion was considered indispensable if one wanted to avoid hypothermia. The hotel in Tréport was on the cutting edge of modernity: "w.c. with boards for writing, just like home—but what they also have are electric lights, which illuminate our work and are turned off afterwards."[29] As for the "leitmotiv of elastic mattresses," a second mattress took care of that.

Jeanne took advantage of her solitude to read Balzac's *Splendor and Misery of Courtesans*. And what distressed her even more than Rubempré's death, she wrote, was the death of Esther, the Jewish usurer Gobseck's daughter, who had become a prostitute.[30] Esther, again and always . . .

Very much in the here and now, pragmatic and efficient, she didn't want anyone else dictating her behavior. Marcel wanted her to stay longer, until October 15, so that he could join her in Tréport. Papa would be much freer for the Russian festivities, he pleaded, referring to the sumptuous ceremonies organized by the French Republic for the arrival of the czar in Paris. President Faure must have reserved special seats for his friend Dr. Proust. But Jeanne held firm:

My darling, you are very kind—and so am I. I will not return on a whim (by the way, your father proposed that I wait until the 1st to return), but I will come back when I tire of the baths—I take them arduously and get all the benefits from them that I can—that's all I can promise you.[31]

She'd come home when she liked. No sooner, no later.

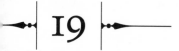

19

The Broken Glass

Jeanne was now an orphan. Committed to black. She was aware of it, even before her father's death, as she threw a spadeful of earth on Uncle Louis's coffin. A strange custom, participating in the burial of one's family, as if the living must be separated from the dead as quickly as possible so that we might continue to live. Nothing embellishes death in Jewish ritual. The nude body is slipped into a white shroud. No flowers. A pebble set on the tomb in lieu of an offering, a Kaddish[32] intoned in Hebrew and in Aramaic. Louis Weil refused any eulogy, even in the press. There was just a simple announcement.[33] The entire family was there, all those who had cherished him for his hospitality and his moral stature. Aunt Frédérique, the widow of Godechaux Weil, and Aunt Amélie de Beauvais ("Mother Weil") walked with difficulty. Jeanne saw that the "Three Graces," her cousins Jenny, Hélène, and Claire, were also mature women. Marcel, his head covered like all the men, had trouble holding back his tears. Nathé stared at the ground to hide his disarray. It tore at Jeanne's heart to see him. He had lost his brother and best friend. Their squabbles were but the modest form their affection took, a sign of their complementarity. He knew his time was coming soon.

Before the funeral procession left for the Père Lachaise cemetery, a tragicomic incident occurred, Louis Weil's last wink. Marcel had informed one of his uncle's former mistresses of his death—the ever-present Laure Hayman, whose good and loyal services to the males of the tribe had raised her to the official rank of friend of the family. The former cocotte was now forty-five and had taken up sculpture, for which she showed some talent. A cyclist brought a floral wreath from her to the home of the deceased at 102, boulevard Haussman, where everyone had gathered before leaving for the cemetery. When he saw it, Marcel burst into tears and had the wreath sent on, though it couldn't be put on the hearse, which was to have no decoration. Jeanne, waiting at the cemetery, was surprised at seeing the flowers arrive with the cortège, a symbol of Louis's innumerable conquests. She asked that they be lowered into the tomb with the old roué. Later, Marcel thanked Laure by sending her one of Louis's tiepins.

With the death of her uncle and her father, Jeanne became very wealthy. Nathé's estate and that of Adèle, in the absence of a will, were divided equally between their two children.[34] Louis left Jeanne and Georges his apartment on the boulevard Haussmann,[35] the house in Auteuil (reduced now to the value of its land),[36] as well as annuities and stocks; nor did he forget his Proust nephews, to whom, in a codicil added in 1887, he bequeathed 100,000 francs, share and share alike, which they would receive at the time of their marriage. This capital, invested in a government bond, would ensure them an annual income of 2,000 francs each. Louis's legendary generosity, which contrasted with his brother's frugality, was unfailing: according to Jewish custom, he donated 5,000 francs to the poor people in the community.[37] No one had ever sought his help in vain.

Jeanne had experienced her uncle's generosity when she interceded for her cousin Hélène. Four years earlier, Hélène had lost her husband, Camille Bessières, who ran an insurance company.[38] With three children to raise, she found herself in need. Jeanne wrote to her:

My dear friend,
I received your letter and I have sent it to Uncle Louis. He answered this morning and told me to come speak to him at three o'clock, which I did,

and here is what he said: "Your aunt and I have always had a soft spot for Hélène; she has not been happy. Here is what I can do for her, since, according to my calculations, she cannot get by with what she has and with the pension that your father and I granted her—from January 1, 1896, onward, I will raise her amount by 1,200 francs; that is, instead of 1,800 it will be 3,000, to be sent to her in four payments of 750 each. As for the future, she won't be disappointed: as long as I live, I will maintain this pension as well as her mother's 2,000-franc pension. After my death, I will leave 100,000 francs to Hélène, and 50,000 francs to her daughter; if her daughter marries during my lifetime, I will see that those 50,000 francs are part of the marriage contract; if she marries after my death, she will inherit them directly. And for now, I will give you a check for two hundred francs to help her straighten things out." My poor dear, I was very happy for you and I could not persuade my uncle to tell you of his good intentions himself—he said, "No, I want neither letters nor correspondence, I've said what I have to say and I insist that you be the one to write it." Now will you help safeguard my responsibility: after you've read this letter, don't waste a minute and send it back to me, but only after you've taken the time to write a note to me on the last page that you've received it and read it. [. . .] My uncle said, "I don't want any correspondence, I don't want any letter, I don't want any thanks," but that last clause I think that you will disobey with a full heart. Much tenderness, my dear friend, and joy over yours.

J. Proust

Answer me simply in one of two lines acknowledging receipt, and mail it without losing a moment so that the remittance is sent right away.[39]

Once again, family solidarity had come into play.[40]

An era was coming to an end. Soon, the property in Auteuil would be sold. The new owner had the house torn down and commercial buildings erected. In the summer of 1897, Jeanne and Adrien rented a chalet at the Parc des Princes. In a scene in *Jean Santeuil,* Marcel shows Monsieur and Madame Santeuil stopping by Auteuil on their way to the Bois. "Keep your eyes shut," Monsieur Santeuil tells his wife each time they approach the new construction. Sometimes she covers her eyes with her hands to hide her tears.[41]

After the sale of the rue La Fontaine, the memories flowed. There was the day Robert arrived late for lunch. He had gone boating on the lake in the Bois de Boulogne. Professor Duplay, his wife, and their son Maurice had been invited for lunch in Uncle Louis's garden. They were eating dessert when Robert appeared. He excused himself pitifully and approached his mother to give her a kiss. She turned her head away. Marcel observed the scene, close to tears. He stood up, trembling, and signaled to his brother to follow him. Jeanne followed on their heels. Was he having an episode, the beginning of an attack? All three of them ended up in the parlor. Marcel had used subterfuge to reconcile his mother with her younger son.[42]

This anecdote confirms Robert Proust's account of a Marcel who looked after his brother "with an infinite, enveloping, and, one might say, maternal sweetness."[43] Each sibling was both big brother and little brother to the other, in a close relationship that inevitably included rivalry. Robert was independent. He had escaped his mother's supervision, refusing to be treated like a child after he reached the age of twenty. How did he view the special bond between his brother and his mother? During his childhood, he must have had some feelings of exclusion. Knowing how moody and possessive Marcel was, Jeanne kept insisting on Robert's affection for him and strove to maintain equilibrium between the brothers. It wasn't easy. In a letter to his mother, Marcel asked her "not to show this letter to my angel of a brother, who is an angel but also a judge, a severe judge and who would infer from my remarks on the Count of Eu a certain snobbery or frivolity that is far from my true feelings rather than the need that makes me tell you what we might chat about and what might amuse us."[44] His possessive character, his obsessive jealousy, can't be understood without keeping in mind the existence of this "little brother," both loved and envied.[45]

After her solitary stay in Dieppe, Jeanne's spirits remained low. True to herself, she didn't complain or reveal her sadness. She confided only in a notebook, read by André Maurois and Philip Kolb but now lost, and whose secrets we so would have wished her to reveal. For each period of mourning, Jeanne committed her thoughts to the notebook, let her memories come to the surface, and looked to her writing to keep alive those she had loved. In her tall, narrow handwriting, she fought in her own way against oblivion and dissolution. Much later, Marcel wrote to his friend Anna de Noailles:

> I just found a notebook in which Mama recounted, hour by hour, the last illnesses of her father, her mother, Papa, accounts which, though without the shadow of an intent to suggest anything whatsoever, show so much distress that one can hardly continue to live after having read them.[46]

To all those around her, she made herself available and offered the mask of her gaiety. Everyone, even Marcel, was taken in.

But one incident, which so marked him that he told it on several occasions, revealed to him the depth of his mother's sorrow.[47] To recover from a
trying summer, Marcel decided to spend a few days in Fontainebleau. He left
on October 19, 1896, and took a room at the Hôtel de France et d'Angleterre,
the most luxurious hotel in town. With its terrace, large garden, and telephone, it promised to provide a pleasant stay. Unfortunately, it was raining
heavily, he almost suffocated when lying in bed, and those few days, despite
the dynamic presence of Léon Daudet, turned out to be an ordeal. Perhaps
never since his childhood had he suffered so from the absence of his mother.
There was no one around him to replace her, just as it had been at Beg-Meil
when he was there with Reynaldo Hahn at the beginning of their love affair.
His correspondence makes no mention of Jean Lazare, a family friend who
lived in Fontainebleau,[48] or of his great-grandfather Baruch Weil, who, as
Marcel may not have known, was buried there.

His letters are a long cry of distress, lamenting his suffering and his guilt.
He wrote to his mother once or twice each day, and she wrote to him at the
same rhythm. Between two letters, they called each other on the phone.
This was the first of those *téléphonages* that would move him so deeply, as he
later told Antoine Bibesco:

> And suddenly, over the phone, I heard her poor broken, tortured voice,
> changed forever from the voice I had always known, now full of cracks
> and fissures; and it was on hearing those bleeding, broken fragments in
> the receiver that I had my first terrible inkling of what had broken forever
> within her.[49]

Did he blame himself for leaving her during this trying time? Could he not
tolerate her sorrow, which he would attribute, in *In Search of Lost Time*, to his
grandmother, presenting it as a warning sign of death? The Prousts didn't
yet own a telephone (they would have one installed on the rue de Courcelles
in 1900). Jeanne took her phone calls at Cerisier's bakery across the street,
but in order to make a call she had to go to the crowded post office, because
the baker was not equipped for intercity calls. Her first letters to Fontainebleau were a pathetic effort to lighten the situation; she was ready with "a
little smile from the home front" when she was called to the telephone; she
would "break into song" if he was well.[50] She didn't realize that her voice
had betrayed her, something she discovered only in a story that Marcel sent
her, part of the novel he was writing.[51] In her subsequent letter, she affected
a light tone, not devoid of empathy, so as to reassure him. These pages, she

wrote, "are very sweet but so sad, my little wolf. They make me unhappy thinking of the sadness you felt. The story of a deported convict's arrival at the Salvation Islands couldn't be more heartbreaking."[52] The lesson wasn't lost on Jeanne, and from then on she doubtless tried to control her inflections, for Marcel wrote to her: "You weren't the same on the telephone yesterday. That's not your voice."[53]

Jeanne's letters, like her voice, failed to mask her worries. Even when she was trying to reassure Marcel, we sense the anxiety constantly gnawing at her. Nothing is worse for a mother than to see her son suffer. And the disease they thought was under control for several years had come back with a vengeance. Marcel had a severe asthma attack in July. He fought it with Espic cigarettes and inhalations of Legras powder; he struggled against insomnia by taking trional, valerian, and amyl nitrate. Since the previous winter, he had gotten into the habit of working at night and sleeping during the day. Jeanne couldn't sleep either. How could she when her son might be suffering far from her? She waited "impatiently for news about each night." Had he been able to "break his pact with that ungodly trional?" "Did you work? What time did you get up? And go to sleep? Be very careful about their cooking and heating in the evening. I think of it every evening."[54]

It's not surprising that the poor wolf gave full details of his nights, his waking up, his digestion. All the more so, since a new worry was torturing him: he had mysteriously lost over thirty francs. "Ravaged by remorse, harried by guilt, crushed by melancholy," he saw no solution other than to come home and abandon any idea of living apart.[55] What could Jeanne do except try to soothe him? Conscious of the gap between Marcel's despair and the actual situation, she tried to restore his sense of reality: "My darling, keep things in order and avoid creating these torments for yourself. [. . .] A thousand tender kisses dear little one, don't be scared and govern your person and your appetite according to the great principles."[56] The great principles . . .

It wasn't long before her son returned. Jeanne was both relieved and discouraged. The "poor exile," as she called him, was twenty-five years old, and he was incapable either of tolerating separation or of adjusting to reality. What would become of him if she didn't look after him? Her worries about his illness overlapped with her feelings for Marcel and his for her. Their reciprocal anxieties fed on each other and became a yoke weighing on both of them.

As for Robert, Marcel's return seems to have been his pretext to leave home for good. He lived his own life.

How could Jeanne not have felt lonely? Her brother Georges had been married for five years to Amélie Oulman, a plump, thirty-eight-year-old widow.[57] He hadn't left his mother until her death. He was forty-four. Now that he was the father of little Adèle, he was no longer the bachelor who used to spend time at his sister's. He seemed more and more like Nathé, irascible and finicky. Since 1889 he had been the titular judge at the Tribunal de première instance of the Seine, the greater Paris region. That same year, he had served as one of the representatives of the French government at an international conference in Washington, D.C., on maritime law.[58] He spoke perfect English. His daughter Adèle would learn the language from earliest childhood. Georges published several books about British institutions and in 1895, a historical work titled *Legislative Elections since 1789*.[59] A passionate reader, he possessed a library of twelve thousand books. The Georges Weils lived in a large apartment at 22, place Malesherbes, the former home of Amélie's first husband. The family gathered for dinner on Sunday evenings in the Henri II–style dining room, in a highly regulated atmosphere. The size of their staff—a cook, a valet, two chambermaids (one to serve meals, the other for laundry), a maid to polish the copper and brass, a governess for Adèle—gives some indication of their standard of living. Later, Amélie would organize sumptuous "white balls" for her daughter, which Emmanuel Berl always remembered with a touch of scorn. Georges's marriage to this young widow, who came from a less assimilated Jewish family than the Weils, further enlarged the family circle. The couple was married at the synagogue on the rue de la Victoire. The Oulmans were among the most visible, active elite families of the Jewish community. "On the occasion of her marriage to Monsieur Denis Weil, Madame Herman, widow of the late William Herman, invited the students of the Neuilly Shelter for Young Israelite Girls to light refreshments and an outing to the Zoological Gardens," the *Archives israélites* reported.[60] It was probably an arranged marriage, because Amélie never got over the loss of her first husband, originally from Frankfurt; until her death, she continued to wear her first wedding ring, which she had set with small stones to transform it into a regular ring. She was famous for her absent-mindedness: people liked to tell about the time she held out her hand to the washerwoman and said "Bonjour, Madame."[61]

Jeanne didn't see much of Adrien either, as he became increasingly absorbed by his life outside the household. No doubt he had given up trying to reform his elder son. Marcel, it must be said, was finally working, if a non-paying position as an assistant at the Mazarine Library could be called work. He had held the position, for which he had competed, since June 1895. After taking one leave after another, he finally resigned in 1900. He wrote. But most of his time was spent with his friends and acquaintances. He was a prisoner of "the icy wastes of social life."[62] Jeanne saw it as a form of dissipation, deploring his lack of will, his frivolousness. His love affair with Reynaldo Hahn, the musician, was followed by another one. Jeanne's affection for Reynaldo was clear. His family was Jewish, originally from Caracas, and he shared with Jeanne and Marcel their classical tastes and passion for music (Mozart, Gounod, Saint-Saëns). So Reynaldo won Jeanne's confidence, despite what Maurice Duplay called his "dark and cruel expression": his appearance seemed to suggest one of Henri III's *mignons* and one of Lucretia Borgia's lovers.

Was Jeanne equally impressed by Lucien Daudet? Lucien was the youngest son of Alphonse and Julia Daudet, "a lovely boy, with curly pomaded hair, made up and powdered, who spoke in a tiny voice that seemed to be coming out of his vest pocket," as Jules Renard wrote in his diary on March 3, 1895. All of Marcel's friends—Robert de Flers, Robert de Billy, Fernand Gregh—attest to Jeanne's warm welcome. Lucien was no exception to the rule. He would dedicate his book *Around Sixty Letters from Marcel Proust* "to the memory of Madame Proust, Marcel Proust's admirable mother." In it he describes his first visit to his friend's house:

> That day, he introduced me to his mother, whom he resembled: the same face, long and full, the same silent laugh when she found something amusing, the same attentiveness to anything you told her, the attentiveness that in Marcel could be mistaken for absent-mindedness because of the impression he gave of being "elsewhere"—when in fact it was, on the contrary, a sign of his concentration.[63]

A few days later, Marcel invited Lucien again, at Jeanne's behest. This time the young man was introduced to Adrien and made the acquaintance of Robert. He was struck by Robert's physical resemblance to his father, but saw his facial expressions as his mother's. "When their mother was there, you realized they were brothers,"[64] he wrote perceptively.

Lucien would be the indirect cause of a dispute—and an equally significant reconciliation—between Marcel and his parents. Marcel had posed with Robert de Flers and Lucien Daudet for the photographer Otto. After seven failed attempts on account of Marcel's uncontrollable nervous laughter, the photographer's final shot immortalizes Flers, nobly contemplating the horizon, and Lucien, apparently in love, casting a caressing eye on Marcel, who is seated. Jeanne and Adrien demanded that the photos be destroyed. A violent quarrel ensued, which Marcel transposes in *Jean Santeuil*. In every family, scenes of this kind crystallize accumulated resentments: "If you don't want to work [. . .] you can do the other thing: you can get out!" decrees Monsieur Santeuil in full view of the horrified servant.[65] Marcel's parents were of one mind with the Santeuils in expressing their discontent. They were exasperated with the general attitude of their son. Sharing the same work ethic, they saw the young man's frivolity as inseparable from his habits and the company he kept. In the novel, the mother writes to her son's friend, asking him to retreat. This abuse of power revolts Jean. "You are both idiots," he utters before leaving the room, slamming the door so hard that the glass panel shatters. As soon as Jean gets to his own room, he explodes, giving full rein to his fury. In his altered state, he seizes a Venetian glass, a present from his mother, and throws it to the ground. It breaks "in fragments that no amount of contrition could mend, put together again, and fuse once more into its ancient unity."[66]

Crying and shaking, Jean walks toward his bathroom and grabs the first piece of clothing he can find, a coat his mother used to wear, which is hanging in his armoire with some other old clothes. Its soft fabric and smell evoke the image of a young and loving mother. With heartrending awareness of the irreversibility of time, his tenderness returns. He rejoins his parents in the dining room and asks his mother's forgiveness, trying to kiss her. But she turns her head away. He forces himself to make the same attempt with his father, who, being "weaker than his wife, more violent and softer," can't resist. He sits down at the table. But then his father notices the coat he's wearing, lined with pink satin: "It's ridiculous to swaddle yourself like that. [. . .] It's quite warm in here, and in any case, that thing belongs to your mother. Take it off this minute!"[67] The story continues:

> His mother however, looking at him with innocent eyes which seemed to grasp without the slightest difficulty all the thoughts that had been working in him for the past two hours, smiled.

Jean then flings his arms around his mother's neck and gives her a long hug.

> But she, happy in the knowledge that she was loved, but not wishing that he should love her with an excess of passion which one day might cause

him pain, said gently, in a tone of blessed common sense, and ceasing to smile: "Now, don't be a little silly: go back to your place, and let us get on with dinner."[68]

Whether or not the second part of the scene actually took place, it sheds much light on the relationship between Marcel and his parents. The end of the story is no less powerful, but this time we'll hear it from Jeanne Proust herself:

My dear boy,
Your letter has done me good—your father and I were feeling very bad. [. . .] Let's never speak or even think of it again. From now on, let the broken glass be what it is at temple—a symbol of indissoluble union.[69]
Your father wishes you a good night and I kiss you tenderly.
J.P.
I have to come back to the subject after all: be sure not to go into the dining room with bare feet, because of the glass.[70]

The same words, or nearly the same, would appear in the novel. All of Jeanne Proust is in these lines: her marital bond ("your father and I") and the indissoluble and sacred tie with her son; the reference to Judaism as law and as symbol—the broken glass of the marriage ceremony; the forgiveness, contradicted by the mock warning; and, above all, love. She says nothing about the distress her son's odious tantrum surely caused her, but merely expresses relief. "Your letter has done me good." Marcel must have apologized by letter, and she responded by letter. Writing had always been a bond between them. Marcel wound up by promising to keep only three copies of the compromising photograph and to give the others to his mother.

Other fights doubtless took place, even though Marcel maintained that this was the only time in his life that he was ever really angry. The expenses he incurred exasperated his parents, who handled their wealth like good bourgeois, aware of the value of money. Marcel tolerated his dependence on them poorly, though he knew there was no way he could support himself on his own. His odd hours, his extravagant social life, his refusal or incapacity to conform to a strict schedule of meals, his longing for freedom, and his illness created tensions that reflected back on the mood of the family. Jeanne was usually the one to exercise authority in the household, Adrien serving as last resort in times of crisis. Sometimes indulgent with an unhealthy son she was so close to, sometimes strict because she was trying to impose rules on their life together, she had lost, with the death of her father and her uncle, the symbolic recourse the two men represented. And she was no longer dealing with a child or an adolescent but with a twenty-five-year-old man, who defended his choices and, despite his culpability, was learning to make those choices acceptable to his mother.

———•••••———

Worries about her own health added to her maternal preoccupations. Jeanne suffered continuously from female ailments that are still difficult to cure. Gynecology was in its infancy. Despite the recent invention of the speculum, a pelvic examination was still rare. Hemorrhages, abdominal pain and swelling, fatigue: after Salies-de-Béarn and Mont-Dore, in 1895, Jeanne tried a treatment at Kreuznach, which had salty waters with the same properties as those at Salies and a cooler climate. For thirty years, this little town on the Rhine in the Nahe Valley had become famous throughout Europe, though its social life was quieter than that of Marienbad. Jeanne and Marcel stayed at Kreuznach on two occasions, in July 1895 and in August and September 1897. During the first trip, the one-day visit of Marcel's friend Robert de Billy and his new wife Jeanne offered a little distraction for Marcel, who gave Robert some literary advice. Jeanne Proust welcomed the young bride, whose father was a board member of the Banque de France, "with her customary goodwill."[71] But during their second trip, which Marcel took on the spur of the moment, perhaps because of his mother's poor health, he was bored to death. He didn't know a living soul, and was reduced to writing long messages to Madame de Brantes, who was taking the waters in nearby Marienbad. Sunny and dry weather did nothing for his asthma, which lessened only at the end of his stay, when it turned cold and rainy. He read Balzac's *Duchess of Langeais* and *The Muse of the Department*. And in the absence of a social life, he worked on his novel *Jean Santeuil*.

Jeanne, with her usual diligence, bathed in double-lined copper and wooden tubs filled with steam. In the late afternoon, after her treatments, she and Marcel went boating on the river, through blue hills and vineyards. When Jeanne was too tired, Marcel relaxed on his own in a row boat among the reeds, walked a little in the forest, or contemplated the Schlossberg Valley. In the evening, in the Kurhof dining room, they would drink a delicious golden wine in long-stemmed glasses and talk about their day. Jeanne would describe the concert in the municipal gardens or fill Marcel in on the latest gossip from the spa or the Orianenhof, the hotel where they were staying. Who knows whether the name of the hotel might have inspired the first name of Oriane de Guermantes, whose in-laws were related to German princes and margraves? The Prousts' Germanic culture made Kreuznach an almost familiar setting, though they were probably unaware that Jeanne's cousins, the Berncastels, had once lived there.[72]

By 1898, Jeanne's health had worsened. She needed an operation, presumably to remove a fibroid tumor.[73] Adrien chose the clinic of the Sisters of the Divine Redeemer, rue Georges-Bizet, in the sixteenth arrondissement. It seems surprising that this freethinker—an opponent of organized religion, a professor of medicine and service chief at the Hôtel-Dieu, Paris's oldest public hospital—should have chosen a private clinic run by nuns. At the time, a battle was raging between nuns, traditionally in charge of hospital care, and secular nurses. In certain clinics, it even came to fistfights! The nuns were criticized for their lack of medical training and dubious hygiene, the secular nurses for being disrespectful of doctors. But the clinic on the rue Georges-Bizet had a story of its own.[74]

In 1887, the mother superior of the community of the Sisters of the Very Sacred Savior, established in 1881 on the hill of Chaillot, fell ill with severe peritonitis. When all hope seemed lost, the doctor who was treating her decided to call in the famous Professor Félix Terrier, one of the pioneers of asepsis, the technique for sterilizing medical equipment and operating with the strictest standards of hygiene. It wasn't for another two years that he managed to impose these standards at Bichat. Nor was it rare at the time for a leading surgeon, like Professor Jules Péan, to operate in street clothes or even evening clothes. The same syringe was used to inject several different women in labor, soiled dressings were reused, and some hospitals were infested by rats and fleas.[75] Félix Terrier obviously took every precaution and only went to the nuns' clinic accompanied by his own nurse and anesthesiologist. But what he found there was a clinic where the rules for asepsis were already practiced; the nuns even sterilized all the sheets by ironing them with a hot iron. Taking the mother superior aside, the professor asked her to make two rooms available to him for his own surgical patients. In 1897, the prefecture authorized the convent to take up to thirty patients.

We can understand, then, why Dr. Proust had his wife operated on by Professor Terrier, the specialist of surgical hygiene, in a clinic that respected the rules to the letter. The operation was long and painful. Not until fifteen years later would Jules Péan perfect the technique of ablating fibroids.

"The operation she underwent was terrible," Marcel wrote to his mother's friend Marguerite Catusse: "It took almost three hours, and we wondered how she could ever come through." No one knew how, he continued. But she was doing well, and "even my poor papa himself, who was out of his mind for days and refused to be reassured by her improvement, is satisfied."[76] Adrien had not shown so much emotion since Marcel's first asthma attack or Robert's accident.

"Soon she'll be as good as new, even better, without this terrible weight. We don't understand how she's been able to bear it," Marcel told Madame Catusse.[77] The day after the operation, Jeanne "made four or five clever remarks, which, with my bias as her son, I found extremely witty," he added. The family was reassured. Still, she wasn't yet allowed to read, and she needed to rest. The seriousness of her condition was kept from her. A month later, a complication arose, requiring a second operation. On August 30, she was still bedridden. She didn't leave the clinic until early September. On August 31, a much-relieved Adrien left for his annual treatments at Vichy. Robert, unable to get an extension, left for his twenty days of military service at the training camp in Châlons. But his mother's illness had a profound affect on him: the subject of his medical thesis was "surgery of the female genital tract." Meanwhile, it was Marcel who looked after the patient.

At the beginning of September, Jeanne, still bedridden, was finally able to receive letters. The details of her operation continued to be kept secret, and she herself "didn't like to think about it"[78]—self-abnegation to the point of denial.

By mid-September, still weak but more or less recovered, Jeanne was finally able to travel to the Les Roches noires at Trouville for her convalescence. Thanks to the elevator, she could leave her room and spend four hours reading in the gardens facing the ocean. Marcel accompanied her; then Adrien came to spell him. At the beginning of October, the weather was still warm enough for her to lounge in a sheltered spot on the beach with her husband. Gabrielle, her chambermaid, brought them letters from Marcel. Jeanne read them to Adrien, and reread them by herself. "I am getting along ADMIRABLY, do you read me?" she wrote to her son, who complained often that he couldn't tell what was going on with her. And she added: "I will make the concession of writing to you only once a day."[79]

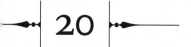

20

On Guard!

Dear Sir,

Yesterday I did not answer the question you put to me about the Jews. For this very simple reason: though I am a Catholic like my father and brother, my mother is Jewish. I am sure you understand that this is reason enough for me to refrain from such discussions. [. . .] But I very much welcome this occasion to say something to you that I might never have thought of saying. For since our ideas differ, or rather, since I am not free to have the ideas I might otherwise have on the subject, you might, without meaning to, have wounded me in a discussion.[80]

This letter lays out succinctly the situation of its author. Addressed to Robert de Montesquiou, who would serve as a model for Charlus, allowing Proust to stigmatize that character's hysterical anti-Semitism, it explains the writer's close ties to as well as his distance from Judaism. His attitude during the Dreyfus affair was inseparable from his position as the son of a Jewish mother whom he adored. Yet his attitude toward Jews in *In Search of Lost Time* was ambiguous. His critical and often ironic take on Jews and Judaism precisely reflected Jeanne's own attitude toward her fellow Jews. But Jewish she was, and Jewish she remained.

Jeanne Weil, as we have seen, was a typical product of a social group, French Israelites who wanted more than anything to integrate, that is, to assimilate. They had acquired citizenship a century earlier. On the Weil side, there had not been a single mixed marriage in the first two generations to live in France—neither in Baruch's generation nor in Nathé's. The same was true of the French branch of the Berncastels. "In Judaism, mixed marriages are considered a plague, and rightfully so," the liberal magazine *Archives israélites* reminded its readers in 1891. Apart from the secret conversion of Amélie Crémieux, it wasn't until the generation born around 1850 that any mixed marriages occurred in the family: Jenny Weil followed by Jeanne and Hélène were the only women to marry Catholics. None of these three converted, and, as we know, they kept close ties to the rest of the family.[81] It was a Jewish family, whose members and in-laws were named Neuburger, Leven, Anspach, Lévy, Nathan, and in the subsequent generations Lange, Eisenschitz, Bergson, Baur, Hauser, Julien-Caïn—and Dreyfus. They were bankers, lawyers, doctors, military officers, engineers, or teachers, trained in the elite schools. They incarnated the successful social mobility of French Israelites, a success founded on their fathers' wealth, on their personal merit, on their work ethic, and on their desire to assimilate. They felt absolute loyalty to France, the first country to give them the right to be citizens. They were French. "The French Revolution was our second Law of Sinai," wrote Isadore Cahen in the *Archives israélites* in 1880. Assimilation for them, Simon Schwarzfuchs has written more recently, was "the best way—perhaps the only way—of ensuring the survival of Judaism."[82] What did being Jewish mean for these often very secular Israelites, who went to synagogue only for marriages and bar mitzvahs and who, like Nathé Weil, knew little of their religion beyond a few mourning rituals? It meant above all a sense of belonging. "A Jew was a person who hadn't left Judaism," says Schwarzfuchs. "Angélique is going to think I'm converting—and Madame Raimbert will be full of hope!" Jeanne joked one Friday as she had her cook prepare a meatless dinner for two Catholic guests.[83] Like Geneviève Straus, she didn't have "enough religion to change religions."

The Israelites were nonetheless attached to their origins. Citizenship, even civil service, didn't prevent them from continuing a number of traditions in private, whether that meant using a few words of Yiddish or, as Louis Weil did, making charitable gifts to the community. Here and there, as Proust notes in *The Prisoner*, they would utter

> one of those terms that are used within families to designate a certain thing [. . .] without the offenders understanding. Such expressions are usually a throwback to an earlier state of the family in question. In a Jewish family, for example, the word will be a ritual term displaced from its original meaning, perhaps the only word of Hebrew that the family, now wholly French in its manners, has retained.[84]

Marcel himself, for example, knew the term *meshores* (servant), and he knew *schlemiel*, a common expression in families of Alsatian origin, taken from a "semi-German, semi-Jewish dialect which delighted Monsieur Bloch within the family circle, but which he thought vulgar and out of place when spoken in front of strangers."[85]

One sees in Jeanne and her entourage both loyalty to their mixed French-Jewish heritage and determination to blend in with everyone else. Like Michel Bréa, Henri Bergson,[86] Joseph Halévy, Théodore and Salomon Reinach, all brilliant intellectuals and part of the same social network, they broke their ties with religious Judaism. They represented Franco-Judaism, "a fusion of Jewish tradition with the ideals of the Nation."[87] Whatever traits might once have distinguished them from the rest of the French had disappeared. They were part of the elite of the Republic. The few bastions of privilege from which they were still excluded—certain salons or the Jockey Club, for example—would have to give in with time, or so they believed. They avoided Jews who were too obvious about it, like the Blochs and the Nissim Bernards of *In Search of Lost Time*,[88] who were still in the first phases of their ascension in French society. Like the wretched Jewish refugees arriving in the thousands from Russia, these people were unpleasant reminders to the established Israelites of what their ancestors must have been like.

"Someone I know likes to tell his son: 'I don't care if you marry a woman who doesn't know who Ruskin is, but I won't be able to stand it if you marry a woman who says *tramvay* (instead of *tramway*),'" Proust wrote in a footnote to his translation of Ruskin's *Sesame and Lilies*.[89] Who, other than Jeanne Weil, would have been more likely to stigmatize the German-Jewish pronunciation of an English word?

In short, the French Israelites "wanted to be Jewish but didn't like being reminded of it."[90] The Dreyfus Affair would take care of that.

Modern anti-Semitism, which had been on the rise since the 1880s, found a spokesperson in Edouard Drumont. The term itself was used for the first time by Wilhelm Marr, one of the founders of the first anti-Jewish political party in Germany in 1878. In 1886, Drumont's book *La France juive* (Jewish France) was phenomenally successful: a year later, it was already in its 145th printing. In a few years, anti-Semitism had become a veritable ideology. In 1892, Drumont launched his newspaper, *La Libre Parole* (Free Speech), which, through a combination of invective and polemic, presented the "tribe of hooked noses" as a menace to the integrity of the French. "Go away Jews!" and "France for the French!" were its principal slogans, reiterated in every possible manner. The financial scandals surrounding the failure of the Union générale bank, the Panama Canal scandal, the doctrines of General Boulanger's populist party, and socialism itself all nourished the polemic against "Jewish capital" and politicians. At a Catholic conference in Reims, in 1896, Albert de Mun urged: "Don't buy anything from Jews!" The Catholic press supported this boycott by publishing lists of Jews and Freemasons.

But the French Israelites used all their force to minimize anti-Semitism, which they considered a German import. France anti-Semitic? Impossible. They responded to Drumont's book with what Théodore Reinach called "the silence of contempt." The only way of defending themselves was to be "good Frenchmen." Or, on a personal level, they responded by appealing to the code of honor: they fought duels. Wasn't this the best way to show their courage?[91] The death of Armand Mayer, a young student of the Ecole polytechnique, an elite engineering school, who was killed in 1892 by the marquis de Morès, raised a public outcry. The immense crowd of Parisians who followed Mayer's funeral cortège seemed to prove the optimists right. "There is no Jewish question, at least in France," claimed Lazare Wogue in 1893, "and we hope there will never be."[92]

Meanwhile, one man spoke out against anti-Semitism: the writer Emile Zola. In an article in the newspaper *Figaro* on May 16, 1896, entitled "For the Jews," in which he referred to Drumont without ever mentioning him by name, Zola lent his support to the Jewish cause. In this vibrant article, he took apart the arguments of anti-Semitism one by one, calling it a "monstrosity" that put France "back centuries." Arguing for the concept of assimilation, he explained, long before Sartre, that it was the anti-Semite who created the Jew. The only safeguard for Jews was total assimilation—in other words, their disappearance as Jews. The Jewish press took note of his plea, which cost Zola both his position as a columnist at the *Figaro* and his election to the venerable Académie française.

While he had long shared Zola's point of view, the anarchist Bernard Lazare would, for his part, castigate the Jewish community for its silence. "They should have risen up, banded together, not allowed for a single minute any questioning of their absolute right to exist,"[93] he proclaimed. He even fought a duel against Drumont and developed the notion of Jewish nationalism. His ideas intersected with those of Theodor Herzl, a Viennese journalist and the founder of Zionism, who was sent to Paris to report on the Dreyfus Affair. For Lazare there was no question: Dreyfus had been accused of treason because he was Jewish.

By casting Captain Dreyfus, born to a family of textile manufacturers in Mulhouse, as a traitor to France, the Affair touched what the Israelites held dearest: their French identity. Who could have been more patriotic than the Alsatians, who accounted for the great majority of Parisian Israelites at the end of the nineteenth century? Can't you be both Jewish *and* French? A whole century of "regeneration"—to use the language of the Enlightenment—was called into question. For these men and women, the Dreyfus Affair was an affliction, probed by Marcel on multiple occasions. It is no accident that Proust granted the Affair so much importance in *Jean Santeuil* and in *In Search of Lost Time*. It shook the very deepest part of his dual identity:

> "It's not a bad thing, if you wish to learn about life," said M. de Charlus when he had finished questioning me about Bloch, "to have a few foreigners among your friends." I told him that Bloch was French. "Is that so?" said M. de Charlus. "I took him to be Jewish."[94]

How could Jeanne not have felt implicated? There is an obvious parallel between the Dreyfuses and the Weils, even if the latter had been Parisians for much longer. Like Baruch Weil, Alfred Dreyfus's father Raphaël had founded a business. Like Uncle Alphonse, Alfred Dreyfus chose the army as his profession. His career began brilliantly, and by age thirty-five he was already serving as an assistant to army headquarters. He married Lucie Hadamard, the daughter of a diamond merchant, and lived on the avenue du Trocadéro, in one of the new neighborhoods that symbolized social success. The Weils and the Dreyfuses were part of the same world.

Always an attentive reader of newspapers, Jeanne kept track of the different stages of the Affair: Dreyfus's arrest on October 15, 1894; his degradation; his deportation to Devil's Island. Most Jews accepted the condemnation of Dreyfus. "For a long time, I believed that my co-religionist was guilty," Bergson admitted.[95] Above all, they worried that any sign of solidarity with Dreyfus would be interpreted as sectarianism. In 1897, Léon Blum later recalled, only a handful of people believed in Dreyfus's innocence. These included his family, Bernard Lazare, and the linguist Michel Bréal, a cousin of the Weils who was convinced that an Alsatian Jew whose family had chosen France over Germany in 1870 could not possibly be a traitor. And if we are to believe Maurice Duplay, Marcel and Jeanne also doubted Dreyfus's guilt from the beginning.

On January 5, 1895, the evening of Captain Dreyfus's degradation,[96] Maurice was still a student at the Lycée Condorcet. His parents gave a large dinner party that night, to which the most illustrious doctors and their wives were invited, including Adrien and Jeanne Proust. Maurice had read in the evening papers an account of the grim ceremony and was struck by the tone of sincerity on the part of the accused. With a touch of rebelliousness, he spoke up at the dinner table: "What if Dreyfus is innocent?" It was a scandalous thing to say. His father gave him a withering look, calling his remark "childish and stupid," and the boy hung his head in shame. But after dinner, as Maurice Duplay later recalled,

> Madame Proust, who had always been so sweet to me and had shown me so many kindnesses, took me aside in a corner of the parlor: "So, you have doubts about Dreyfus's guilt? Well, can you imagine! Marcel feels the same way. He read the report in *Le Temps,* and claims that Dreyfus doesn't sound at all guilty."[97]

The mocking tone with which Jeanne wrote to her son in October 1896, that "the story of a deported convict's arrival on the Salvation Islands couldn't be more heartbreaking,"[98] may have been addressed to a Marcel despairing in his room at Fontainebleau, but it shouldn't fool us. She was on Dreyfus's side.

It was one of the very first Dreyfusards, Joseph Reinach, who convinced Marcel and Jeanne of Dreyfus's innocence. Born in 1856, this outspoken member of the French parliament was close to Gambetta, a former protégé of Adolphe Crémieux. A member of the Opportunist party, he took the lead in opposing General Boulanger's populist movement. His hero was the British prime minister Disraeli, "doubly a foreigner to England, as a Venetian and as a Jew," yet "from the first to the last day of his public life, the most English of the English."[99] Reinach, next to Dreyfus and Alphonse de Rothschild, would become the most hated Jew in France. Still, as he saw it, taking Dreyfus's side amounted to fighting for the integrity of the French Republic.

In August 1897, at the Clos des Mûriers in Trouville, Reinach shared his conviction with Madame Straus, whom he had always adored. In October, she gathered her entourage in her salon for a presentation by Reinach. From then on, Marcel was convinced. He later boasted that he had been "the first of the Dreyfusards," alluding to the role he played in supporting the petition in favor of Zola in January 1898, just after the brouhaha created by Zola's pro-Dreyfus editorial "J'accuse." Marcel is said to have been responsible for getting Anatole France to sign. Gathering signatures with Daniel and Elie Halévy, attending Zola's trial, just as Jean Santeuil and Bloch do in his fiction, "taking with him no more than a few sandwiches and a small flask of coffee, and [staying] there, fasting, excited, emotionally on edge, until five o'clock,"[100] Marcel became deeply involved in the Affair. It was yet another bond with his mother.

Jeanne had the satisfaction of seeing both her sons take her side, for Robert was no less passionate, and unlike the majority of medical students, who sided with the anti-Dreyfusards, he joined the partisans of Dreyfus in street fighting that threw the Latin Quarter into a ferment. "Tell Robert to stay calm," Marcel advised his mother on September 10, 1899, after Dreyfus had been found guilty for the second time at the trial in Rennes. "He should bear in mind that any encouragement of disorder would greatly embarrass the government, which would be obliged to punish his friends." Each brother acted according to his nature: Robert through action, Marcel through his relationships. Like all Dreyfus supporters, their disappointment equaled their certainty that his innocence would eventually be recognized. "Don't be too sad about the verdict," he wrote in the same letter to his mother, who was deeply affected. Summing up the reactions of the press, he was constantly exchanging information with her. A few days later, he added, "I shudder to think how you must have laid yourself open to Antoine when he brought you the news."[101] If Jeanne, always in control of her feelings, might have "laid herself open" to the concierge of her building, she was clearly overwhelmed with emotion.

Adrien, however, was on the other side, which must have been painful for

Jeanne. In this respect he was merely conforming to the majority opinion and in particular to his social class and his status as a doctor and a member of the grande bourgeoisie. With his official responsibilities, he was on the side of power and the law. The government and the army could not be wrong. Jeanne, surrounded as she was by her family and her sons, must have felt the gap separating her from her husband even more acutely. As for Jeanne's brother-in-law in Illiers, Jules Amiot, he added Drumont's *La Libre Parole* to his regular reading of the newspaper *L'Intransigeant*, which tells us a lot about the way Adrien's Jewish wife must have been perceived among her in-laws.[102] No doubt there were plenty of animated discussions around their dinner table.

The Dreyfus Affair not only put into question the idea of justice and the responsibility of the French state. It also brought to the surface, to the astonishment of all those involved, a deep-seated hatred and rejection of Jews. In Marseille, Lyon, Rennes, Versailles, Clermont-Ferrand, La Rochelle, Poitiers, Angoulême, and Saint-Flour, crowds marched, chanting "Death to the Jews!" The demonstrations turned into riots. Stores were pillaged, shop windows broken, synagogues vandalized. In Paris, gangs of anti-Semites lead by Jules Guérin spread terror.[103] In Algeria, the riots resulted in bloodshed. Jews fought to their death. Elected officials were overwhelmed by the situation. On April 29, 1898, Gaston Thomson, a deputy from Constantine and one of Jeanne's cousins, was physically attacked by anti-Semites.[104] The affair was hitting close to home. Did she secretly regret having married a non-Jew? Or, on the contrary, was she reassured by the fact that her sons had been baptized?

———◆———

Jeanne was caught up in her own contradictions. She was very close to Madame Félix Faure and her daughters Antoinette and especially Lucie. She frequented Madame Faure's weekly salon at the Elysée (the presidential palace), where, "in an atmosphere of perfect tedium, the conversation was all about the health of the parents, children, and cousins of the visitors."[105] Félix Faure, then president of the Republic, was fervently opposed to overturning the verdict on Dreyfus. Jeanne and her husband were invited to the Elysée and to the presidential box at the Opéra. In October 1897, the Prousts entertained Félix Faure at Rambouillet. Marcel, that same year, invited his friend Constantin de Brancovan into the president's gallery in the Chamber of Deputies. The Prousts and the Faures had other traits in common.

Like Adrien, Félix Faure came from modest origins. Son of a small furniture maker in the Faubourg Saint-Denis, a district largely inhabited by artisans, he had worked for a while as apprentice to a tanner. He was self-taught and had forged his own path, first as a businessman in Le Havre, then in politics. Having become a wealthy bourgeois with endless vitality and virile energy, he was determined to endow his presidency with a pomp and splendor worthy of France. The political cartoonists nicknamed him "Félix le Bel" because of his taste for ceremony, protocol, and luxury. A Freemason and a freethinker, he was also a fervent defender of the armed forces. For him, Dreyfus's innocence mattered less than the prestige of the army. Though he took sides against Dreyfus, he nonetheless condemned the excesses of what he called "the chauvinist party." Faure's wife, said to have been a naive but good-hearted woman, had personal reasons for resenting Drumont: the editor of *La Libre Parole* had tried to create a scandal by publicizing the fact that her father had been convicted and sentenced in absentia to twenty years in prison for shady business dealings.

Adrien's anti-Dreyfus sentiments must still have been moderate, more like a principled stand than a deeply felt conviction. In the thick of the Affair, Marcel wrote to him: "Now for a piece of gossip. The painter Rolle, who is a friend of the Elysée, claims that Madame Faure is a strong Dreyfusard and shuts herself up with him to read the good newspapers, but that M. Faure and Lucie are very much against."[106] A few weeks earlier, indeed, the counterfeit documents forged by Colonel Henry and added to Dreyfus's dossier—the false documents that led to his unjust condemnation—had finally been revealed to the public. Adrien Proust then crossed over to the camp of the Revisionists—those who wanted the guilty verdict changed. Marcel wrote to his mother: "Please ask Papa to try and find out from Dr. Pozzi if Dreyfus is really a dying man, what is wrong with him, whether he (Pozzi) is still convinced of his innocence, and the names of the two officers who voted for acquittal."[107]

Throughout this period, the Affair was a major preoccupation for Jeanne and Marcel, as their correspondence shows. Even the servants were involved: "Remember me to Eugénie and the Gustaves," Marcel wrote to his mother, "and tell them I haven't misled them about the Affair, that if Dreyfus were a traitor those hostile judges wouldn't have modified the sentence of '94, taking so many years off his prison term and making the conditions of confinement less severe—and that two of them are said to have been opposed to his rehabilitation."[108]

All their relationships passed through the sieve of the Dreyfus Affair and the Jewish question. Not that the two issues were necessarily connected, as we see from Madame Sazerat's sarcastic remark in *In Search of Lost Time:* "Monsieur Drumont has the nerve to put the Revisionists in the same bag as the Protestants and the Jews! What a charming coterie!"[109] There were those who were "on the right side"; those who, like the former notary Monsieur Cottin and his wife in *In Search of Lost Time,* hadn't compromised themselves, though it's clear that they were "anti"; and those "with prejudice," as Bloch's father put it.[110] Marcel described the father of his friend Pierre de Chevilly as an "old fool" and a "brutal maniac."[111] At the Daudets', he tried "not to push too many anti-[Dreyfusards] down the stairs."[112] The Daudets were certainly in the vanguard of anti-Dreyfus activism—which didn't prevent Marcel from keeping company with the rabid anti-Semite Léon Daudet and uttering platitudes about his genius as a novelist.

Did this mean that Marcel favored people who were Jewish? Not necessarily. Although he was totally sympathetic to the elevator operator who was forced to resign because his pro-Dreyfus position made him too many enemies at the luxury hotel where he worked ("I think he's a co-religionist," Marcel wrote his mother), the attitude he shared with Jeanne toward Jews was often caustic, to say the least. They were both fond of ironically referring to Jews as "the syndicate,"[113] or "the Semitic element." Writing from Evian in 1900, Jeanne reported:

> The Semitic element is represented here, apart from the Weisweillers, by the Paul Heilbronners, the Mayers [. . .], and the Levyliers, with whom we've apparently been afflicted since last evening although I haven't met them yet. Just enough time to unpack the trunks and after that![114]

Her remarks are echoed by her son's mentioning "the arrival of the syndicate."[115]

This distancing, this critical glance cast upon one's own kind, is a well-known phenomenon: the difficulty of seeing oneself reflected in the gaze of others, or *Selbsthasse* (self-hatred). "Every aging Jew turns into either a prophet or a boor," Marcel confided to Emmanuel Berl, his distant cousin.[116] Proust's character Bloch also had "the habit of referring ironically to his Jewish origin, to the side of his family that came from somewhere near Sinai."[117] Thus the narrator of *Swann's Way* tells how his grandfather sang, "Archers be on your guard!" and cried out, "On Guard! On Guard!" every time his grandson invited a Jewish friend to the house—Proust couldn't resist this nod to his own grandfather Nathé Weil, who had doubtless reacted that way when Marcel came home with a Robert Dreyfus or a Daniel Halévy. The scene in *Swann's Way* is made even funnier by the fact that the grandfather is quoting a line from the opera *The Jewess* by Fromenthal Halévy, Daniel Halévy's uncle.[118]

Baptized but a member of an important Jewish family, Marcel, a well-brought-up boy, had attended Jewish marriages, had celebrated bar mitzvahs, had sat shiva. He went to the synagogue on the rue de la Victoire or the rue Notre-Dame de Nazareth for the weddings of his cousins and his uncle Georges. His familiarity with Jewish ritual was apparent, for example, when after the death of his mother's cousin, Daniel Mayer, he noted: "There won't be any prayers at home and only a few words at the cemetery."[119] How could we imagine even for a moment that his involvement with the Dreyfus Affair had nothing to do with his Jewish origins? His fawning toward Daudet, Barrès, and Montesquiou changed nothing: the *stain* doesn't get erased just like that.[120] It's striking that the names of two characters in *In Search of Lost Time*—Rachel, the Jewish prostitute who becomes a lady of the theater, and Bloch, the archetype of the obnoxious Jew—constitute the name of his paternal great-grandmother, Rachel Bloch.

In a letter to Robert Dreyfus, Marcel recalled that *La Libre Parole* had once referred to him as being among "the young Jews" demonstrating against Barrès. "To rectify this statement I should have had to say that I wasn't a Jew and I didn't want to do that," he added firmly.[121]

"By the time I had taken my first communion, prim and proper ladies were being confronted, to their astonishment, with elegant Jewesses in some of the houses they frequented," he wrote in *In Search of Lost Time*.[122] Jeanne knew as well as he how difficult it was to be received in society when you were Jewish. She too was faced with what Bernard Lazare referred to as "the moral ghetto": "This animosity is commonly hidden, yet the intelligent Jew perceives it. He feels a resistance before him, he has the impression of a wall that adversaries have built between himself and the people in the midst of whom he lives."[123]

Jeanne had heard young girls say starchily, like Albertine, "I'm not allowed to play with Israelites."[124] Her marriage to Adrien Proust might have given her the illusion that she was a Frenchwoman, like everyone else. But the Dreyfus affair lifted the veil. In *The Fugitive*, Proust writes:

Forcheville, who like any self-respecting nobleman had drawn from family discussions the certainty that his name was more ancient than that of La Rochefoucault, considered that in marrying the widow of a Jew he had acted with the same charitable spirit as a millionaire who picks up a prostitute in the street and saves her from poverty and the gutter.[125]

Which reveals a lot about how high society viewed his mother's "co-religionists."

Among certain French Israelites, this wave of anti-Semitism provoked a sudden burst of Jewish identity. Nowhere was it better demonstrated than in Proust's characters Bloch and Swann, whose pro-Dreyfus passions ended up blurring their critical judgment. In a famous comparison of homosexuality and Jewishness, Proust makes the self-hating Jew a metaphor for the invert. While obsessed with both conditions, admitting his inversion was as impossible as recognizing what was Jewish in him. Yet he didn't deny it. "Nine times out of ten, when someone identifies a Jewish character trait in me, it's something I've inherited from my father, and when it's supposed to be a Christian character trait, it comes from my mother," he told his young cousin Emmanuel Berl.[126] Things were probably easier for Jeanne. She knew who she was and accepted it with her usual realism. She was the Jewish mother of Catholic sons. "Even a bigoted peasant girl would have felt that the soul of so perfect a Jewess must be more pleasing to the Lord than all the Christians, Priests and Saints in the world."[127]

Jeanne would never forget Racine's *Esther*, "the play she loved best," for which Reynaldo Hahn wrote choral music based on the words "He is appeased, he pardons." Hahn sang it for the first time at the Prousts' apartment, accompanying himself on the piano near the fireplace. Marcel, not feeling well, was lying down. Adrien arrived late and sat quietly on an armchair. Jeanne remained standing. She "tried over a solo part, diffidently, as though she were one of the young girls at Saint-Cyr rehearsing before Racine; and her beautiful Jewish features stamped with Christian sweetness and Jansenist fortitude made her a [true] Esther,"[128] her son would write.

A Jewish heroine and a Christian virgin.

 **21**

The Soul of Venice

Jeanne Proust was her son's first reader. It was clear that Marcel was going to be a writer. His first book, however, *Pleasures and Days*, published in 1896, was scarcely noticed. It would be a long time before his talent was recognized. Since 1895 he had been working on the novel *Jean Santeuil*, but he was having trouble giving form to the accumulating pages. He read passages to his mother. She must have identified with his evocations, his rather transparent re-creation of moments in their life together. But her classical education also helped her realize how dense and unfinished the project was. Marcel wrote articles, gathered information. He went out a lot. She encouraged him to work more regularly. Like Madame Santeuil, she may have dreamed of another future for her son. Still:

She was fully aware that his sole occupation at present seemed to consist in paying visits and leading a social existence, that meditating, using his imagination, writing—even that—would have represented, in the way of achievement, a great deal more than he had to show. If that was all she could get from him now, then it was her duty to try to get at least that.[129]

She would make her son into a real writer.

For a number of years he'd been interested in the work of the British philosopher and aesthete John Ruskin, whom he'd discovered through journal articles. In 1897 he had read the newly published study by Robert de la Sizeranne, *Ruskin and the Religion of Beauty*, and in the following months he discussed Ruskin's work with Robert de Billy, then a diplomat in London. This interest would turn into a passion, taking "precisely the same course as his love affairs or ardent friendships [. . .] except that it brought him joy unspoiled by suffering,"[130] as Painter remarks. Ruskin had a hundred and sixty books to his name.[131] As his translator, Marcel sought to transmit Ruskin's thought in France. Instead, Ruskin would transmit Proust's thought to Proust himself.

Jeanne was inseparable from that undertaking. Her collaborative work with her son was both a gesture of maternal love and an expression of deep understanding. By encouraging him, participating in his work, she offered him a tight net of constraints, sustained effort, rigor, and the asceticism required for any far-reaching enterprise. For the first time, Marcel experienced genuine discipline in his work. His mother worked with him. The hours they spent together on Ruskin's texts were certainly among the happiest of Jeanne's life. She had the feeling of being useful, of participating in a work in progress. Here we get a glimpse of the kind of person she might have become if she'd lived in an era when women were no longer confined to traditional roles. Yet we shouldn't imagine that she was dissatisfied. In her work on Ruskin, Jeanne saw not an outlet for personal potential, but rather the happiness of collaborating with her son. In that way, she greatly resembled her favorite author, Madame de Rémusat, who "seems to have said yes to everything, seems to have internalized everything regarding the canonical representation of women,"[132] but who was vigilant about the education and the reading of a son she adored.

Jeanne, like her brother Georges, had a perfect grasp of English. The same couldn't be said of Marcel. His friend Constantin de Brancovan expressed surprise when he learned about Proust's plan to translate *The Bible of Amiens*.

"How are you doing it, Marcel, since you don't know English?"[133] Beginning in December 1899, it was Jeanne who made the first draft of Ruskin's translation, a literal, word-by-word version that her son shaped into literary form. Although Marcel, according to Geroges de Lauris, "would have had a terrible time even ordering a chop in an English restaurant" (which in fact he never had to do), he "knew Ruskin's English in all its nuances."[134] In his composition notebooks with the yellow, green, and red covers, we find two hands, the son's corrections inserted into the mother's text.[135]

At times the handwriting is intermingled—Jeanne's somewhat rigid shapes, Marcel's messier, more fluid letters—and at times one is superimposed on the other. Certain pages are totally rewritten, others barely touched. Sometimes Jeanne has trouble with a technical term in architecture; sometimes she trips over Ruskin's obscure English. But her translation is faithful and covers the whole of the text.

Jeanne's wording, "The true date to remember is 481, when Clovis himself arrived on the throne, a fifteen-year-old young man," becomes, after Marcel's editing, "The true date to remember is 481, Clovis's accession to the throne at the age of fifteen."[136]

Jeanne didn't merely translate *The Bible of Amiens* and excerpts from *Sesame and Lilies* and *Mornings in Florence*. She took notes and summarized or copied excerpts from books she'd borrowed from the library, such as W. G. Collingwood's *The Life and Work of John Ruskin* (1893). She was a zealous collaborator, absorbed by her task. A fire burned in the fireplace in the dining room with its mahogany reflections. On the oval table, covered with a red cloth, mother and son, in turn, pored over papers and books. She worked by day, he wrote by the soft light of an oil lamp at night. A chaise longue allowed him to rest. Sometimes, Jeanne stayed up with him and dozed off in an armchair. Before going to bed with the first morning light, Marcel left written instructions for his mother. In these notes, household details and work are combined, reflecting the intimate character of their collaboration:

My dearest Mama,
From midnight to 12:15 I stood guard at the door, hearing papa blow his nose but not reading the paper, so I didn't dare come in.

Tomorrow morning, will you be good enough to translate for me on the large format paper I've left you, without writing on the back; without leaving any blank space, tightening up what I showed you from *Seven Lamps* . . .

Also I'd appreciate it if you could copy the attached page circled in blue pencil (I started to circle the back of it in blue pencil, but that doesn't count). Start with the first word (which is: in our view), finish with the last (which is: to find you, for) without worrying that the meaning is cut off; don't copy anything from the back. But keep your copy as well as the attached page for me, which I will need to consult.

I have the feeling I'm doing better and in any case I'm smoking a good deal less. I'm getting to sleep without taking anything. I'm the one who opened the bottle of Vichy water.

A thousand tender kisses,
Marcel[137]

And here is another, similar letter written while they were working on the translation of chapter four of *The Bible of Amiens:*

My dearest Mama,
Do the end of the *Bible* just as before, make a clean copy. Do a rough draft only of the prophets and the months of the year.

[. . .] I'll put the blank paper for you next to my note. I left everything in the parlor except for the copy of my manuscript, which I'm taking with me so that the pages won't get misplaced again. [. . .] Since I've set aside your pages, your book, and your dictionary for you, it would be best not to touch the mess in the parlor or in Robert's room, there's no reason to.

A thousand tender kisses,
Marcel[138]

Even when other collaborators came to Marcel's aid, replacing Jeanne, she never stopped helping him, supporting his efforts and struggling to see him follow through, once his initial enthusiasm had dampened. She had spent days and days translating hundreds of pages. Happy days, without a doubt, when, in the large parlor on the rue de Courcelles or in the dining door on the boulevard Malesherbes, she and her son exchanged points of view on a detail of the translation, or reread a page of Ruskin. Jeanne's goal was merely to serve as the modest technician of language, facilitating her son's work. He was the master, skilled at taking advice from various experts, people like Marie Nordlinger and Robert d'Humières. But without Jeanne's groundwork, without her immediate assistance, aided by their proximity, without the discipline she brought him through her example, would he ever have taken on this task, and would he have seen it through to completion? And who other than Jeanne would have persisted for so long, translating

word by word? Jeanne's role was indispensable. "From the novel to the translation of Ruskin," Jean-Yves Tadié has noted, "the aesthetic relationship of
mother and son was thus reinforced: she watched over his writing just as she
had watched over his sleep."[139]

She would watch over it until her death, knowing that her son's salvation
lay in writing regularly. She didn't confuse translation with creation—but
she knew that translation gave him a structure he needed. The organization
of his work compelled Marcel to stick to a schedule. Compared to the literary pastiches he excelled in, translation was a less entertaining but equally
fruitful constraint. Short of imagining, as Buffon did, that genius could be a
question of patience over the long haul, Jeanne realized that the qualities her
son lacked most were willpower and perseverance. She persisted in helping
him acquire them. And for this, the translations of Ruskin provided excellent training. Her faith in Marcel, her confidence, her vigilance, her intelligence, her demands, and her love were the crucibles forging the iron will
that would one day enable Marcel to go the distance. She would never see
her efforts crowned. Imagine how proud she would have been to witness
Marcel's drive in finishing his great work! But would she have allowed him
to sacrifice his life to it? Her presence was indispensable; perhaps her disappearance was equally so.

In John Ruskin, Marcel found the fertile reflection on art and religion that
served as a foundation for his own aesthetic and spiritual search. Far from
being a waste of time, his translations, as well as the prefaces to his translations of *The Bible of Amiens* and *Sesame and Lilies*, were essential steps in the
maturation of his thought and the development of his own work. His exten-
sive notes show the progression of his reading, and his correspondence confirms that for nearly two years Ruskin was the centerpiece of his intellectual
life and the reason for most of his travels.

In December 1901, Marcel finally delivered the manuscript of his translation to his editor Ollendorff. He was thirty years old. In his acknowledg-
ments of the translators who had helped him, he didn't cite his mother. She
probably didn't want him to. Her son's name would live on in posterity without her.

Together, Jeanne and Marcel visited Venice in May 1900. In March of that
year, Marcel had been indefinitely relieved of his position at the Mazarine
Library—a job that had never much interested him. Given his absences—in

1896, he had gone in once to give copies of *Pleasures and Days* to his colleagues, and he had had no trouble renewing his request for a leave of absence every December—the administration insisted that he resign, which
suited him fine. Even his father was no longer under any illusion.

Jeanne was more worried than ever about her son's health. In April 1900
he fell prey once again to violent asthma attacks that kept him awake and
in distress for nights on end. In the early hours of morning, exhausted, he
wrote her: "You can stay a moment facing me, it seems as though this keeps
me from suffocating. I'm in awful shape."[140] Jeanne stood at the foot of the
bed, her eyes full of tears. She hoped she could soothe him with her presence, at least. Gone were the days when she had tried to toughen him up. If
only she could comfort him just a little.

Marcel's asthma, combined with the flu, didn't prevent him from continuing to work on Ruskin or to write about it to Marie Nordlinger, Reynaldo
Hahn's charming English cousin, whom he had met four years earlier. Marie
was born in Manchester and had attended the School of Fine Arts there. For
two years she studied painting in France. A woman of great learning and culture, she shared Marcel's admiration for the author of *The Bible of Amiens*. In
April, he sent her the issue of *Mercure de France* in which his article "Ruskin at
Notre-Dame d'Amiens" had appeared—an article she had helped him with
by translating texts for him. She was in Italy at the time. It so happened that
Marcel and his mother were planning to go to Venice. The Baedeker Guide
recommended the city to people with ailing lungs because of the absence of
dust, but discouraged those with arthritis from going, because of the humid-
ity. Jeanne, who suffered from arthritis, was confined to bed on their return.
In *In Search of Lost Time*, Proust made the trip his mother's idea.

Adrien did not accompany them. Venice, for him, was a city of international conferences. He had gone there twice, in 1892 and in 1897, to argue for
cooperation on matters of public health; he had even indulged in the ritual
feeding of the pigeons on the Piazza San Marco. He congratulated himself
that Venice would now have a supply of drinkable water. But it's hard to
imagine him on an aesthetic pilgrimage. Prudently, he abstained. Now age
sixty-five, he had retired from his hospital duties at the Hôtel-Dieu just a few
months earlier, and he was suffering from kidney stones. Mother and son
would commune together in their Ruskinesque fervor.

After carefully studying the train schedules and packing their trunks and
suitcases, Jeanne and Marcel were ready by early May to board the train that
would take them through the Alps to Venice, via Turin and Padua.[141] They

probably took the night train. A twenty-four-hour journey in bumpy train cars, even in first class, surrounded by black coal fumes, was a trial for an asthmatic young man just recovering from an attack. Jeanne looked after him as though he were ten years old. She had provisions of hard-boiled eggs, bottles of water, newspapers, and books, which she doled out along the way as surprises to keep him occupied. Just before arriving in Venice, after the train had already passed Mestre, she read him a passage from *The Stones of Venice*, in which Ruskin compares the city to the coral of the Indian Ocean and to an opal. John Ruskin would guide them "like the column of fire that led the way for the Israelites."[142]

Marcel and his mother stayed at the Danieli, a stone's throw from the Piazza San Marco. "From a window of his hotel room at the Danieli (from the other side you could see the Riva dei Schiavoni), the gold angel of the bell-tower of San-Marco held out her arms to him," noted Marie Nordlinger.[143] As at the Roches noires in Trouville, Marcel's room was located at one corner of the Danieli.[144] This luxury hotel, located since 1822 in the Palazzo Dandolo, the former headquarters of the French ambassador to the Serenissime Republic, had been the site of the tempestuous love affair of George Sand and Musset, as well as the locale for a calmer stay by Charles Dickens.

Shortly after the Prousts' arrival, they met Marie Nordlinger, chaperoned by an aunt, and her cousin Reynaldo Hahn, who were staying at the Palazzo Fortuny Madrazzo, a family fiefdom. Marcel and Jeanne discovered Venice in their company.

Although still suffering from asthma, Marcel woke at a more reasonable hour than in Paris. His blinds were open by ten in the morning. Jeanne loved seeing him go out, a little later, into the Venetian light. She herself, out of habit and taste, was happy to remain in the hotel in the morning. She wandered about, did her correspondence, read, studied a map of the city. She liked to wait for him on her balcony, her black dress brightened by a summer hat:

> Her face [. . .] surrounded by a light veil of tulle (as heart-rendingly white for me as her hair) which I sensed that my mother, on drying her eyes, had pinned to her straw hat partly in order to seem "properly dressed" in the eyes of the hotel residents, but above all to seem to me to be less in mourning, less sad, almost consoled for the death of my grandmother.[145]

This is a highly fictionalized portrait of a *mater dolorosa*, since Jeanne, who had just turned fifty-one, did not have white hair, and her mother had been dead for ten years.

Marie Nordlinger also recalled Jeanne's silhouette set against the window frame, reading as she waited for her son, her shawl hanging over the marble balustrade, this "mother who, in his lifetime, was the caryatid, the one and only."[146] Years later, Proust recalled how, as his gondola was passing by San Giorgio Maggiore,[147] this maternal face turned toward him, framed like an oriental miniature by the ogive of the window illuminated by the noonday sun, radiating the gentle sweetness of what he would elsewhere call "the soul of Venice."

If Jeanne sometimes let her son take a ride in a gondola or visit churches and museums without her, it may have been so as not to intrude upon his time alone with Marie. With her round face, her full lips and dark eyes, her pensiveness, her kindness, her tastes so similar to Marcel's, her culture, her good manners, even her mildly bohemian appearance—she was a perfect candidate for marriage. I find it hard to believe that Jeanne never imagined a union of her Marcel with the compatible young Englishwoman. One afternoon, during a storm, the two young people took shelter in a baptistery to escape the rain and the lightning, and read *Stones of Venice*, which Marie translated for him. But Marie remained a friend and nothing more.

At the lunch hour, Jeanne met her son in the hotel lobby, with its extravagant decor of marble and crystal chandeliers, dominated by a monumental arched staircase. In the afternoon, as Marie later recalled, Jeanne and Marcel "called a gondola and went off to explore the *campi*, the canals, the wharfs and the lagoons, outings moored in the pages of *The Fugitive*."[148] Marie often joined them during her own ten-day sojourn. They followed Ruskin's footsteps as they toured Venice: they studied the mosaics and inscriptions on the baptistery, visited the Carpaccio of San Giorgio degli Schiavoni, the palazzo of the Grand Canal. They were amateur art historians, attentive to the slightest detail. One day they even asked for a ladder so as to examine a bas-relief to which Ruskin had drawn their attention. Gondolas took them from one palazzo to another, from churches to "those delightful rose-colored, semi-erect buildings that loom out of the waters."[149] In the cool of the Basilica San Marco, notebook in hand, Marcel lost track of time while studying the mosaics representing Christ's baptism. Jeanne, afraid he would catch cold, threw a shawl around his shoulders. Later, he wrote:

> The time has now come for me when, on remembering the baptistery, facing the waters of the Jordan where St. John immersed Christ while the gondola awaited us by the Piazzetta, I cannot remain indifferent to the

fact that there was by my side in this cool twilight a woman clothed in mourning, whose respectful but enthusiastic fervour matched that of the elderly woman who can be seen in Venice in Carpaccio's *St. Ursula*, and that nothing can ever remove this red-cheeked, sad-eyed woman, in her black veils, from the softly lit sanctuary of St. Mark's where I am certain to find her, because I have reserved a place there in perpetuity, alongside the mosaics, for her, for my mother.[150]

In the early evening, when they'd finished visiting the museums and churches, they relaxed on the terrace of the Florian café, eating sorbet, sipping *limonata* or hot chocolate. They ran into people they knew, exchanged niceties. Once again, socializing took over. Flower vendors hawked their bouquets. Marcel would turn away from them, no doubt preferring the red velvet banquettes, the marble, and the mahogany woodwork of the hotel lobby where Jeanne could dream of George Sand and Musset. Perhaps they paid homage to the little *pensione* along the Guidicca canal where Ruskin, abandoning the Gritti, had written the second part of *Stones of Venice*. The owners of the modest bar that Ruskin frequented had agreed to rent him a room there, then a second room for a friend.

Marcel and Jeanne also spent a day in Padua; in the Arena Chapel, they discovered Giotto's frescoes depicting the Virtues and the Vices, reproductions of which Charles Swann gives to the narrator of *In Search of Lost Time*.[151]

They usually dined at the Danieli, although from time to time they sampled the cuisine of some other highly reputed palazzo, enjoying mullet and risotto, like the marquise of Villeparisis and her old lover Monsieur de Norpois.[152] After dinner, Marcel would go out with his friends, exploring the dark alleys of Venice. Jeanne, left to herself, would read for a while before retiring.

One shadow hovered over the memory of this trip, though it's unclear whether it had its foundation in reality or was merely the product of Marcel's extreme sensitivity. In any case, he described the scene in several places,[153] and it reveals much about the relationship of mother and son at that stage of their lives. In *The Fugitive*, the scene takes place just after Marcel, following his nocturnal wanderings through the narrow *calli* of the city, imagines the possibility of hours of carnal pleasure and the arrival of a woman, the mere thought of whom excites him. But it was time to leave Venice. He asks his mother if they can postpone their departure. She refuses, not seeming to take him seriously. He digs in his heels, taken with "my old desire to resist a fictitious plot hatched against me by my parents."[154] His mother doesn't respond. When she is about to leave for the train station, he orders a drink on the terrace overlooking the canal. No one makes a scene. Without a word, his mother leaves for the station, dismissing her son's attempt at resistance as mere childishness.

Left to himself, Marcel watches the sun set, and the thought of staying in Venice without her, knowing he has upset her and without her presence to console him, turns the city from a magical place into an inferno. As at the Deligny pool, where he used to watch his mother swim without him, the black water of the canal fills him with horror. He is incapable of moving, of making the slightest decision. Across from the hotel, a musician sings "O sole mio." But that cheerful ode to the sun sounds desperately sad, proclaiming his irrevocable sorrow in a city reduced to shards. Without his mother, "the soul of Venice has drained away." Finally he takes action, running to the train station as fast as he can. The doors of the train are already closed, and his mother, flushed with emotion, convinced he isn't coming, can barely hold back her tears.

This masterfully constructed episode recounts yet again how impossible separation was for this mother and son, dramatizing their interlaced feelings, churned together like the waters of the lagoon.[155] "The unbearable recollection of the distress I had caused her plunged me into anguish that only her presence and her kiss could heal," the narrator concludes:[156] "There are times when hatred meanders through a vast stretch of love and appears to be lost in it."[157]

In October 1900, Marcel returned to Venice alone. He stayed at the Hôtel Europa[158] in the Palazzo Guistiniani, across from the Basilica of Santa Maria della Salute. Who knows? Perhaps on that trip it wasn't only the city's soul he tried to embrace.

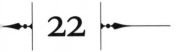

22

Jeanne's Address Book

Jeanne's address book came from Schneider's stationery store on the boulevard Haussmann. It had a brown marbled paper cover and red corners, and its lined pages were filled with the names and addresses of guests, organized according to the date they were invited to the Prousts'. As time went by, and Jeanne's hands became swollen or arthritic, the handwriting was distorted. A few names were written in pencil; some were crossed out. Here and there a death or a change of address was noted. Today, the paper has yellowed, certain pages are loose from the bindings, and the black ink has faded.[159]

The four hundred and thirty names in Jeanne's address book give us some idea of the Prousts' social life around 1900. The last entries were made in 1899, as if to round out the century.[160] The book shows Jeanne's talent for organization and planning, her concern for social conventions, her role as wife and mother. It takes us right to the heart of the Third Republic bourgeoisie, a network of social, political, professional, and family groups that remained stable over several generations. Social homogeneity was the rule: no socializing with the aristocracy of the Faubourg Saint-Germain or with the working class. A baron, a countess, a viscount, the few aristocratic names from this segment of society—the Chimays, the Noailles—were all Marcel's connections.

As a good doctor's wife, Jeanne carefully noted at least sixty of her husband's colleagues. It was by far the largest category on the list, for a woman's social life was often an extension of her husband's professional life. A number of those listed were members of the Academy of Medicine, to which Adrien had belonged since 1879. Among physicians included in the notebook are Professor Brissaud, "handsome and charming," author of *Hygiene for Asthmatics*—"you have to fight with him to get him to talk about medicine"[161]—the model for the doctor at Boulbon who examines the narrator's grandmother in *In Search of Lost Time;* Professor Dieulafoy, who recorded Jeanne's mother's death; the dashing Samuel Pozzi, who was murdered by one of his patients; Professors Trousseau and Fernand Widal; and Dr. Robin, famous for his love affair with Liane de Pougy. They invited one another to dinner parties in couples; the ladies left their calling cards at the homes of the other wives or stopped by long enough to sample a few petits-fours and exchange the day's gossip. Madame Brissaud received guests on Tuesday in her apartment at 5, rue Bonaparte, as did Dr. Georges Brouardel's wife on the rue de Lille—not to be confused with the wife of Professor Brouardel, who received her visitors on Fridays on the rue de l'Université. In *Swann's Way,* Proust describes Dr. Cottard's wife, who never hesitates to climb the stairs of twenty-five different houses in a single day and who holds out her gloved hand to Swann on the omnibus, after which "she courageously makes her way up the rue Bonaparte, her plume high, lifting her skirt with one hand, holding in the other her sunshade and her card case."[162]

Adrien's official functions often led him to call on highly placed officials, ministers, and persons in the public eye. Some thirty such names appear in the address book, often accompanied by titles or functions, perhaps to avoid faux pas: members of parliament; members of the Conseil d'Etat like the young Jacques Helbronner, who in 1939 authored a decree condemning anti-Semitism; consuls and governors; plenipotentiaries from the Netherlands or Sweden; diplomats like Camille Barrère, the French ambassador to Rome; prefects like Jules Lépine; former ministers like Jules Siegfried; Alexandre Ribot, who was president of the Conseil d'Etat in 1895; and Jean Casimir-Piere, former president of the Republic. These were only outranked by ministers then in power, such as Georges Leygue, in education; Waldeck-Rousseau, president of the Conseil d'Etat; Armand Fallières, president of the Senate; and the president of the Republic himself, Emile Loubet, elected on February 18, 1899. Félix Faure, the previous French president, had died several days earlier in notorious circumstances.[163] Jeanne continued to call on his widow, one of her best friends, who had moved from the Elysée to the avenue d'Iéna, where she received visitors on Saturday, a fashionable day for receiving, also favored by the baron James Rothschild's wife, by the prince and princess of Caraman-Chimay, and by Madeleine Lemaire. Fleshing out this picture of a respectable social milieu were notaries; lawyers; judges; the president of the Compagnie des chemins de fer de l'Est, Monsieur van Blarenberghe, whose wife was murdered by their son Henri, who then took his own life; magistrates from Limoges or Besançon (whom Jeanne had met at the spa); consultants to the treasury; and bankers. The list is faithful to the definition given by the annual *Tout Paris* of the Société parisienne in 1886: "Aristocracy, foreign colony, civil servants, diplomatic corps, political world, magistracy, army, clergy, sciences, literature, beaux-arts, high finance, real estate, etc."[164]

One had to keep up with these networks, and Jeanne did her part, organizing dinner parties, calling on people, having special days for receiving visitors, doing favors, giving presents, sending flowers, writing thank-you notes and letters of condolence—a string of minor but unavoidable social obligations. She excelled in writing condolence letters, something that appeared to be a family specialty. Her table was set with damask tablecloths, crystal, silver, fine German china, floral arrangements from Dechaume's. When the Prousts gave receptions, the butler had extra servants to assist him, and everything took place according to impeccable protocol. Just as for Monsieur de Norpois, the diplomat in *In Search of Lost Time,* elite guests were served beef with carrots in aspic and a salad of pineapple and truffles, followed by a Nesselrode pudding with chestnuts and fruit *confit,* a veritable "feast of Lucullus." The marquis would need a treatment at the Carlsbad spa to recover! Unless Félicie had decided that evening to prepare one of her light soufflés and her Yorkshire ham, which she "sent down to the oven of the local baker, looking like pink marble inside its coating of breadcrumbs."[165] The society pages reported some of those dinners, such as the party given on Monday, April 24, 1899, to which the Prousts invited their son's friends Anatole France, Madame Arman de Caillavet, Madeleine Lemaire—one of the models for Madame Verdurin—and the Count and Countess Mathieu de Noailles, the latter also known as the poet Anna de Noailles, an icon of the Belle Epoque. It was a literary dinner at the highest level. Anna de Noailles, a tiny brunette with enormous eyes beneath her bangs, dazzling with her witty, almost frenzied chatter, her hands extended in front of her as if catapulted, "the floor around her strewn with her veils, her scarves, necklaces, Arabian rosaries, muffs."[166] Her husband, "tall, thin, with a pointy mustache, every bit the thoroughbred, did not utter a word, though he smiled."[167] Laparcerie quoted poetry by Anatole France, Anna de Noailles, and Robert de Montesquiou. The report in next day's *Le Matin* didn't mention whether Dr. Proust had enjoyed the evening.

Dr. Proust and his wife were often acknowledged in the society pages, which also noted their arrival at vacation resorts or their presence at parties where they rubbed shoulders with the very best people. On Tuesday, April 14, 1896, for example, the couple attended a performance of Dufresny's *L'Orme de Lucrèce* at the home of some friends of Marcel's, Georges and Jeanne Arman de Caillavet; it was "a charming play," reported *Le Figaro*.

Though not a socialite, Jeanne obeyed the social conventions of her milieu. She knew many people and adored gossiping with her son, who often looked to her for "the full biography."[168] Madame Derbanne and Madame de Saint-Marceaux, two renowned hostesses, were on her list. Even if she socialized primarily to advance her husband's career or to help one of her sons, she seems not to have minded doing so. She appeared at a reception at the Ecole centrale, at the Opera, at the Elysée palace; in Venice, Marcel introduced her to Anna de Noailles's sister, Hélène de Brancovan, the princess of Caraman-Chimay; with Adrien she was invited to attend a presidential hunting party at Rambouillet; and so on.

But illness and mourning would gradually limit her social life. Jeanne remained absolutely faithful to those she loved. Family and friends held a place of honor in her address book. The Prousts' oldest friends, the Bénacs, were noted there as receiving guests on Thursdays.[169] Some thirty relatives were listed, from both the Weil side and the Berncastel and Crémieux side, not counting the Amiot family, carefully noted on a page headed "Outside Paris"—Jules in Illiers, Fernandin Blinic and Alphonse in Algiers. All the relatives were catalogued, including those related by marriage, such as the Oulmans and the Hechts. The only name missing is Gustave Neuberger, perhaps because his wife Laure Lazarus, Jeanne's cousin, had died in 1898, and Jeanne didn't keep in touch with the banker afterwards. The many Jewish last names indicate the Prousts' ties to the Jewish community. The Nathans are on the list; Laure, née Rodriques-Ely, was one of Jeanne's best friends, as we have seen. A tall brunette with a strong personality and a great sense of humor, she remained close to Jeanne to the end. With no children of her own, she extended her affection to her nephews and second cousins; everyone called her Aunt Laure. Helbronners, Weisweillers, Heymans, Oulifs, Lévys, Oppenheims, Revels, Cohns, Dreyfouses, Lippmanns, and Halphens appear in Jeanne's book alongside the great financiers Finaly, Romilly, Pereire, and Rothschild. It's clear that Jeanne maintained bonds with "the Semitic element"—sometimes long-lasting ones, as with Madame Levi-Alvarès.[170]

Some of her friendships were made at spas. While Adrien regularly went alone to Vichy, after 1899 he also accompanied Jeanne to Evian, on the southern banks of Lake Geneva. They arrived there in mid-August and took the waters for the standard three weeks. The beauty of the spot and its modern facilities attracted a rich and famous clientele. Dressed in white, with large veiled hats, and parasols in hand, the elegant ladies would stroll along the pier or in the gardens of the casino, accompanied by mustached gentlemen in straw boaters.

The Hôtel Splendid, where Jeanne and Adrien stayed, was the most luxurious hotel in Evian. Opened two years earlier, and surrounded by an immense park, its classic facade looked out over the lake. With electric lighting, an elevator, and over one hundred rooms with thin walls, it made for a comfortable but noisy stay, and Jeanne discouraged her son—in vain—from joining her there. There were bellhops everywhere, taking orders from a demanding set of guests whose tips were rarely as generous as Marcel's. Every year the Prousts met both relatives and friends at Evian, such as Monsieur Cottin, the notary who had married them, and his wife, whom Jeanne nicknamed "Anne of Brittany," or Dr. Cottet, who the previous year had "gone overboard" about Marcel. "You realize (and I only add this stupid remark because of my mother's imagination), I say overboard in a good sense, so don't go imagining that it's an evil connection, great gods!!!"[171] Marcel wrote his mother, proving once again that the unspoken truth between them was a question of degree and that they could joke about it.

Jeanne also gave free reign to her caustic wit in letters that "amused and enchanted" her son, including "astonishing" revelations about the Oulif couple, who appeared so serious, or a merciless portrait of Nisard, the old ambassador to the Vatican: "Very amiable but very deaf. He doesn't hear anything you tell him and since he speaks so quietly you don't hear anything he says either."[172] As for Madame Armand Brun, the wife of an avid club-goer whose path she crossed in 1903, "if she is as irreproachable in her life as in her outfits, she is a woman of quality."[173] Sometimes it was Jeanne's turn to ask Marcel for information:

> What kind of composer is Lepneveu: god, basin, or table? I know nothing about him—a vague memory of a cantata—for the visit of the czar?—tell me something in case I end up face-to-face with him—and it's a miracle it hasn't happened yet (he's part of the group with Ployer, Silhol, Chauveau, etc.—) so I might say, "There's really nothing more beautiful than your . . ."?[174]

As far as Jeanne was concerned, she and Adrien were "not allied with any group"; along with their friends the Duplays, they constituted an "independent republican party."[175] "As to politics I'm like you, a member of the great 'liberal conservative intelligent' party," she had written to her son, back when he was eighteen.[176] They awaited the daily arrival of newspapers from Paris and analyzed the news: in 1899 it was the Dreyfus Affair, in 1900, the attack on the European colony in Peking. They played dominoes with the Duplays, who were amused by the passion Dr. Proust put into the game. In the evening they went to the theater by way of an electrical funicular linking the Hôtel Splendid to the pavilion.

Jeanne paid careful attention to her treatment, and made the most of it by accompanying her husband back to the spa in June after he had undergone a painful operation for kidney stones. While Adrien "devoted his entire attention to examining the light and dark shades of his urine,"[177] Jeanne sat down at the Cachat fountain, where patients filled their glasses with mineral water, and wrote to Marcel:

> Your Mama—doing things on a grand scale—takes a bath every other day. This morning I took it at nine, and beforehand I drank from the fountain—I got out at ten—and drank a second glass—and finally I'm sitting at one of the tables with paper, ink, etc.—[. . .] and while I'm writing to my son the second glass will have time to make way for a third.[178]

Her light tone and somewhat feigned gaiety shouldn't fool us. Her principal worry remained Marcel, whose letters she awaited impatiently. Every morning, she wrote him before the mail went out at eleven. When he joined her in 1899, their "embrace on the terrace" was witnessed by a "stern and ironic" Adrien.[179] Her husband found these public displays of affection childish and inappropriate. In August 1902, Marcel's protestations—"I don't miss you"—proved nothing, for they were accompanied by pathetic bleating that he was alone, abandoned, and sick. He confided in Antoine Bibesco: "Since Mama has left I'm lonely and so sad."

The following summer, Adrien and Jeanne extended their visit to the Swiss spa by going on to Zermatt, where they stayed at the Hôtel du Mont-Cervin. Jeanne walked ten hours a day in hopes of losing weight. In 1903, they traveled to Interlaken and returned to Evian via Ouchy ("The Hôtel d'Ouchy is to this one what Mme Cahen d'Anvers's wardrobe would be to mine"), where they encountered the usual crowd. Jeanne, true to form, had scarcely arrived in Evian than she demanded a full report:

> My darling, will you please answer my household questions:
> Are all your clothes from head to toe in perfect shape? Whatever needed washing—cleaning—looking at—resoling—marking—taking in—hemming—changing collars—fixing buttonholes, etc. Not counting holidays, Marie had six days for all of that. I would like to know if they were well spent. Try to make sure that everything is done carefully (I know that you're capable of giving directions without my preaching). [. . .]
> A thousand hugs—though I'm wearing gloves, which makes my writing somewhat illegible.
> A thousand tender kisses.[180]

We might expect that her son, now thirty-two, would have wanted even a rough warning of when she would be returning home. However, Maurice Duplay tells us that

> one evening, near dinner time, while the tuxedos and evening dresses gathered on the terrace, the hotel omnibus arrived with new guests; among them was a young man all bundled up as though he were freezing on the coldest day in winter. This newcomer was Marcel Proust.[181]

For him, better yet to be right on the spot.

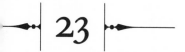

23

A Wedding and a Funeral

Jeanne was now fifty-two. She had gained weight, and in her brown hair, drawn back into a chignon, a few strands of silver marked the passing years. She still dressed with discreet elegance. In a photograph taken in 1904, still in mourning, she was wearing a black suit, a silk blouse with a lace jabot, diamond earrings, and an antique silver necklace with a medallion. Her gaze, her face with its full features, were tinged with sadness despite the hint of a smile. There was nothing bitter in her expression, though she certainly had worries. She felt tired; her operation had aged her. The spa visits no longer helped her aching joints. She had begun to suffer from uremia, the kidney disease to which her mother had succumbed. Her feet and hands were swollen, she had trouble walking, and on some days she could scarcely hold a pen or play the piano.

Jeanne still worried about Marcel. She didn't regard his illness as an excuse for the eccentric life he led or for his strange schedule, incompatible with family life. Even though there had been tensions between them of late, she knew how much he needed her. If only he could find a wife who would eventually look after him.

Instead, Robert was the one getting married. And his marriage was also a source of unhappiness for his mother. Everything had come easy for her second son: a dedicated student, charming—he was known as "the handsome Proust"—a connoisseur of women, and adept at sports of all kinds, he had become a doctor like his father. Or rather, he became the doctor his father wanted him to be. He would have preferred to study mathematics or architecture, but this time, Adrien did not back down. He made Robert his sentimental heir: the younger child found himself in the role of elder son. When Jeanne looked at Robert, with his freewheeling elegance, his confident posture, it was like seeing a younger version of her husband, the same body language, the same way of talking—although his large dark eyes and black hair clearly came from the Weil side. In 1901, Robert was the first surgeon in France to remove a prostate. He took his *agrégation* in 1904 and defended a thesis on surgery of the female genital tract.[182] He was also interested in the study of androgyny. For Adrien, Robert made up for Marcel's deficiencies. Professor Proust was proud of his son.

How could Jeanne not be proud as well? Despite his irritability, Robert, in his way, was more docile than Marcel, who always said yes but did as he liked.

Robert's marriage too was the work of Adrien Proust. His son was to marry Marthe, the daughter of Madame Suzanne Dubois-Amiot, with whom Professor Proust had—or so it was said—a very "personal" relationship.[183] Nathé Weil had done business with Suzanne's father, Monsieur Favier, a banker, and Adrien had been called to her bedside when she was sick.[184] So there was a family connection of sorts. Adrien must have felt that this arranged marriage with a wealthy young woman couldn't help but advance his son's career. For Jeanne, such a union, concocted in the boudoir of one of her husband's mistresses, was a slap in the face. She knew what was going on. She may also have guessed that the marriage would not be a happy one.

If we are to believe Marcel, the marriage plans were kept secret, even from the bride's brother Louis. On January 24, 1903, an engagement party took place at the Prousts' elegant apartment at 45, rue de Courcelles, where they had been living for three years. The wedding, first planned for March 1, was moved up to February 2. Why such a hurry? There were many worries. Half of the invitations were lost. Everyone was feeling irritated. Because of a death in the Amiot family, the contract was signed privately, *en famille*. According to last-minute modifications, Robert brought to the marriage a regular income of 3,000 francs and 100,000 francs in the form of an advance on his inheritance. This sum was taken from the revenue of Jeanne's own dowry, with her authorization, of course, as we see from her handwritten letter to her notary.[185]

Ailing and unable to leave her bed, Jeanne couldn't attend the civil marriage ceremony on January 29. Nor was Marcel present. There was distress both moral and physical: the mother of the groom was taken by ambulance to the Eglise Saint-Augustin, where the religious ceremony took place, attended by a large crowd. Robert, an atheist like his father, was married in a church. The bond with the Weils was broken.

Marcel, obsessed by the fear that he would burst out laughing, hadn't been able to sleep for three nights. The ceremony was an ordeal for him. As best man, he was supposed to accompany his cousin Valentine Thomson (the great-granddaughter of Adolphe Crémieux) as she took up the traditional collection for the poor. The young lady, dressed to the nines and proud of the bouquet of orchids that Jeanne had given her, was horrified to find Marcel looking deathly pale, bundled up in three overcoats, his shirtfront bulging from layers of woolen undergarments and his neck swathed in woolen scarves. He couldn't even negotiate the pews. Valentine decided to do it alone. He followed her along the aisle, announcing as he stood at the end of each row that he hadn't been able to dress any other way because he was sick and that it was not his fault.

Poor Marcel! It took him ten days to recover. Robert's wedding "literally killed him."[186] And so he concluded that getting a brother married was almost as fatiguing as getting married oneself.[187]

Jeanne's illness probably prevented her from attending the elegant reception and lunch that the Dubois-Amiot family gave at their apartment on the avenue de Messine. Marthe's relationship with her in-laws remained distant. After Robert's death, she unburdened herself of her collection of Marcel Proust's papers, burning some and selling others.

———◆◆◆———

Marcel, having turned thirty, seemed ready for independence. Alone at home with his parents, he must now have felt the weight of their authority even more intensely. It was a second adolescence. His letters to his mother revealed an aggressiveness which, though not new, had never been expressed so clearly. The feeling was mutual. His complaints were often more than Jeanne could bear. She pointed out to him that plenty of people with ailments still had to work in order to feed their families. She criticized his frivolousness, his late-night outings. His health was bound to suffer from his irregular habits. At times her tone was bitter, and she despaired of ever making him see reason. She was also tired of his promises to get down to work or improve his habits. She could be sharp, even hurtful.

They fought constantly over household issues. Jeanne wanted to force Marcel to respect the household schedule. But he went to bed in the morning and rose in late afternoon, sometimes only in the evening. He allowed no one to make the slightest noise or even to open the windows. He was not to be disturbed.

> "Mama, my pet, you know it's late. I don't need to remind you about noises. [. . .] Perhaps it would be as well if you would leave a little note for Robert, to make sure he knows, and doesn't walk straight into my room."
>
> "Walk straight into your room?
> *Can he be unaware how strict a law*
> *Fences our Monarch here from men in awe.*
> *And that for mortal rash enough to come*
> *Unbidden to his sight, death is the doom?"*

It should be noted that Marcel suspected Robert of coming in on purpose to wake him. But like Ahasuerus, Marcel only deigned to offer his golden scepter to his Esther, Mama:

> *What fear you? Were these laws for you designed?*
> *Do I not love you with a brother's mind?*[188]

The reality was far less poetic. The servants had to tend to Marcel at all hours. Jeanne ordered them to refuse his requests, putting them in an embarrassing situation and infantilizing Marcel. On one occasion, when he had to invite his friends to visit in a room with no fire in the hearth, he took out his anger on his love of the moment, Bertrand de Fénelon, stamping on his new hat and tearing it to shreds. Such behavior might be considered mere childishness if there were not also elements of real despair and real violence.

He accused Jeanne: "The truth is that as soon as I feel better, the life that makes me feel better exasperates you and you demolish everything until I feel ill again." And he concluded, "It's sad, not being able to have affection and health at the same time."[189] This comment, written in a fit of anger, was right on the mark—far truer, perhaps, than he realized. And it was all the more cruel for being addressed to his mother.

Marcel's bedtime hours became a constant duel. Jeanne tried to protect him, but by imposing an orderliness that didn't agree with him. He responded by using sickness as blackmail. Sleep was the bedrock of their conflict, a source of anxiety from the beginning: "To think that I never succeeded at the only thing I wanted—to teach myself to sleep when I still had Mama, which was the only thing she wanted,"[190] he wrote Lucien Daudet, many years after Jeanne's death.

Jeanne would criticize Marcel for preventing her own sleep by returning home so late. Sometimes she had to wait until eleven o'clock to have dinner with him. In March, there was a real fight: Marcel accused his mother of sabotaging the "triple reform" he was planning to adopt.[191] He held her responsible for his indecisiveness. But Jeanne wasn't to be outdone: "Change your habits, or you won't get your dinner party," she threatened when he asked her to organize a reception for his literary connections. With tensions raised, they communicated by letter. "A dinner party for cocottes" was how she referred to what Marcel conceived of as a professional event, as useful for him as dinners given by Robert or his father. She used the word deliberately. The pejorative term conveyed her real feelings on the subject, and perhaps her unconscious rejection of her son's values—as if her customary indulgence was yielding to her anger. Let him invite his friends out to a restaurant, and let him pay for it.[192]

She kept up the pressure. She insisted that he get back to work and finish his translation of Ruskin, the work that *she* desired, as he pointed out to her, and whose limits he already understood. She was convinced that work would save him. How could he possibly meet her demands? He felt so weak, "racked." How could he escape this maternal will? How could he satisfy her? Jeanne imposed this dilemma on her son, certain that it was for his own good and that she must not give in. Give to him, yes, but demand from him in return. The three first chapters of *The Bible of Amiens* had just been published in a literary magazine. She must have been proud of him. But Marcel complained: "You'll continue to disapprove of everything I do until I fall ill again as I did two years ago."[193]

And then there was money. It was hard for Jeanne to give this spoiled child a sense of the value of money earned. He was expected to pay for his powders for fumigating his room, and his parents asked him to keep a budget. Again, it was his mother, not his father, who bore the brunt of Marcel's ill humor. She, who had never counted pennies over her son's studies—paying liberally for classes in philosophy, law, and Latin—was now refusing to let him travel to London or Rome. Marcel couldn't stomach his financial dependence. He used to joke about his mother's "instinct for concision and economy." But when Antoine Bibesco, in front of Adrien and Jeanne, referred—accidentally?—to his extravagant tipping, Marcel burst into tears.[194] He longed to support himself, to live in a "separate house"; even if it meant visiting his mother "twenty times a day," he would do it, he was ready.[195] But Jeanne smiled. She knew he wasn't leaving.

She did, however, make concessions. On April 1, 1903, Marcel invited Paul Hervieu and Abel Herman, Antoine Bibesco, Emile and Geneviève Straus, Constanin de Brancovan, Anna de Noailles, and Hélène de Caraman-Chimay to dine at the Prousts'. In July, she relapsed again, giving a dinner party in honor of Caston Calmette, Marcel's boss at *Le Figaro*. He thanked her tenderly, saying he would "deal with the financial question another time."[196]

One morning she received a note from her son in which he described "the paroxysm of emotion" that he felt once again in thinking about her, after the disappointments of the past few months due to her sarcasm and harshness. Was this "surge of his true spiritual nature" a result of his illness—what he called his "real physical nature"?[197] As he was drifting off to sleep, he wrote a second note, a terrible confession: "I'd rather have asthma attacks and please you than displease you and not have any."[198] She agreed to wake him up at half past five that afternoon, as planned: "Please don't make any noise or open the windows, Monsieur Marcel is sleeping."

Jeanne knew her son well enough to understand that his love life was far from happy. Bertrand de Fénelon seemed indifferent. Louis d'Albufera was a connoisseur of good-looking women like the actress Louisa de Mornand, whom Marcel appeared to be courting. Illan de Casa-Fuere, Francis de Croisset, Léon Radziwill, his new friends, shared his tastes but did not reciprocate his feelings. One after the other, they all married, even Léon (nicknamed Loche), who claimed he was doing it to please his mother. "You couldn't do anything more certain to hurt her, sooner or later, and I'm sure your mother is fond enough of you to put her pleasure in your happiness, and not in your leading a life of self-sacrifice," advised Marcel, who knew what he was talking about.[199] He wasn't wrong: Loche left his wife a week after they were married. With Gabriel de La Rochefoucault and Armand de Gramont, duc de Guiche,[200] Proust was socializing with the high aristocracy—and his brother gave him plenty of grief about it. All these young men would gather on the rue de Courcelles, just as they used to gather on the boulevard Malesherbes. Jeanne couldn't ignore them—any more than could Madame Cocteau or Madame Rostand, mother of the indescribable Maurice, with his eyeliner and powdered face. But Marcel, thanks to his earlier experiences in his days at the Lycée Condorcet, had learned to keep up a fiction that everyone pretended to believe. There was nothing effeminate about his looks. To his family, he didn't need to appear to be a *salaïste* (his term for a homosexual),[201] since he was nothing of the kind, he explained to Antoine Bibesco, who must have been highly amused by the denial. But as we've seen, Jeanne wasn't easily fooled, and her silence on the subject amounted to acceptance. "Love teaches us much, but also it much corrupts us," Proust wrote in *Jean Santeuil*.[202] Perhaps Jeanne, like Jean's mother, learned to tolerate what had once repelled her.

Reynaldo Hahn, the closest of all of Marcel's friends, wrote much later that "there was nothing that Madame Proust needed to forgive in her son, whom she valued more than anything else and whom she never took it upon herself to judge or try in any way to penetrate."[203] It was a half-truth or a half-lie, depending on your perspective.

———◆··◆———

Adrien too had aged. He was almost seventy. Although his health had declined, he had scarcely slowed his professional activity since retiring from the Hôtel-Dieu in 1899. He had had a few setbacks: he had twice failed to be elected to the august Académie des sciences morales et politiques, which he had longed to join, and, more disturbing, there had been a public debate over a system of quarantine he had ordered as inspector-general of sanitary services.[204] He defended his actions, but the struggle was clearly exhausting. In October 1903, he took an active role in an international public health conference in Paris. On November 23, he was present at the annual meeting of the International Association for the Fight against Tuberculosis, and even saw a few patients at his home.

With the passing years, Adrien Proust had become less pompous and more human, if we're to believe *Jean Santeuil*. He spent time with his wife; he was tender, solicitous. He had also grown closer to his elder son, with whom he shared a few moments of close collaboration when Marcel helped him write the speech inaugurating the monument in honor of Pasteur in Chartres, as well as the speech he gave a few weeks later, in July 1903, for the end-of-the-year prizes at his former school in Illiers.

In a beautiful passage of his unfinished novel, Marcel describes Jean's parents in their old age. The mother limps a little; the father's shoulders stoop as he walks, and he is short of breath. They rent a canoe and go boating on the lake in the Bois de Boulogne, an extraordinary expense for this frugal couple who, despite their wealth, have no car and travel only by omnibus or rental car. They savor this unusual treat, and while Monsieur Santeuil explains everything he sees, as is his habit, Madame daydreams, happy to have her husband by her side, happy with this new intimacy, now that the children are grown.

The real-life Prousts' contentment didn't last long. At 4:00 P.M. on November 24, 1903, Jeanne picked up the telephone: Adrien had collapsed at the medical school. Her first thought was to alert Marcel gently, through the open door: "Forgive me for disturbing you, but your father has taken ill at the School."[205] Soon afterwards, a grim procession arrived: Adrien, unconscious, lay on a stretcher carried by two nurses, followed by Robert. Robert had been worried by his father's pallor when Adrien stopped by his son's place on the boulevard Saint-Germain to visit Marthe, who was about to give birth;[206] the young doctor had then accompanied his father to the medical school, where Adrien was to chair a dissertation defense. Adrien excused himself from the examination room, and didn't return. An assistant alerted Robert in his lab before forcing open the door of the toilet where Adrien lay unconscious, felled by a cerebral hemorrhage.[207] He never regained consciousness, and died two days later, on November 26, 1903.

The funeral rites took place on Saturday, November 28. Beneath the windows of number 45, boulevard de Courcelles, in front of the entryway draped in black, the Fifth Battalion performed a fanfare to honor the remains of Professor Proust. Friends filed through the apartment to pay their last respects. In full sight of Jeanne, who seemed not to notice, a woman no one knew placed a bouquet of violets next to the body. A procession of hearses covered in flowers made its way to the Saint-Philippe-du-Roule church, where members of the medical, diplomatic, and political establishments and Paris high society rubbed shoulders with the Faubourg Saint-Germain aristocracy, who had come to support Marcel. Pale and faltering, he walked beside Robert, leading the mourners. Jeanne was surrounded by the Weil family. A succession of funeral orations paid homage to "a good, helpful colleague whom everyone admired." Adrien was buried in the Père-Lachaise cemetery in a family plot he had recently purchased.[208] The dean of the medical school, Professor Debove, described him as "enough of an epicurean to enjoy things without waxing tragic about life's little woes; enough of a skeptic to be patient with those who didn't see eye to eye with his version of the right way to do things; enough of a stoic to conceive of death with strength." Adrien had recently confided to his colleague: "I've been happy all my life, and I have only one wish: that I go gently and without suffering."

Jeanne never recovered from her husband's death.

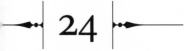

24

La Vie à Deux

Jeanne was shattered, but it wasn't obvious. Not yet. Everyone admired her energy, her courage. Nothing about her seemed to have changed. The same calm, the same determination. But Marcel knew that the drama was being played out at such a deep level and so violently that they should fear for the worst. Perhaps the shock wave hadn't yet reached the surface; perhaps her husband's sudden death still seemed something of an abstraction to her: an absence, slightly longer than his other absences. At first there was so much to do: the funeral, the thank-you notes, the papers.

She had always feared for Marcel's life, and it was Adrien who had died. "She gave him every minute of her life," Marcel wrote to Madame de Noailles.[209] She had lived only for her husband, he protested later to Maurice Barrès, who had written him, thinking it would please him, that Marcel had been his mother's favorite.[210] What would become of Jeanne's existence now? To whom would she devote herself? The response was obvious: to Marcel.

Living under the same roof, they were both alone, and it's tempting to imagine their tête-à-têtes, like the idyllic days enjoyed by the mother and son in *Jean Santeuil* when the father is away. But reality is always more nuanced. Marcel, conscious of his responsibility, made serious plans to "reform his life." Several days after his father's death, he wrote her:

> I would so much like, I so much want, to be able soon to get up at the same time as you do and drink my breakfast coffee with you. To feel our sleep and waking distributed over the same hours would be, will be, such a delight to me.[211]

Sadly, it's easier to get from the conditional to the future on paper than in real life. As much as he dreamed of sharing life with his mother "by the same timetable, in the same rooms, at the same temperature," his grand resolutions ended with his asking her to "make Marie and Antoine keep quiet and keep the kitchen door closed, so their voices don't come through."

Although Jeanne retained few illusions, one area in which she would not give up was work. Learning that Marcel had abandoned his Ruskin project (he claimed he couldn't find his page proofs), she got right back on his case, with the perfect argument: his father had been waiting eagerly for this publication, which had been his dearest hope. Marcel had to go on. We should admire the subtlety of this maternal strategy: it wasn't for her but for his father that Marcel needed to finish his translation project. He returned to work. In the meantime, he had begun his translation of Ruskin's *Sesame and Lilies*. *The Bible of Amiens* came out in February 1904 with this dedication: "To the memory of my father, struck down at his workplace on November 24, 1903, died November 26, this translation is affectionately dedicated."[212]

But for the time being he was preoccupied with his health, his friends, his articles, and his frequent trips, often taken on a whim. Jeanne wanted him to leave without her in January 1904. She herself left Paris for the countryside (perhaps Saint-Cloud, where Robert and his wife had rented a house). But she soon returned home, stricken with nephritis. She managed to hide her pain from her son; Marcel had no idea. Still, symptoms of the illness that would eventually kill her were increasing. She walked with difficulty, her legs and hands swollen with edema.

The following summer she joined Robert and his family in Etretat while Marcel cruised on a yacht belonging to Robert de Billy's father-in-law. After pages of meticulous details concerning his schedule, his health, his activities—he even accused his mother of not reading his letters—he devoted a few lines to their separation ("when I'm tucked away in your heart and have you perpetually within reach of my thoughts and my affection") and to Robert and Marthe: "I'm so glad they are such nice children for you, nicer than I am."[213] A touch of jealousy, or guilt, or relief? He didn't ask her a single question about her own health.

Doubtless, as he said, he spoke to her in imagination a hundred times a minute, but their relationship was all about him; he was the center. Loving his mother had always, from the very beginning, amounted to an obsessive report of his every move, proof that he was ailing but alive. "It gives me so much pleasure to complain to you," he admitted in all innocence.[214] It never occurred to him to spare her. But she knew he meant it when he expressed regret that she couldn't be there with him, admiring the sea she so loved, breathing the cool fresh air, for she had always suffered terribly in hot weather. Robert was on hand to attend to her health, and Marcel recommended that she talk to him in detail about her fatigue. Robert had grown gentler, less "acid." "His intelligence and his kindness will combine to advise you,"[215] Marcel told her, adding: "I live in close proximity to you with my eyes closed." Did Jeanne realize that if his eyes had been open, he couldn't have borne watching her die, week by week?

In any case, she opted for solitude. After endless equivocations, Marcel decided to stay in Paris in September. Jeanne made up her own mind: she was old enough to do as she liked.[216] On September 20, she left for Dieppe, where she used to go as a child with her parents. The Hôtel Royal was closed, so she stayed at the Hôtel Métropole et des Bains. "I think I did well for *myself* by coming here."[217]

It was bitterly cold, though without that wind from the sea that "you have to struggle with mightily, but emerge ennobled." Her bedroom was icy. She put on two nightdresses, piled on four extra blankets and an eiderdown, and left the electric light on all night so as not to have to go to the other end of the room to turn it off ("which shows you that the lighting is included," she joked). She walked bravely along the esplanade, stopped by the post office, bought a newspaper. There was scarcely anyone at the hotel, and the dining tables were set up in the same room as the communal table for local guests. Just as she had done after the deaths of Louis and Nathé, she attempted to regain her strength alone and in Dieppe.

Taking advantage of her absence, Marcel tried to implement his great plan for reform, which he described to her with an abundance of details. Struck with a sudden insight, he exclaimed: "My dear little Mama, I realize how boring it must be to hear all this talk of my health."[218] His dear little Mama may well have thought, "And how!" But she protested: "You are wrong, darling, your letters are *all* charming, *all* appreciated by me as I appreciate my little wolf from every point of view."[219] An admirable mother, if sometimes importunate, Jeanne seized the opportunity to remind her thirty-three-year-old son that he needed a haircut: "Your hair gets in my eyes when I think of you. I hope by the time I finish this you'll have had it done."

Jeanne never dwelled on her own pain. In her letters she commented on the news and on society gossip and directed Marcel in his supervision of the domestics. She continued to joke: Julia Daudet, having visited Lourdes, became "Julia de Sacré-Coeur."

After Jeanne returned from Dieppe, she was faced with the innumerable chores her son imposed upon her—various errands, wedding presents for friends. It was she who dropped off a copy of *The Bible of Amiens* at Léon Daudet's, she who took Marie Norlinger to Auteuil. Marcel's reforms were taking their time. He still went out at night, except when he was sick, which was often, or on the days commemorating his father's death. This anniversary ritual, like the one Jeanne had followed after her mother's death, was for her an expression of fidelity, a rendezvous with the departed that she respected scrupulously. Marcel kept her company on Tuesdays, because Adrien had suffered his stroke on a Tuesday; on the 24th day of each month, for the same reason; on the 26th, the day of his death; on the 28th, the day of his funeral; and, of course, on November 26, 1904, when Jeanne went to Père-Lachaise cemetery with both of her sons. Meanwhile, she asked Marie Nordlinger to sculpt a medallion in Adrien's likeness to be placed on his tomb.

She was worried about her brother Georges. Increasingly neurasthenic, he suffered from severe abdominal ailments. The doctors were reassuring: there was nothing wrong with him, it was purely psychological. Yet he would die of renal failure just a few months after Jeanne,[220] who had to be hospitalized for her own kidney condition from December 1904 until early January 1905.

In a handwritten will, Adrien Proust left her his entire estate. The document, dated May 26, 1896, written after Louis Weil's death and in anticipation of Nathé's, specified: "I name as my sole beneficiary, for all my property and with no exception, my wife, Madame Jeanne Weil." The amount of the inheritance came to 1,430,613 francs, not including Jeanne's own personal property, dowry, and inheritances. Jeanne was now extremely wealthy. So were her children. Marcel received 194,582 francs, a small fortune.[221]

But Jeanne made no changes in the way she lived, remaining careful with her expenses, doubtless wanting to ensure the best possible future for her son. For while Robert had a profession, Marcel was far from being able to support himself by his writing, despite his efforts. In a questionnaire sent to him by Maurice Le Blond, Zola's son-in-law,[222] who was campaigning against state funding for the Ecole des Beaux-Arts in the name of artistic freedom, Marcel defended the principles that had been inculcated in him from early childhood: "the pernicious effect of sloth, sickness, or conceit" and the "benefits of discipline, as important for the neuropath as for the artist," adding that "discipline is something fruitful in itself, whatever the value of what it prescribes."[223] Jeanne couldn't have said it better.

Despite his asthma attacks, Marcel was working. He asked his mother to help him unravel his preface to *Sesame and Lilies*. Nothing could have pleased her more. But this time, Marie Nordlinger was in charge of the translation.

——•••——

Marcel and Jeanne gradually settled into their ménage as a twosome. At the beginning of 1905, Marcel gave a large dinner party in honor of Bertrand de Fénelon, who was passing through Paris, then a tea for his aristocratic friends. He patiently constructed his career, his network of connections; his ambition was membership in the Cercle de l'Union, a club less selective than the Jockey Club but still too restrictive for a former Dreyfusard. Jeanne noticed his efforts. He read a great deal and took notes. He wrote to his childhood friend Robert Dreyfus: "I lead a very quiet, restful life of reading and very studious intimacy with Mama."[224] This studious intimacy may have had something to do with the preface, titled "On Reading," that he was working on for *Sesame and Lilies;* many pages of that preface evoke his childhood, in a foretaste of Combray. The descriptions of the house at Illiers, the memory of Easter vacations and the time he spent alone, reading, emerged from this period of mourning as a kind of adieu to his father. He must have recalled those places with Jeanne, asked her for details, compared their memories. I hope she read this text. It was Marcel's first step toward his great work, the consciousness of "the inviolate place of the Past: the Past familiarly risen in the midst of the present."[225]

With her illness progressing, Jeanne walked with increasing difficulty, was short of breath and easily exhausted, and suffered ever more frequently from nausea. In June of 1905, though ailing himself, Marcel gathered the strength to visit the Whistler exhibit at the Ecole des Beaux-Arts. Wildly enthusiastic, he sketched a map of the exhibit for Jeanne, pointing out which paintings she needed to see, so as to save her too much walking. With Marcel's note in hand, Jeanne, in turn, gazed up at the "little scenes of Venice, streets, squares, rios," that they had once visited. His instructions were detailed:

> Go into the room and turn around so that the door next to the staircase by which you entered is facing you, and you will see on the wall in front of you (separated by the door onto the staircase), to your left and to your right, two paintings of sailboats in a port, at evening.[226]

He spared her no detail, leading her as if by the hand; the words of this ailing son guided a mother soon to die.[227] She saw with his eyes, loved what he loved.

Marcel's condition too was deteriorating; he had to take to his bed for several days after every outing. After consulting his doctors, he seriously considered going to the hospital. His mother continued to do countless favors for him—sending mail or books, making various purchases. Twice it was she who, despite the heat, had to go to Neuilly to get news of Yturri, Robert de Montesquiou's secretary, who was seriously ill with diabetes. To spare Marcel the shock, she broke the news of Yturri's death very slowly.

On September 8, 1905, mother and son decided to visit Evian. Jeanne had not been back since her husband's death. Two hours after arriving, she fell ill. One attack of uremia followed another, with dizziness and vomiting. Jeanne's kidney disease had reached the terminal stage. She could no longer eliminate either water or toxins. The edema was spreading, poisons were diffusing throughout her body. Gray, exhausted, her lungs filling with liquid, Jeanne could neither eat nor walk without help. She nonetheless insisted on going downstairs in the morning to the hotel parlor, supported on either side so as not to fall. Marcel phoned his friend Madame Catusse, by whom his mother wished to be photographed, though Jeanne was hesitant, fearing to leave behind too sad an image. She refused all tests and didn't want to see a doctor. Robert was informed and came hurrying to her side; he insisted on taking her back to Paris. He had to drag her onto the train, along with Madame Catusse. In a final effort, Jeanne demanded that Marcel remain in Evian, to spare him from suffering through her own death throes, which she knew were close at hand. She had seen her own mother die of the same disease. Until the end she would protect her son, choosing to deprive herself of his presence.

Marcel waited in Evian, returning to Paris only several days later. Jeanne was already refusing all food and medicine—as her mother and father had done and, later, as her son would do. She could hardly be persuaded to see Dr. Landovski. She had never had much faith in doctors. What had they ever done to cure her son? Despite her weakness, she insisted on getting up, washing, dressing. Marcel, in despair, knew that what hurt his mother most was the idea of leaving him alone in the world, vulnerable, incapable of living without her. The nun who took care of Jeanne told Marcel later that to his mother, he was still a four-year-old. Until the very last moment, despite the nascent paralysis and aphasia with which she was stricken, Jeanne struggled to hide her condition from her son.

Georges understood without being told. He simply disappeared. He didn't return until his sister's funeral.

Speaking with difficulty as she lay dying, Jeanne quoted Labiche and Molière—her final eloquence: "My little lad mustn't be afraid, his Mama won't leave him. It would be a fine set-out if I were at Etampes and my spelling at Arpajon!" And then, Marcel tells us, "she became unable to talk. Once only, when she saw I was constraining myself to keep back my tears she made a grimace at me, half frowning, half smiling; and though by then she could not speak plainly, I caught the words, 'Though not a Roman, act the Roman's part.'"[228] *Sursum corda:* lift up your heart, little wolf!

At her bedside was her cousin Laure Nathan, "Aunt Laure." Marcel, sick himself, was in the next room. Jeanne could no longer speak or move. Her face betrayed acute anxiety; she seemed to be trying to mouth the word "Marcel." Laure understood and tiptoed away. As she must have told it afterwards, when Marcel came into the room, Jeanne's face suddenly radiated contentment. Marcel was fine. She could die in peace. Those were her last living moments.[229]

Jeanne died Tuesday, September 26, 1905. She was fifty-six. For two days, Marcel stayed by her side, "weeping and smiling through his tears at her body."[230] Thin from her illness, her hair still dark, her face unlined, she looked thirty.

Jeanne had never converted and remained faithful to the religion of her parents. There were to be no prayers in her home, for her burial, like those of her parents, was organized by the Jewish Consistory of Paris.[231] Her hearse was covered with flowers, but it was a rabbi—the ultimate gesture of a son for his Jewish mother—who recited the prayer for the dead before a crowd of Parisian society.

Esther had gone to meet her Ahasuerus.

Epilogue

"My life has now forever lost its only purpose, its only sweetness, its only love, its only consolation," wrote Marcel.[232] His descent into hell would last two years, with remissions, relapses, and crises. When his mother died, Marcel recognized, she took little Marcel with her.

Little Marcel may have died, but he gave birth to the writer, Marcel Proust, who would spend the rest of his days constructing a work of art that would have made his mother proud. Perhaps his most touching acknowledgment of her occurs in the very first line of *In Search of Lost Time:* "For a long time I used to go to bed early." Jeanne would have loved those words.

ACKNOWLEDGMENTS

This book is the result of an encounter. My thanks go first of all to my good fairy—she'll know whom I mean. My thanks also to the following:

Nathalie Mauriac, who allowed me to consult Jeanne Proust's precious address book
Madame Claude Heuman, Georges Weil's granddaughter
Nicole Rodrigues-Ely, for speaking with me about Aunt Laure
Mireille Naturel, general secretary of the Société des amis de Marcel Proust, for her patience in answering my questions
Anne Borrel, who speaks Proust fluently
Pierre-André Meyer, a generous genealogist
Jean-Pierre Kleist, who helped me decipher Alsatian script
My friend Malika Mokedeem, for consulting long distance
Marina Gasperi at Sotheby's, Monaco
Monsieur and Madame Monier at Illiers-Combray
Anne-Marie Bernard, for the Nadar photos

Philippe Landau, archivist of the Central Consistory
Valérie Sueur, of the Bibliothèque nationale de France
Isabelle Arcos, of the Bibliothèque de Trouville
André Trillaud, with his eagle eye

Finally and always, I thank my dear editor, Manuel Carcassonne. And I thank you, Pierre.

Translator's thanks: I am grateful to the author, Evelyne Bloch-Dano, for her gracious assistance with sources; to Selin Ever, Gerry Canavan, and Jaimee Hills for their research assistance; and to Margaret Mahan, for her keen eye.

Appendixes

APPENDIX I:
QUESTIONNAIRE SENT TO THE
JEWISH ELITE IN 1806

* Are Jewish men allowed to marry several women?
* Is divorce permitted under Jewish law? Is divorce valid without having been decreed by the courts and by virtue of laws contradictory to those of the French code?
* Can a Jewish woman marry a Christian man, and can a Christian woman marry a Jewish man? Or does Jewish law require that Jews only marry among themselves?
* In the eyes of Jews, are Frenchmen brothers or foreigners?
* In either case, what kind of relations with Frenchmen who are not of their faith does their law prescribe?
* Do Jews born in France and treated as citizens under French law consider France their own country? Do they have an obligation to defend France? Are they obliged to obey the laws and follow all the aspects of the civil code?
* Who appoints rabbis?

✤ What kind of policing do rabbis exercise among Jews? What kind of policing do rabbis exercise among themselves?

✤ Are these appointments and this policing demanded by their law or
merely established by custom?

✤ Are there certain professions forbidden to Jews by Jewish law?

✤ Does Jewish law prevent Jews from lending at interest to their brothers?

✤ Does Jewish law prevent Jews or allow them to lend money at interest to
foreigners?

Source: Archives of the Consistoire de Paris.

APPENDIX 2:
NAPOLEON AND THE
CENTRAL CONSISTORY

The emperor took a personal interest in the integration of Jews, as we can see from this dialogue with the representatives of the Central Consistory in December 1808, which tells us as much about his attitude toward them as it does about his conversational style.

The Emperor:
— Your name?
— Lazard, Sire.
— And you?
— Cologna.
— Surely a rabbi.
— Grand Rabbi, Sire.
(To Lazard): Are you one of the principals? Are you from Paris?
— Sire, I am from Paris and a member of the Central Consistory.
— From Paris proper?
— Yes, Sire, from Paris.

— Well then, how is it going?

— Sire, we are getting organized.

— Have you begun to correct the bad ones?

— Sire, they shall all be worthy of being subjects of Your Majesty.

— That's good . . . that's good . . . Do just as they did in Bordeaux . . . Like the Portuguese.

Source: Proceedings of the Central Consistory, December 12, 1808. Archives of the Consistoire de Paris.

Genealogical Charts

THE WEIL FAMILY

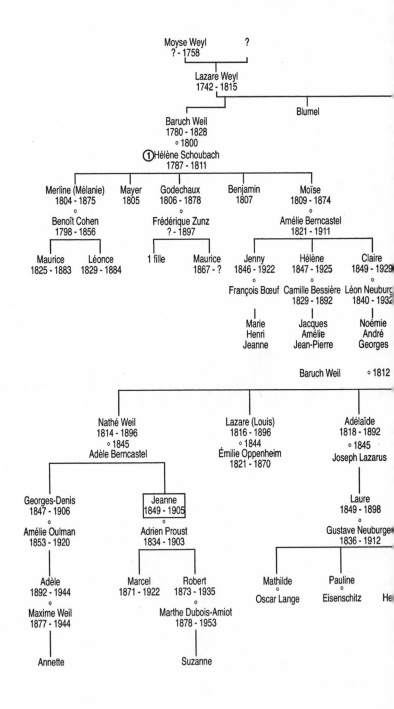

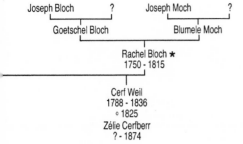

```
Joseph Bloch        ?        Joseph Moch        ?
       └──────┬──────┘             └──────┬──────┘
        Goetschel Bloch              Blumele Moch
               └──────────────┬──────────────┘
                         Rachel Bloch ★
                          1750 - 1815
                               │
                           Cerf Weil
                          1788 - 1836
                            ∘ 1825
                         Zélie Cerfberr
                           ? - 1874
```

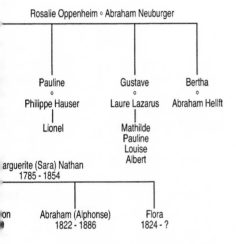

```
Rosalie Oppenheim ∘ Abraham Neuburger
   ┌───────────────────┼───────────────────┐
Pauline             Gustave             Bertha
   ∘                   ∘                   ∘
Philippe Hauser    Laure Lazarus     Abraham Hellft
   │                   │
Lionel              Mathilde
                    Pauline
                    Louise
                    Albert
arguerite (Sara) Nathan
     1785 - 1854
              ┌───────────────┬───────────────┐
on      Abraham (Alphonse)         Flora
          1822 - 1886             1824 - ?
```

* Rachel Bloch's family was affluent. Her father, Goetschel, was the son of Joseph Bloch, provost to the Jews and a merchant, one of the creditors of Samson Ferdinand de Landsberg. Joseph Bloch had also acquired the valuable right to retail salt: He was a *Salzhandel,* a salt merchant. At his death, in 1761, his widow ceded this right to Meyer de Strasbourg in the form of a twelve-year lease. Upon the marriage of his son Goetschel, Joseph Bloch offered 1,200 florins and a house in Niedernai. The dowry paid to the family of the fiancée, Blumele (little flower), daughter of Joseph Moch d'Obernai, amounted to 2,500 florins. Blumele's personal dowry amounted to 3750 florins. Sadly, she did not live long, and Goetschel took another wife seven years after his first marriage. Reichel, then aged three, had a stepmother named Judith. This may be why the fiancée of Lazare (a son from Goetschel's first marriage) received such a small dowry.

THE BERNCASTEL FAMILY

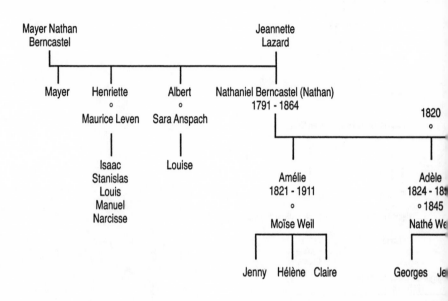

See Weil Family

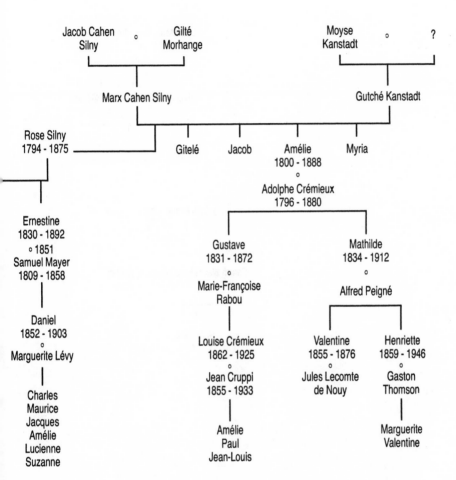

Jacob Cahen Silny ∘ Gilté Morhange

Moyse Kanstadt ∘ ?

Marx Cahen Silny

Gutché Kanstadt

Rose Silny
1794 - 1875

Gitelé   Jacob   Amélie
1800 - 1888
∘
Adolphe Crémieux
1796 - 1880

Myria

Ernestine
1830 - 1892
∘ 1851
Samuel Mayer
1809 - 1858

Gustave
1831 - 1872
∘
Marie-Françoise
Rabou

Mathilde
1834 - 1912
∘
Alfred Peigné

Daniel
1852 - 1903
∘
Marguerite Lévy

Louise Crémieux
1862 - 1925
∘
Jean Cruppi
1855 - 1933

Valentine
1855 - 1876
∘
Jules Lecomte
de Nouy

Henriette
1859 - 1946
∘
Gaston
Thomson

Charles
Maurice
Jacques
Amélie
Lucienne
Suzanne

Amélie
Paul
Jean-Louis

Marguerite
Valentine

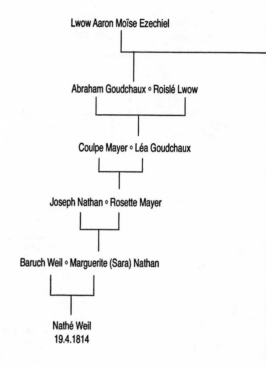

Lwow Aaron Moïse Ezechiel

Abraham Goudchaux ∘ Roislé Lwow

Coulpe Mayer ∘ Léa Goudchaux

Joseph Nathan ∘ Rosette Mayer

Baruch Weil ∘ Marguerite (Sara) Nathan

Nathé Weil
19.4.1814

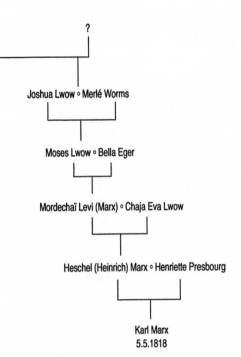

?

Joshua Lwow ∘ Merlé Worms

Moses Lwow ∘ Bella Eger

Mordechaï Levi (Marx) ∘ Chaja Eva Lwow

Heschel (Heinrich) Marx ∘ Henriette Presbourg

Karl Marx
5.5.1818

NOTES

For works cited by author and title only, the bibliography furnishes details.

Notes to Part One

1. Yiddish for servant.
2. Claude Bernard, *An Introduction to the Study of Experimental Medicine*, trans. Henry Copley Greene (New York: Macmillan, 1927).
3. In 1900, when they were looking for an apartment to rent, the Prousts were rejected by a landlord who didn't want a doctor or lawyer for a tenant. And that was a period when Proust devoted himself primarily to scientific research and didn't see any patients at home. See Marcel Proust to Pierre Lavallée, April 29, 1900, letter no. 246, *Correspondance*, 2:394.
4. On Adrien Proust's career, see Panzac, *Le Docteur Adrien Proust*.
5. For his part, Adrien contributed clothing, furniture, and his library, valued at 20,000 francs; 2,000 francs in cash; 4,000 francs owed to him by creditors, and approximately 7,000 francs in various obligations—all solid values.

6. An addendum to the marriage contract dated October 22 and October 29, 1870, testified to the good use of the dowry.

7. Archives nationales LXXXV, 1235.

8. There was no reciprocal arrangement, since the dowry belonged to Jeanne. This final clause of the contract must have been the subject of last-minute negotiations, since every mention of reciprocity was crossed out (Contrat de mariage, Archives nationales).

9. Nor was she the object of a papal dispensation (Registre des dispenses, Archives de l'Archevêché de Paris).

10. Police archives. For the same reasons, Professor Robin, founder of the field of histology and a fervent positivist, was excluded in 1868 from the list of jury members for the Seine district. (Darmon, *La vie quotidienne du médecin parisien en 1900*).

11. Fragments of Proust's semiautobiographical first novel have been assembled under the title *Jean Santeuil*. "Can I call this book a novel?" he wondered. "It is less perhaps, and much more, the very essence of my life, gathered with nothing mixed in, in these broken hours from which it has flowed. This book was never made, it was harvested." Epigraph from the manuscript of *Jean Santeuil*, from a draft of an unfinished introduction, reproduced in *Jean Santeuil*, ed. Clarac and Sandre, p. 41.

12. Proust, *Jean Santeuil*, trans. Hopkins, p. 738.

13. Ibid.

14. First quoted by André Maurois in his *A la Recherche de Marcel Proust*, p. 14. Maurois does not specify his source, which was probably an unpublished letter written during the last years of Proust's life. The source of this oft-quoted passage remains a mystery.

15. État nominatif des recettes du Judenschirmgeld, no 581 (Archives du Bas-Rhin). The spelling of proper names was inconsistent; Weyl was later listed as Weil.

16. André Aaron Fraenckel, *Mémoire juive en Alsace, contrats de marriage au XIIIe siècle* (Editions du Cédrat, 1997) and Rosanne and Daniel N. Leeson, *Index*. Available through the Cercle de généalogie juive (CGC), 14, rue St Lazare, 75009 Paris.

17. The census accounted for 3,942 families, or 19,624 individuals, across 150 different communities (*Dénombrement des Juifs d'Alsace*).

18. Fraenckel, *Mémoire*. In 1701, Louis XIV required all Alsatian Jews to file with notaries [the attorneys in charge of contracts] an account of marriage contracts made in the presence of a rabbi. In Jewish law, the wife cannot be heir to her husband, whose property goes directly to the children or the nearest descendant. To protect the future (and eventual) widow despite this rule, the contract guaranteed to her a *douaire* or *ketouba*, equal to one and a half times her dowry.

19. See the genealogical chart of the Weil family. Lazare and Reichel were married on July 28, 1774.

20. There were 178 Jews in Niedernai, divided into 37 households—approximately 17 percent of the population of the village (*Dénombrement des Juifs d'Alsace*).

21. These names are all taken from the municipal registers of Niedernai. Jews weren't included until 1792 (Mairie de Niedernai, Bas-Rhin).

22. According to the 1836 census, in addition to thirty-one Jewish households there were also a rabbi and a cantor, twenty-one retailers, three butchers, one cattle merchant, one rag dealer, and a man who sold feathers for beds (Claude Ruscher, "Niedernai in 1836 . . . Un état des lieux," *Bulletin communal*, 1998).

23. Judeo-Alsatian word for synagogue.

24. Blessing the name of God over wine (from the Hebrew *kaddosh* meaning saint).

25. From the German *Milch* (milk), referring to all dairy products.

26. From the German *Fleisch* (meat).

27. Potato dumplings.

28. Henri Grégoire, *Essai sur la regénération physique, morale et politique des juifs* (Paris: Flammarion, 1988).

29. The Assemblée nationale constituante was formed during the first stages of the French Revolution, governing France from July 9, 1789, to September 30, 1791.—Trans.

30. Death certificate for Cerf Weil dated September 27, 1836 (Archives de Paris), reconstituted by public decree from 1861 (Archives nationales): "Cerf Weil, a porcelain manufacturer, chevalier of the Légion d'honneur, age 48 years, 7 months, born in Bürgel, principality of Isembourg." Today Bürgel is a part of greater Offenbach-am-Main.

31. *Die Judengemeinden in Hesse* (Frankfurt/Main: Societäts-Verlag, 1971), 2 vols.

32. The following details are taken from Rosine Alexandre's privately published pamphlet, *Fontainebleau, naissance d'une communauté juive à l'époque de la Révolution (1798–1808)*.

33. Jacob Benjamin was the future brother-in-law of Cerf Weil; he married Zélie Cerfberr, the sister of Cerf's wife, in 1825.

34. Lazare Weyl died in Fontainebleau in 1815.

35. In a France where cemeteries had long been under the auspices of religious authorities, finding places of burial was no small issue for Jews. The Jewish community in Fontainebleau asked for permission to enclose the parcel of the cemetery that had been granted to them in 1794. Baruch and Lazare signed this petition. The reply had to be addressed to Baruch at the factory, which indicates that, despite his relative youth, he was already playing a leadership role in the community.

36. Information provided by P. A. Meyer. For Marx, the Jewish people were the very essence of bourgeois society: "The Jew has emancipated himself in Jewish fashion, not only by taking to himself financial power, but by virtue of the fact that with and without his cooperation, money has become a world power, and the practical Jewish spirit has become the practical spirit of the Christian nations" [Karl

Marx, "On the Jewish Question" (1844) in *Selected Essays,* trans. H. J. Stenning (Freeport, NY: Books for Libraries Press, 1926; reprinted 1968), pp. 89–90]. "This judeophobic tone isn't hard to find in the writing of Karl Marx, a Jew emancipated by a philosophy that called for the emancipation of the Jews through material wealth," comments Michel Winock in *Les Voix de la liberté* (Paris: Seuil, 2001), p. 315. Marx's ambivalence is interesting to compare with that of Marcel Proust. See the genealogical chart "Karl Marx and Marcel Proust."

37. The information on Baruch Weil's career is from Régine Plinval de Guillebon, *Porcelain of Paris 1770–1950,* trans. Robin R. Carleston (New York: Walker and Company, 1972).

38. He exhibited, among other pieces, two large, sky-blue vases with the Sèvres eyelet motif and a seventeen-piece breakfast set with a beige background.

39. These two plates represent, respectively, "the inhabitants of the realm of Andalusia, Spain" (green raised borders with flowers and gold wreaths) and the "port of Le Havre seen from a builder's office" (green raised border decorated with patterns of flowers and red and gold leaves), according to Horace Vernet. They are listed in the sales catalog for Sotheby's Parke Bernet (Monaco) in 1977, nos. 31 and 38.

40. Proust, *In the Shadow of Young Girls in Flower,* trans. Grieve, p. 483. The narrator of *In Search of Lost Time* is himself interested in antique porcelain services, of which the Verdurins possess a number of rare pieces. See Proust, *The Prisoner,* trans. Clark, p. 207.

41. See Appendix 1.

42. The third decree, later labeled "infamous," expressed the negative side of this acknowledgment. The Jews once again experienced political discrimination. But the Weils, as "Parisian Jews," were not part of that decree. A final decree issued later stipulated that Jews had to register their names with the state and could not change them. They were forbidden to take biblical personal or place names, as they had done in the past. They were to take French first names. These registration lists constitute a precious source of information today. They account for 46,054 French Jews—2,733 in Paris. Just before the Revolution, there were fewer than five hundred Jews in the French capital.

43. The consistories were composed of one or two rabbis and three secular members.

44. His fee was fixed at 1,500 francs. Meeting of the Consistoire central, February 27, 1809.

45. Baruch Weil was the treasurer of the temple located on the rue du cimetière Saint-André des Arts and of the Committee for Charities, of which he was one of the first underwriters and one of the presidents. He was president of the Society for Encouragement and Aid to Indigent Israelites. He administered the *Hevra* (society for mutual aid) of the Jewish Cemetery of Montrouge and Père Lachaise. He was

also a member of the committee for the boys' school (Frédéric Viey, *Des Juifs à Fontainebleau*, information gathered for the September 17, 2000, exhibit at Fontainebleau, available online at www.alliancefr.com/culture/fontaine).

46. Ibid. Michel Beer was secretary and recorder for the March 1807 Grand Sanhedrin.

47. Letter to Monsieur Rey, member of the General Council of Manufacturers and of the Central Jury for 1827, regarding his text on the need to construct a building devoted to general exhibits of the products of industry (Paris: Donde-Dupré, September 1827, Bibliothèque nationale de France, VP-5349 in-8°, 23 pp.).

48. "It is therefore not in nationality that the future of our industry lies, and what wiser method is there for maintaining the sacred flame than to encourage meetings of the industrialists, to regulate with a single agreement the interests of each branch, to set the price of merchandise and the wages of workers, to inform new enterprises, to improve national products, to share details about the solvency of buyers, and, finally, to bring respect to a trade we see prostituting itself to strangers who come to Paris with 50,000 francs and carry off over 100,000 crowns' worth of merchandise, the fruit of French workers' sweat, of the manufacturer's financial ruin, and often of the merchant's dishonor." Ibid.

49. Family council for the children of Baruch Weil's second marriage (Archives de Paris). Appearing on the paternal side: Godechaux Weil, the children's half-brother; their uncle Cerf Weil; and the banker Michel Goudchaux, a close friend of Baruch and one of the first Jewish members of the Chamber of Deputies, who became minister of finance during the Second Republic. Appearing on the maternal side: Benoît Cohen, Baruch's son-in-law, married to Baruch's eldest daughter Merline; Aron Schmoll, an old friend; and the merchant Moïse Schoubach, the father of Baruch's deceased first wife, Hélène. All of them lived in the same neighborhood, with the exception of the banker, who resided on the rue de Vendôme.

50. Merline and her husband Benoît Cohen acquired the store and at first were partners with their uncle Cerf Weil, whose second wife was Zélie Théodore Cerfberr, and their stepbrother Godechaux. The Fontainebleau factory was sold in 1833. Godechaux and his uncle Cerf eventually founded a competing factory on the rue de Bondy.

51. Nathaniel was born October 7, 1791, in Trèves, in the Saar region.

52. Merl, Braiudel, Himel, Abraham, and Hyman. Henriette (Himel) Berncastel later married Maurice Leven; and Albert (Hyman) Berncastel married Sara Anspach, the daughter of an "enlightened Israelite" from Metz. Her uncle Soloman, a watchmaker, moved to England, where he changed his name to Berncastle. Later, other Berncastel cousins emigrated to Great Britain, and their descendants moved to the United States and Australia (information provided by Pierrre-André Meyer and Jan Lees).

53. Naturalization file for Nathan Berncastel (Archives nationales).

54. This extremely humiliating oath made Jews into separate citizens and required them to swear on a Bible, in the synagogue, in the following infamous terms that assumed their duplicity: "In case I commit any kind of fraud, may I be eternally damned, devoured and annihilated by the fires that destroyed Sodom and Gomorrah and beset by all the curses described in the Torah." The *more judaico* was not abolished until 1848.

55. A monk, Father Thomas, and his servant disappeared. The crime was attributed to Jews. Suspects were accused of a ritual crime and torture; the charge was supported by the head of the French government, Adolphe Thiers.

56. From a speech given on June 10, 1845, quoted by Amson in *Adolphe Crémieux, l'oublié de la gloire.*

57. Fonds Crémieux (Archives nationales 369 APr).

58. "On June 25 of the year 1837, I, the undersigned priest of Mortefontaine in the arrondissement and canton of Senlis, department of the Oise, hereby baptize a girl named Claire Mathilde, born December 13, 1834, of the legal marriage of Monsieur Isaac Crémieux and Madame Louise Amélie Silny, both residing in Paris; the godfather is Monsieur Paul Dabrin, stockbroker, and the godmother the Baroness of Feuchères, née Sophie Saws, who have cosigned this document with me" (ibid.).

59. An homage offered in 1840 by the Frankfurt lodge, signed by Monsieur Oppenheim of Frankfurt, shows other ties to the Weil family: Louis Weil, Nathé's brother, married Emilie Oppenheim, the daughter of a banker from Hamburg. Nathan Berncastel's aunt, Blume, had also married a Jacob Oppenheim.

60. *In the Shadow of Young Girls in Flower,* trans. Grieve, p. 116.

61. In 1845, the sum total of his contributions (272.20 francs) tells us quite a bit about the flourishing nature of his business, even if that sum is substantially inferior to the 1,034.50 francs paid by a banker like Michel Goudchaux (Archives de Paris).

62. Proust, *Sodom and Gomorrah,* trans. Sturrock, p. 506.

63. Nathé Weil brought to the marriage 4,000 francs in clothing, linen, personal effects, jewelry, and furniture, and 43,000 in cash and stocks, "all of it from his own earnings and savings," which implied that he had not inherited it. Adèle Berncastel's trousseau was valued at 3,000 francs, and she brought to the marriage 30,000 francs in cash, which, according to the law, would be transferred to her husband after the marriage ceremony. Nathé's witnesses were his mother, Marguerite, and his brothers Moïse and Godechaux. Signing on Adèle's side were her sister Amélie, Moïse's wife; Adolphe Crémieux; a cousin, Edouard Kann; and her sister Ernestine, who at the last moment replaced Nathé's sister Flora, still unmarried (Archives nationales XXX 851).

64. Ernestine's dowry (20,000 francs) was less than Adèle's, probably because her husband also contributed less (Archives nationales XXX 877).

65. Proust, *The Guermantes Way,* trans. Treharne, p. 341.

66. April 21, 1849, at 11:00 P.M.

67. April 19, 1814, the day before Napoleon left for Elba Island.

68. Archives de Paris.

69. *Jean Santeuil*, trans. Hopkins, p. 37.

70. Marcel Proust to Nathé Weil, April 2, 1879, letter no. 386, *Correspondance*, 21:539. [The French has spelling mistakes as well as lack of punctuation.]

71. Georges Baruch Denis Weil was born October 26, 1847.

72. The line is a quotation from Madame de Sévigné. See Jeanne to Marcel, April 23, 1890, in *Marcel Proust: Selected Letters*, 1:28.

73. Ernest Feydeau, *Mémoires d'un coulissier* (Paris: Librairie nouvelle, 1873).

74. Emile Zola, *Carnet d'enquêtes* (Paris: Plon / Terre humaine poche, 1986), p. 70.

75. Soupault, *Marcel Proust du côté de la médecine*.

76. André Jardin and André-Jean Tudesq, *Restoration and Reaction 1815–1849*, trans. Elborg Forster (Cambridge: Cambridge University Press, 1983), p. 174.

77. Proust, *Swann's Way*, trans. Davis, p. 17.

78. Henri Raczymow, *Swan's Way*, trans. Robert Bononno (Chicago: Northwestern University Press, 2002).

79. Their nephew, Lionel Hauser, advised Marcel on his investments, which were often rather chancy.

80. Zola, *Carnet d'enquêtes*, pp. 91, 92.

81. Marcel Proust, draft 3 for *Du côté de chez Swann* (untranslated material), in *A la Recherche du temps perdu*, ed. Tadié, 1:669.

82. *Swann's Way*, trans. Davis, p. 17.

83. *In the Shadow of Young Girls in Flower*, trans. Grieve, p. 62.

84. Uncle Adolphe, a connoisseur of beautiful women, owned another apartment on the rue de Bellechasse, where the narrator finally met "the lady in pink"—the first appearance of Odette de Crécy.

85. *Sodom and Gomorrah*, trans. Sturrock, p. 443.

86. Commissioned to construct the Seminary at Beauvais, he was solemnly thanked by the bishop in these terms: "The era of veritable tolerance begins the day that the Christian clergy can commission an Israelite architect to design a Catholic seminary" (*L'Univers israélite*, July 1845).

87. Service historique de l'Armée de terre, Vincennes.

88. Confined to a dozen from the turn of the century until 1845, conversions of Jews increased to 75 between 1845 and 1849 (out of a total of 381 conversions from any religion) and experienced a spectacular increase between 1853 and 1855; then, around 1860, such conversions ceased almost entirely (Registre des abjurations, Archives de l'Archevêché de Paris).

89. Information furnished by Philippe Landau, archivist of the Consistoire de Paris.

90. Viey, *Des Juifs à Fontainebleau*.

91. Proust, *Jean Santeuil*, ed. Clarac and Sandre, p. 702. Note how strange the name Friedel sounds in the context of the Santeuil family.

92. Viey, *Des Juifs à Fontainebleau.*

93. Moïse and Louis Weil were known to be Freemasons. Nathé may have been one also, though we have no proof.

94. Quoted by Proust in "Talking to Mamma," in *By Way of Sainte-Beuve,* trans. Warner, p. 70.

95. The description of the play was gleaned from the archives of the Comédie-française.

96. "Talking to Mamma," in *By Way of Sainte-Breuve,* trans. Warner, p. 70. Esther, the Queen of the Jews, is ordered by her uncle Mordecai to intervene with her husband Ahasuerus, king of Persia, to save his people, threatened by the minister Haman. The feast of Purim commemorates this episode, which has come to symbolize victory over persecution.

97. Hassine, *Marranisme et hébraïsme dans l'oeuvre de Proust.*

98. Jeanne to Marcel, April 23, 1890, letter no. 15, in *Marcel Proust: Selected Letters,* 1:28.

99. Favart had played Marianne in *Les Caprices,* Camille in *On ne badine pas avec l'amour,* and Elsbeth in *Fantasio;* she had even played the Muse in *La Nuit d'Octobre* (Archives of the Comédie-française).

100. We have no original documents other than identity papers and photographs. Adèle Weil's portrait can only be read between the lines, through her daughter's or her grandson's writing.

101. *In the Shadow of Young Girls in Flower,* trans. Grieve, p. 253.

102. Ibid., p. 223.

103. Many young girls were still educated this way up until 1950. This was the case for Adèle, Jeanne's niece (interview with Annette Heuman, Georges Weil's granddaughter).

104. Report on the inspection of private schools ordered by Victor Duruy in 1867 (Archives nationales AJ16 515).

105. This is perhaps why the narrator's mother pretends to hesitate whenever she quotes from the Latin.

106. Proust, *Jean Santeuil* (Gallimard/Pléiade edition), p. 250.

107. Report to the minister of public instruction, Archives nationales.

108. In Jeanne's day, the average age for marriage among Jewish women was twenty-two. See Anne Lifschitz-Krams, *Les Mariages religieux juifs à Paris 1848–1872* (Paris: Cercle de généalogie juive, undated).

Notes to Part Two

1. Information provided by Monsier Monier, who was kind enough to provide me with a photocopy of the invitation.

2. *Journal des Goncourt*, March 26, 1860, quoted by Anne Martin-Fugier, "Bourgeois Rituals," in Perrot, *A History of Private Life*, 4:322.

3. This chapter draws largely from the following sources: an article by Denise Mayer, "Le jardin de Marcel Proust," *Les Cahiers Marcel Proust*, no. 12; Proust, *Jean Santeuil*; Proust, "Preface to Blanche," in *Against Sainte-Beuve*, trans. Sturrock, pp. 245–60; and Proust, *Swann's Way*.

4. The firm of Trelon, Weldon & Weil owned a factory at 246 rue de Bercy-Saint-Antoine and a retail store at 14 *bis*, boulevard Poissonnière.

5. *Jean Santeuil*, trans. Hopkins, p. 113.

6. See the Weil family tree in appendix 3.

7. *Jean Santeuil*, trans. Hopkins, p. 102.

8. Valentine Thomson, "My Cousin Marcel Proust," *Harper's Magazine* 164: 711.

9. *Swann's Way*, trans. Davis, p. 6.

10. *Jean Santeuil*, trans. Hopkins. p. 91.

11. This episode, which Proust recounted to Céleste Albaret, may have been a source for the cruelty of Françoise, Aunt Léonie's cook, who persecuted her scullery maid—Giotto's charity, as Swann called her—a young woman who was pregnant and allergic to asparagus.

12. Proust, "Preface to Blanche," p. 248.

13. *Jean Santeuil*, trans. Hopkins, pp. 137–38; translation modified.

14. Berl, *Interrogatoire par Patrick Modiano*.

15. *Swann's Way*, trans. Davis, p. 13.

16. See *Jean Santeuil*, trans. Hopkins, p. 135.

17. Proust, "Preface to Blanche," p. 250.

18. Myosotis. See chapter 17 for *Vergiss mein nicht* and other German terms.

19. *Swann's Way*, trans. Davis, p. 124.

20. Ibid., p. 190.

21. Draft 2 for *Swann's Way* (untranslated), in *A la Recherche du temps perdu*, ed. Tadié, 1:642.

22. *Jean Santeuil*, trans. Hopkins, p. 33.

23. Proust, *Pleasures and Days*, trans. Brown, p. 6.

24. *Jean Santeuil*, trans. Hopkins, p. 25.

25. Marcel to Maurice Barrès, ca. January 19, 1906, letter no. 6, *Correspondance*, 6:28.

26. Ibid.

27. "The death of Baldassare Silvande," "The End of Jealousy," and "A Young Girl's Confession," from, respectively, *Pleasures and Days*, *Jean Santeuil*, and *In Search of Lost Time*.

28. *Jean Santeuil*, trans. Hopkins, p. 29.

29. *Swann's Way*, trans. Davis, p. 36.

30. Ibid., p. 38.

31. Ibid., p. 37.

32. Ibid., p. 39.

33. Draft 10 for *Swann's Way* (untranslated), in *A la Recherche du temps perdu*, ed. Tadié, 1:677.

34. *Swann's Way*, trans. Davis, p. 49.

35. Cf. the scene in *Swann's Way*, trans. Davis, p. 64.

36. *Jean Santeuil*, trans. Hopkins, p. 86.

37. Ernestine was one of the models for Françoise. But she was born in 1855 and was only thirty-one when her mistress died. See Jeanne Monier, "Tante Léonie et sa maison dans la réalité d'Illiers," in *Bulletin de la société archéologique d'Eure-et-Loir*, no. 69 (2001): 1–14.

38. *Swann's Way*, trans. Davis, p. 51.

39. Monier, "Tante Léonie," p. 13.

40. *Jean Santeuil*, trans. Hopkins, p. 108.

41. Distribution of prizes at the Illiers school, excerpted from the *Progrès d'Eure-et-Loir*, April 4, 1903.

42. Homais is the pharmacist in Flaubert's *Madame Bovary*.—Trans.

43. *Swann's Way*, trans. Davis, p. 49.

44. Albaret, *Monsieur Proust*, p. 162.

45. *Jean Santeuil*, trans. Hopkins, p. 141.

46. Ibid.

47. Fifth and sixth readings for Good Friday Mass, before the reforms of Vatican II. The text quoted here is translated from the French Roman Catholic missal, *Missel quotidien des fidèles par le Père Feder* (Tours: Maison Mame, 1964).

48. *Jean Santeuil*, trans. Hopkins, p. 142.

49. The name Pré Catelan refers to part of the Bois de Boulogne in Paris, reflecting Uncle Jules's pride in his own park.—Trans.

50. *Jean Santeuil*, trans. Hopkins, p. 103.

51. Information provided by Monsier Monier.

52. *Swann's Way*, trans. Davis, p. 127.

53. Marcel Proust, "Preface to *Sésame et les Lys*," p. 101.

54. *Jean Santeuil*, trans. Hopkins, p. 121

55. Ibid., p. 101

56. *Swann's Way*, trans. Davis, p. 128.

57. Ibid., p. 117.

58. From Proust's 1908 notebook. The story was included in only one French edition of *Contre Sainte-Beuve*, in Collection Idées (1965), pp. 346–54.

59. Quoted in Tadié, *Marcel Proust*, p. 38.

60. *Contre Sainte-Beuve*, Collection Idées (1965), p. 356.

61. Jeanne to Marcel, October 20, 1896, letter no. 73, *Correspondance*, 2:135.

62. Albaret, *Monsieur Proust*, p. 162.

63. Morris columns are the thick, round, green columns seen on the streets of Paris, covered in posters for plays and other advertisements.—Trans.

64. See the treatise by César Daly, *L'Architecture privée sous Napoléon III: Nouvelles maisons de Paris et des environs* (Paris: A. Morel, 1864).

65. Proust, *The Guermantes Way*, trans. Treharne, p. 10.

66. Details from Soupault, *Marcel Proust du côté de la médecine*.

67. Gregh, *L'Age d'Or*, p. 154.

68. R-H. Guerrand, "Private Spaces," in Perrot, *A History of Private Life*, 4:369.

69. Marcel to Madame Catusse, November 5, 1906, letter no. 160, *Correspondance*, 6:278.

70. *The Prisoner*, trans. Clark, p. 358.

71. Marcel to Madame Straus, May 21, 1911, letter no. 24, *Marcel Proust: Selected Letters*, 3:38–39; translation modified.

72. Berl's aunt, Mathilde Alange, was the daughter of Gustave Neuburger.

73. Michelle Perrot, "Roles and Characters," in Perrot, *A History of Private Life*, 4:270, quoting from a guide for housewives.

74. *Jean Santeuil*, trans. Hopkins, p. 742; translation modified.

75. Ibid., p. 743.

76. "The Sunbeam on the Balcony," in *By Way of Sainte-Beuve*, trans. Warner, p. 54.

77. *In the Shadow of Young Girls in Flower*, trans. Grieve, p. 17.

78. Céline Cottin's *boeuf mode* was no competition, as Marcel Proust's letter to his mother's last cook showed.

79. *Jean Santeuil*, trans. Hopkins, p. 141.

80. Albaret, *Monsieur Proust*, p. 172.

81. Ibid., pp. 134–35.

82. Jeanne to Marcel Proust, August 28, 1890, letter no. 37, *Correspondance*, 1:158.

83. Jeanne to Marcel Proust, July 14, 1890, letter no. 26, *Correspondance*, 1:144.

84. Albaret, *Monsieur Proust*, p. 76.

85. Marcel to Jeanne, September 11, 1899, in *Marcel Proust: Letters to His Mother*, trans. Painter, p. 77; translation modified.

86. *Jean Santeuil*, trans. Hopkins, p. 127.

87. Ibid., p. 125; translation modified.

88. Jeanne referred to another visit in a letter to Lucie Faure and asked her for information about Van Dyck's Duke of Richmond, "that Marcel is raving about": Jeanne to Lucie Félix-Faure, August 10, 1894, *Bulletin de la Société des amis de Marcel Proust*, no. 7 (1957): 276–77.

89. Jeanne to Marcel Proust, August 23, 1895, letter no. 271, *Correspondance*, 1:422.

90. Jeanne to Marcel, July 1890, letter no. 26, *Correspondance*, 1:144.

91. Jeanne to Marcel, August 1, 1890, letter no. 27, *Correspondance*, 1:145.

92. Quoted by Mona Ozouf in "Claire or Fidelity," in *Women's Words: Essay on French Singularity*, trans. Jane Marie Todd (Chicago: University of Chicago Press, 1997), p. 90.

93. Paul de Rémusat, Preface to Rémusat, *Memoirs of Madame de Rémusat 1802–1808*, p. iv.

94. Quoted by Ozouf, in *Women's Words*, p. 100.

95. Berl, *Interrogatoire par Patrick Modiano*.

96. Proust, "Preface to Sésame et les Lys," p. 102.

97. André Maurois mentions the notebook in *A la Recherche de Marcel Proust*, and Philip Kolb, who appears to have consulted it, in the *Correspondance*, 1:130, note 3. An excerpt is reproduced in Cattaui, *Marcel Proust: Documents iconographiques*. The notebook was not burned by Proust at his mother's death, as some have claimed.

98. *Jean Santueil*, trans. Hopkins, p. 214.

99. Quoted by Amson in *Adolphe Crémieux*, p. 380.

100. Ibid., p. 369

101. Archives nationales, 369 APr3.

102. Isaac Adolphe Crémieux died on February 10, 1880.

103. Amson, *Adolphe Crémieux*, p. 379.

104. Ibid., p. 380.

105. Ibid., p. 379.

106. Anaïs Beauvais (?–1898), a student of Carolus Duran's and of Henner's, first exhibited her work in the 1868 Salon. She specialized in portraits and war scenes. She was also known as Anaïs Landelle.

107. Albaret, *Monsieur Proust*, p. 136.

108. *Jean Santeuil*, trans. Hopkins, p. 56.

109. Jeanne to Marcel, September 1889, letter no. 17, *Correspondance*, 1:129.

110. Robert Proust, "Marcel Proust intime," Hommage à M. Proust, *Les Cahiers Marcel Proust*, no. 1 (1927), p. 24.

111. Marcel Proust, "L'Indifférent," trans. Alfred Corn, *Grand Street 40*, vol. 10, no. 4 (1991): 52 ff.

112. Edouard Brissaud, *L'Hygiène des asthmatiques* (Paris: Masson, 1896).

113. See Panzac, *Le Docteur Adrien Proust*.

114. Marcel to Jeanne, September 22, 1899, letter no. 161, *Marcel Proust: Selected Letters*, 1:205.

115. Quoted by Péchenard, *Proust et les autres*, p. 368.

116. Proust, "Talking to Mama," in *By Way of Sainte-Beuve*, trans. Warner, p. 68; translation modified.

117. Marcel to Robert de Montesquiou, September 28, 1905, letter no. 152, *Marcel Proust: Selected Letters*, 2:208.

118. Soupault, *Marcel Proust du côté de la médecine*.

119. Jeanne to Marcel, September 6, 1888, letter no. 9, *Correspondance*, 1:111.

120. Wallon, *La vie quotidienne dans les villes d'eaux 1850–1914*.

121. Dépôt le Masle, Bibliothèque nationale de France.

122. Max Durand-Fardel, *Traité des eaux minérales de la France et de l'étranger* (Paris: 1883). Even today, fibroids, recurrent infections and pelvic pain are treated at Salies-de-Béarn, along with arthritis and growth problems in children.

123. Jeanne to Marcel, August 17, 1892, letter no. 56, *Correspondance*, 1:179; quoted in Tadié, *Marcel Proust*, pp. 22–23.

124. Maurice Duplay, "Mon ami, Marcel Proust," *Les Cahiers Marcel Proust*, no. 5 (1972), p. 55.

125. Marcel to Adèle Weil, August 1886, letter no. 392, *Correspondance*, 21:544.

126. Ibid.

127. Marcel to Adèle Weil, summer 1885 or 1886, letter no. 2, *Marcel Proust: Selected Letters*, 1:6.

128. Marcel to Adèle Weil, August 1886, letter no. 392, *Correspondance*, 21:544.

129. Jeanne to Marcel, September 6, 1888, letter no. 9, *Correspondance*, 1:111.

130. Jeanne to Marcel, September 12, 1888, letter no. 18, *Correspondance*, 1:133.

131. Jeanne to Marcel, September 7, 1889, letter no. 16, *Correspondance*, 1:126–27, quoted in Tadié, *Marcel Proust*, p. 22.

132. Jeanne to Marcel, September 7, 1889, letter no. 16, *Correspondance*, 1:126.

133. Marcel to Adèle Weil, summer 1885 or 1886, letter no. 2, *Marcel Proust: Selected Letters*, 1:5–6.

134. Marcel to Nathé Weil, September 1886, letter no. 393, *Correspondance*, 21:548.

135. Jeanne to Marcel, September 6, 1888, letter no. 9, *Correspondance*, 1:111.

136. Jeanne to Marcel, September 1889, letter no. 17, *Correspondance*, 1:129.

137. Jeanne to Marcel, September 12, 1889, letter no. 18, *Correspondance*, 1:133.

138. Marcel to Nathé Weil, September 1886, letter no. 393, *Correspondance*, 21:548.

139. Marcel to Jeanne, September 24, 1887, letter no. 4, *Marcel Proust: Selected Letters*, 1:9–10.

140. Marcel to Adèle Weil, August 1886, letter no. 392, *Correspondance*, 21:543.

141. Jeanne to Marcel, September 6, 1888, letter no. 9, *Correspondance*, 1:111.

142. Marcel to Jeanne, September 5, 1888, letter no. 7, *Marcel Proust: Selected Letters*, 1:15.

143. Ibid.

144. George Sand to Hippolyte Chatiron, mid-February 1843, in Sand, *Correspondance* (Paris: Garnier, 1969), 6:43.

145. Alain Corbin, "Backstage: Intimate Relations," in Perrot, *A History of Private Life*, 4:564.

146. Jeanne to Marcel, August 14, 1890, letter no. 31, *Correspondance*, 1:150–51.

147. *Jean Santeuil*, trans. Hopkins, p. 739; translation modified.

148. Quoted in Tadié, *Marcel Proust*, p. 33.

149. George Sand to Casimir Dudevant, November 8, 1825, in Sand, *Correspondance*, 1:268.

150. Jeanne to Marcel, August 14, 1890, letter no. 31, *Correspondance*, 1:150.

151. Ibid.

152. Jeanne to Marcel, August 18, 1890, letter no. 32, *Correspondance*, 1:151–52.

153. Jeanne to Marcel, August 1895, letter no. 76, *Marcel Proust: Selected Letters*, 1:100; translation modified.

154. Tadié, *Marcel Proust*, p.32.

155. Albaret, *Monsieur Proust*, p. 168.

156. J.-E. Blanche, "Souvenirs sur Marcel Proust," *La Revue hebdomadaire*, July 21, 1928.

157. Marcel to Laure Hayman, December 11, 1903, letter no. 264, *Marcel Proust: Selected Letters*, 1:361.

158. Ibid.

159. Corbin, "Backstage: Intimate Relations," p. 589.

160. Péchenard, *Proust et les autres*, p. 359.

161. Dr. Louis Seraine, *De la santé des gens mariés* (1865), quoted by Zeldin, *A History of French Passions*, 1:303.

162. Marcel to Nathé Weil, May 17, 1888, letter no. 395, *Correspondance*, 21:550. We note in passing that Marcel, then age seventeen, uses a capital "M" for Mama [French *Maman*], but a small "p" for papa.

163. *Jean Santeuil*, trans. Hopkins, p. 35.

164. Ibid., p. 725.

165. Ibid., p. 36.

166. Soupault, *Marcel Proust, du côté de la médecine*, pp. 122–23, quoted in Tadié, *Marcel Proust*, p. 32.

167. Draft 49 for *Le Temps retrouvé* (untranslated), in *A la Recherche du temps perdu*, ed. Tadié, 4:977.

168. Ibid., p. 978.

169. Corbin, "Backstage: Intimate Relations," p. 593.

170. Jeanne to Marcel, October 23, 1896, letter no. 80, *Correspondance*, 2:150.

171. *Jean Santeuil*, trans. Hopkins, pp. 723, 732.

172. Ibid., p. 739.

173. Corbin, "Backstage: Intimate Relations," p. 496.

174. Adrien Proust and Gilbert Ballet, *Hygiène du neurasthénique* (Paris: Masson, 1897), p. 154.

175. Draft 2.3 of *Swann's Way*, in *A la Recherche du temps perdu*, ed. Tadié, 1:643, quoted in Tadié, *Marcel Proust*, p. 48.

176. Charles Nathan was born in Lunéville in 1830 and died in Paris in 1905. His father, Abraham Nathan, was the brother of Marguerite Nathan, Baruch Weil's

wife. In 1874, Charles married Laure Rodrigues-Ely, who became one of Jeanne's best friends.

177. Marcel to Robert Dreyfus, August 28 (?), 1888, *Marcel Proust: Selected Letters*, 1:14.

178. Draft 3 of *Swann's Way*, in *A la Recherche du temps perdu*, ed. Tadié, 1:646, quoted in Tadié, *Marcel Proust*, p. 48.

179. A series of questions in the form of a parlor game that has since become the basis for many celebrity interviews: Where would you like to live? What is your idea of happiness? Your favorite painter and musician, etc.—Trans.

180. Marcel to Jacques Bizet, June 14, 1888, letter no. 399, *Correspondance*, 21:554–55.

181. Ibid.

182. Ibid., trans. Edmund White, quoted in White, *Marcel Proust*, p. 29.

183. Maurice Duplay, "Mon ami, Marcel Proust."

184. The phrase is from "'Talking with Maman" in *By Way of Sainte-Beuve*, trans. Warner, p. 71. See also Michel Schneider, *Maman*, who makes it one of the keys of Jeanne and Marcel's relationship.

185. *Sodom and Gomorrah*, trans. Strurrock, p. 16.

186. I'll leave it to the psychoanalysts to explain, according to their various theories, the possible connections between Marcel's attachment to his mother and his homosexuality. Castrating mother, seductive mother, too good a mother, identification, incestuous love (including, according to some, love for his brother Robert)—there has been no lack of interpretations. See, on this subject, *Marcel Proust visiteur des psychanalystes* (Paris: PUF/Quadrige, reprint of the 1999/2 issue of *La Revue française de psychanalyse*). The problem is outlined clearly in the introduction by Andrée Bauduin and Françoise Coblence.

187. Marcel to Jacques Bizet, spring 1888, letter no. 5, *Marcel Proust: Selected Letters*, 1:10–11.

188. Marcel to Robert Dreyfus, August 28(?), 1888, letter no. 6, *Marcel Proust: Selected Letters*, 1:11–13.

189. Proust, *Ecrits de jeunesse, 1887–1895*.

190. Marcel to Robert Dreyfus, September 10(?), 1888, *Marcel Proust: Selected Letters*, 1:19.

191. Ibid.

192. Marcel to Jeanne, September 5, 1888, *Marcel Proust: Selected Letters*, 1:15–16.

193. Mademoiselle Vinteuil pleasured herself with her woman friend in front of a portrait of her dead father, the musician Vinteuil, whom she adored.

194. *Swann's Way*, trans. Davis, p. 180.

195. *Ecrits de Jeunesse, 1887–1895*, p. 123.

196. *Swann's Way*, trans. Davis, p. 166.

197. The document was sold at Drouot in June 1988 (no. 56 in the Boisgirard catalogue, letter dated October 26, 1888).

198. "The Confessions of a Young Woman," in *Pleasures and Days*, trans. Brown, p. 94.

199. Gerard Bonnet, J.-M. Charcot, and Victor Magnan, *Inversion du sens génital et autres perversions sexuelles* (Paris: Frénésie, 2003); Richard von Krafft-Ebbing, *Psychopathia sexualis* (1885; New York: Rebman, 1922); Havelock Ellis, *Studies in the Psychology of Sex*, vol. 2: *Sexual Inversion* (Philadelphia: A. Davis, 1902).

200. Tamagne, *Mauvais genre?* p. 98.

201. Michel Foucault, "Sex, Power, and the Politics of Identity" (1982 interview in English, Toronto), reprinted in *Ethics: Subjectivity and Truth*, ed. Paul Rabinow (New York: New Press, 1997), p. 171.

202. Proust, "Before the Night," in *Complete Stories of Marcel Proust*, trans. Neusgroschel, p. 183.

203. *Jean Santeuil*, trans. Hopkins, p. 655.

204. *Ecrits de Jeunesse, 1887–1895*, p. 25.

205. Daniel Halévy: Journal (unpublished), carnet no. 1 (1886–88) in Proust, *Ecrits de Jeunesse, 1887–1895*, p. 53.

206. Georges Hérellé, quoted by Philippe Lejeune in *Romantisme*, second trimester (Paris: CDU-SEDES, 1987), p. 90.

207. *Ecrits de Jeunesse, 1887–1895*, p. 149.

208. Marcel to Daniel Halévy, autumn 1888, letter no. 12, *Marcel Proust: Selected Letters*, 1:24.

209. Ibid.

210. *Ecrits de Jeunesse, 1887–1895*, p. 152.

211. Gregh, *L'Age d'or*, p. 154.

212. "Talking to Mama," in *By Way of Sainte-Beuve*, trans. Warner, p. 70.

213. Gregh, *L'Age d'or*, p. 159.

214. Jeanne to Marcel, August 17, 1892, letter no. 56, *Correspondance*, 1:179.

215. Jeanne to Marcel, August 1893 (date uncertain), letter no. 96, *Correspondance*, 1:227.

216. According to a document provided by Monsieur Monier.

217. Jeanne to Marcel, September 7, 1889, letter no. 16, *Correspondance*, 1:127.

218. Jeanne to Marcel, December 14, 1889, letter no. 14, *Marcel Proust: Selected Letters*, 1:27.

219. Jeanne to Marcel, August 11, 1890, letter no. 30, *Correspondance*, 1:148.

220. Jeanne to Marcel, December 14, 1889, *Marcel Proust: Selected Letters*, 1:27.

221. Jeanne to Marcel, April 28, 1890, letter no. 23, *Correspondance*, 1:139.

222. Jeanne to Marcel, August 28, 1890, letter no. 37, *Correspondance*, 1:158.

223. Ibid., p. 157.

224. Ibid.

225. Jeanne to Marcel, April 23, 1890, letter no. 15, *Marcel Proust: Selected Letters*, 1:29.

226. Jeanne to Marcel [first semester] 1890, letter no. 21, *Correspondance*, 1:135.

227. Jeanne to Marcel, June 8, 1890, letter no. 24, *Correspondance*, 1:141.

228. Jeanne to Marcel, August 14, 1890, letter no. 31, *Correspondance*, 1:150.

229. Jeanne to Marcel, September 1889, letter no. 17, *Correspondance*, 1:128. [*Tausend Küsse:* a thousand kisses.]

230. Jeanne to Marcel, December 14, 1889, letter no. 14, *Marcel Proust: Selected Letters*, 1:27; translation modified.

231. Ibid.

232. Uremia, like diabetes or polycystic disease, can be transmitted genetically.

233. Jeanne to Marcel, April 23, 1890, letter no. 15, *Marcel Proust: Selected Letters*, 1:29.

234. Ibid.

235. Jeanne to Marcel, June 26, 1890, letter no. 25, *Correspondance*, 1:142, quoted in Tadié, *Marcel Proust*, p. 103; translation modified.

236. *The Guermantes Way*, trans. Treharne, p. 314.

237. Ibid.

238. Ibid., p. 315.

239. Ibid., p. 316.

240. Ibid., p. 320.

241. Ibid., p. 337.

242. Ibid., p. 335.

243. Ibid., p. 340.

244. Ibid.

Notes to Part Three and Epilogue

1. Guide Conty, *De Paris à Trouville et ses environs: Guide pratique et illustré*, quoted in Culot, *Trouville*.

2. Jeanne to Marcel, September 3, 1893 (?), letter no. 98, *Correspondance*, 1:229.

3. Proust, *Sodom and Gomorrah*, trans. Sturrock, p. 167; translation modified.

4. Ibid., p. 168.

5. Ibid. An *en-tout-cas* was a parasol.

6. Details concerning the hotel are taken from Emmanuelle Gallo, *Les Roches noires* (Paris: Cahiers du Temps, 2000).

7. Proust, "Souvenirs," *La Revue blanche*, no. 26 (December 1893), reprinted in *Jean Santeuil* (Pléiade ed.), p. 171.

8. The hotel was remodeled yet again in 1925 by the architect Robert Mallet-Stevens, who also built the Noailles villa in Hyères. Maguerite Duras, who lived at the Roches noires after it was converted into residential housing, made the great hall famous as a location for several of her films.

9. *Jean Santeuil*, trans. Hopkins, p. 26.

10. Marcel to Adrien, September 28 (?), 1893, letter no. 40, *Marcel Proust: Selected Letters*, 1:57–58.

11. They were both born in 1849, Geneviève on February 26 and Jeanne on April 21.

12. Gregh, *L'Age d'or*, p. 168, quoted in Tadié, *Marcel Proust*, p. 143.

13. Bischoff, *Geneviève Straus*.

14. Marcel to Louisa de Mornand, July 14, 1905, letter no. 148, *Marcel Proust: Selected Letters*, 2:201.

15. Marcel to Reynaldo Hahn, September 22, 1894, letter no. 190, *Correspondance*, 1:331.

16. Jeanne to Marcel, September 11, 1894, letter 54, *Marcel Proust: Selected Letters*, 1:73.

17. Marcel to Madame Catusse, June 5, 1915, letter no. 71, *Correspondance*, 14:150.

18. Bibliothèque nationale de France, Fonds Pierre Lavallée.

19. Louis Weil died on May 10, 1896, and Nathé on June 30 the same year.

20. Marcel to Paul Morand, June 16, 1922, letter no. 212, *Marcel Proust: Selected Letters*, 4:379.

21. Billy, *Marcel Proust*.

22. Archives of the Consistoire de Paris, registry of deaths.

23. Marcel to Jeanne, July 6, 1895, letter no. 99, *Marcel Proust: Selected Letters*, 1:130.

24. Marcel to Reynaldo Hahn, July 3 (?), 1896, letter no. 98, *Marcel Proust: Selected Letters*, 1:129.

25. Marcel to Jeanne, July 1896, *Marcel Proust: Letters to His Mother*, trans. Painter, pp. 55–56; translation modified.

26. Marcel to Jeanne, September 2 (?), 1896, *Marcel Proust: Letters to His Mother*, trans. Painter, p. 61.

27. Jeanne to Marcel, September 24, 1896, letter no. 70, *Correspondance*, 2:131–32.

28. Dieppe and Trouville were well equipped with warm baths, but Jeanne seems to have opted for bathing in the sea.

29. Jeanne to Marcel, September 1896, letter no. 71, *Correspondance*, 2:133.

30. An allusion, of course, to Oscar Wilde's comment, "One of the greatest tragedies of my life is the death of Lucien de Rubempré," and a sign of Jeanne's Anglophone culture.

31. Jeanne to Marcel, September 1896, letter no. 71, *Correspondance*, 2:133.

32. Prayer of sanctification, particularly after a death.

33. *L'Univers israélite,* the "newspaper representing the conservative principles of Judaism," noted his death, as well as the death of Nathé Weil—additional proof of the ties the Weils had maintained with the Jewish community—in nos. 34 and 42 of the year 1896. Louis Weil chose a fourth-class funeral, out of the eight proposed by the Consistory.

34. Nathé Weil left an inheritance consisting in stocks appraised at 506,000 francs. Louis Weil's fortune was appraised at 1,540,000 francs. For details, see Panzac, *Le Docteur Adrien Proust*. For approximate present-day monetary values, see footnote on p. 13 above.

35. The apartment was appraised at 568,119 francs.

36. The Auteuil property was now worth 75,000 francs.

37. Duchêne, *L'Impossible Marcel Proust*, p. 308.

38. Camille Bessière died May 9, 1892.

39. Jeanne to Hélène Bessières, August 28, 1895, *Bulletin de la Société des amis de Marcel Proust*, no. 24 (1974): 1800–1801.

40. It will be recalled that Hélène was the daughter of Moïse Weil, an architect in Beauvais and the half brother of Nathé and of Louis.

41. *Jean Santeuil*, trans. Hopkins, p. 726.

42. The story is based on Maurice Duplay's recollections in "Mon ami, Marcel Proust," *Cahiers Marcel Proust*, no 5 (1972): 55.

43. Did this attitude depend, as one psychoanalyst claims, on Marcel's identification with his mother, the only outlet for the guilt he experienced at his younger brother's birth? Was this relationship at the origin of his attraction to young boys? Milton Miller, in *Nostalgia*, suggests this was the case.

44. Marcel to Jeanne, September 14, 1899, letter no. 208, *Correspondance*, 2:320.

45. Note that the narrator of *In Search of Lost Time* is an only son.

46. Marcel to Anna de Noailles, June 3, 1912, *Correspondance*, 11:137

47. *Jean Santeuil*, trans. Hopkins, pp. 365–70 ("Jean at Megmeil: He Telephones to His Mother"); "Days of Reading (II)," in *Against Sainte-Beuve*, trans. Sturrock, pp. 227–33; *The Guermantes Way*, trans. Treharne, pp. 126–30. For an analysis, see Tadié, *Marcel Proust*, pp. 482–83.

48. Jean Lazard (1854–1922) was the second son of Simon Lazard, the founder of the famous bank Lazard Frères. Jean's own career was in agriculture; he married an heiress.

49. Marcel to Antoine Bibelsco, December 4, 1902, letter no. 205, *Marcel Proust: Selected Letters*, 1:277.

50. Jeanne to Marcel, October 20, 1896, letter no. 72, *Correspondance*, 2:134.

51. Excerpts of which were gathered under the title *Jean Santeuil*.

52. Jeanne to Marcel, October 21, 1896, letter no. 108, *Marcel Proust: Selected Letters*, 1:145.

53. Marcel to Jeanne, October 22, 1896, letter no. 109, *Marcel Proust: Selected Letters*, 1:145

54. Jeanne to Marcel, October 22, 1896, letter no. 77, *Correspondance*, 2:146. Both mother and son used the term *cuisinage* rather than *cuisine* (cooking); their suffix *-age* being a shared affectation.

55. Marcel to Jeanne, October 22, 1896 (evening), letter no. 78, *Correspondance*, 2:147; quoted in *Marcel Proust: Selected Letters*, 1:148.

56. Jeanne to Marcel, October 23, 1896, letter no. 81, *Correspondance*, 2:151.

57. The wedding took place on April 20, 1891, in the seventeenth arrondissement of Paris.

58. Viey, *Des Juifs à Fontainebleau* (see pt 1, n. 47, for details).

59. Georges-Denis Weil, *Elections législatives depuis 1789: Histoire de la législation et des moeurs* (Paris: Félix Alcan, 1895).

60. Mathilde, Amélie's sister, married Albert Hecht, and their daughter Suzanne married Pontrémoli, the director of the Ecole des Beaux-Arts. Amélie's brother and another of her sisters were related by marriage to the Bensaude family, of Portuguese descent.

61. Interview with Annette Heuman, Georges-Denis Weil's granddaughter.

62. In French, "des glaces de la vie mondaine," a phrase from *Jean Santeuil* (Gallimard/Quarto ed.), p. 41, from an unpublished fragment of Proust's preface that is not a part of the English translation.

63. Lucien Daudet, *Autour de soixante lettres de Marcel Proust*.

64. Ibid.

65. *Jean Santeuil*, trans. Hopkins, p. 209.

66. Ibid., p. 213.

67. Ibid., p. 218.

68. Ibid.

69. Allusion to the ritual practiced in Jewish marriage ceremonies, where the couple breaks a glass from which they've drunk as a symbol of the permanence of their bond.

70. Jeanne to Marcel, late 1896 or early 1897, letter no. 115, *Marcel Proust: Selected Letters* 1:153; translation modified.

71. Billy, *Marcel Proust*.

72. Wilhelmina Berncastel, born in 1803 in Trèves, married Mayer Levy, a doctor who converted to Catholicism. Their children (of the same generation as Adèle Berncastel) were given the last name Berncastel. One of them became a priest, one a language teacher in Kent, England. The others also settled in England.

73. This is the most likely hypothesis, though it might also have been an ovarian cyst. The medical records exist, but I was denied access to them.

74. Brochure published upon the hundredth anniversary of the Bizet clinic (1887–1987), in my possession.

75. Darmon, *La vie quotidienne du médecin parisien en 1900*.

76. Marcel to Madame Anatole Catusse, July 6, 1898, letter no. 139, *Marcel Proust: Selected Letters*, 1:178.

77. Marcel to Madame Catusse, July 1898, letter 153, *Correspondence*, 2:238.

78. Marcel to Madame Catusse, September 1898, letter no. 162, *Marcel Proust: Selected Letters*, 1:251.

79. Jeanne to Marcel, October 11, 1898, letter no. 144, *Marcel Proust: Selected Letters*, 1:184.

80. Marcel to Robert de Montesquiou, letter no. 92, *Marcel Proust: Selected Letters*, 1:121. This letter is not dated. Kolb proposes May 19, 1896, in which case it would

come after the publication of Zola's article "For the Jews" (described later in chapter 20).

81. From 1807 to 1914, only 877 Israelites were listed among the 10,820 conversions (i.e., 8 percent) registered with the archbishop of Paris. The number increased during the Third Republic, and from 1895 to 1906 there were 193 cases, usually women who married a Catholic, or men whose ties to Judaism were already weak. In many cases, the conversion resulted in a break with the family (Philippe Landau in *Archives juives*, no. 35, 1st semester, 2002).

82. Simon Schwarzfuchs, *Du Juif à l'Israélite* (Paris: Fayard, 1989, p. 265).

83. Jeanne to Marcel, August 1 (?), 1890, *Correspondance*, 1:145.

84. *The Prisoner*, trans. Clark, p. 301.

85. *In the Shadow of Young Girls in Flower*, trans. Grieve, p. 355.

86. The philosopher Henri Bergson married Louise, the daughter of Laure Lazarus and Gustave Neuburger. Marcel had been best man [*garçon d'honneur*] at his marriage in 1892.

87. The concept of Franco-Judaism was developed by James Darmesteter, graduate of the Ecole normale and director of the Ecole pratique des hautes études. He died October 19, 1894, ten days before the arrest of Dreyfus. See Marrus, *The Politics of Assimilation*.

88. But let's remember that in the last volume of *In Search of Lost Time*, Albert Bloch, who has become Jacques du Rozier and wears a monocle, marries one of his daughters to a Catholic. As for Swann's family, claims the nay-saying Madame de Gaillardon, it converted two generations earlier, which explains its success in society.

89. John Ruskin, *Sesame et les lys*, trans., notes, and preface by Marcel Proust (Paris: Mercure de France, 1906), p. 89, note 2. See also *The Fugitive*, trans. Collier, p. 623: "'And yet,' my mother asked me, 'would you believe that old father Swann, although it is true that you never knew him, could have thought that one day he would have a great-grandson or a great granddaughter in whose veins would mingle the blood of old mother Moser, who used to say, "Goot mornink, Chentlemen," and the blood of the Duc de Guise!'"

90. Schwarzfuchs, *Du Juif à l'Israélite*, p. 329.

91. Marcel too resorted to dueling several times, not to respond to anti-Semitic attacks but, on one occasion, to defend his "virility," cast into doubt by Jean Lorrain in February 1897.

92. L. Wogue, "Une séance memorable," *L'Univers israélite*, July 1, 1893.

93. Bernard Lazare, Preface, *Contre L'Antisémitisme: Histoire d'une polémique* (Paris: Stock, 1896).

94. *The Guermantes Way*, trans. Treharne, p. 282. See also, ibid.: "This compatriot of your friend would have committed a crime against his country if he had betrayed Judaea, but what has that got to do with France?"

95. G. Maire, *Bergson mon maître* (Paris: Grasset, 1935), quoted by Tadié, *Marcel Proust*, p. 128.

96. After his conviction, in an 1895 ceremony at the Ecole militaire in Paris, Dreyfus was stripped of his braid and buttons; his sword was broken in half.—Trans.

97. Duplay, "Mon ami, Marcel Proust," pp. 64–66.

98. Jeanne to Marcel, October 21, 1896, letter no. 108, *Marcel Proust: Selected Letters*, 1:145. Devil's Island, where Dreyfus was deported, is one of the Salvation Islands.

99. Joseph Reinach, *Essais de politique et d'histoire* (Paris: Stock, 1899), pp. 108–9, quoted in Marrus, *The Politics of Assimilation*, p. 140.

100. *Jean Santeuil*, trans. Hopkins, p. 320.

101. Marcel to Jeanne, September 10, 1899, letter no. 158, *Marcel Proust: Selected Letters*, 1:198; and Marcel to Jeanne, September 12, 1899, letter 159, pp. 199–201.

102. As described in Marcel's letter to Georges de Lauris, July 29, 1903, letter no. 251, *Marcel Proust: Selected Letters*, 1:342–46. *L'Intransigeant*, founded by Henri Rochefort, was inspired by the spirit of the Paris Commune but later veered toward the right, via the doctrines of Boulanger.

103. Hannah Arendt considered those paramilitary organizations a first manifestation of modern totalitarianism.

104. Gaston Thomson was married to Henriette, Adolphe Crémieux's granddaughter.

105. Georges Poisson, *Histoire de l'Elysée* (Paris: Perrin, 1997).

106. Marcel to Adrien Proust, September 1898, letter no. 142, *Marcel Proust: Selected Letters*, 1:182.

107. Marcel to Jeanne, September 13, 1899, *Marcel Proust: Letters to His Mother*, trans. Painter, p. 83.

108. Marcel to Jeanne, September 12, 1899, letter no. 159, *Marcel Proust: Selected Letters*, 1:200. According to Philip Kolb, Gustave Clin and his wife, concierges at 9, boulevard Malesherbes, had also been at 40 *bis*, rue du Faubourg-Poissonnière, when the Weils were living there.

109. *The Guermantes Way*, trans. Treharne, p. 284; translation modified.

110. Ibid.

111. Marcel to Jeanne, letter no. 160, September 15, 1899, *Marcel Proust: Selected Letters*, 1:202–3.

112. Marcel to Lucien Daudet, 1899, letter no. 191, *Correspondance*, 2:288.

113. "The syndicate" was the term used by the anti-Dreyfusards to designate Jews.

114. Jeanne to Marcel, August 17, 1900, *Correspondance*, 2:407–8.

115. Marcel to Jeanne, September 17, 1899, letter no. 211, *Correspondance*, 2:329–30.

116. Emmanuel Berl, "Proust devant le judaïsme," *Concordances*, no. 4 (July

1971), p. 20. Emmanel Berl's maternal uncle was Oscar Lange, who was married to Mathilde, the daughter of Gustave and Laure Neuburger.

117. *The Guermantes Way,* trans. Treharne, p. 241.

118. *Swann's Way,* trans. Davis, p. 93.

119. Marcel to Jeanne, March 18–19, 1903, letter no. 149, *Correspondance,* 3:275.

120. I'm borrowing the expression from Philip Roth's novel *The Human Stain* (New York: Houghton Mifflin, 2000).

121. Marcel to Robert Dreyfus, May 29, 1905, letter no. 140, *Marcel Proust: Selected Letters,* 2:187–88.

122. *In the Shadow of Young Girls in Flower,* trans. Grieve, p. 91.

123. Bernard Lazare, "Le nouveau ghetto," *La Justice,* November 17, 1894.

124. *In the Shadow of Young Girls in Flower,* trans. Grieve, p. 482; translation modified.

125. *The Fugitive,* trans. Collier, pp. 539–40.

126. Berl, "Proust devant le judaïsme," p. 20.

127. *Jean Santeuil,* trans. Hopkins, p. 285; translation modified.

128. "Talking to Mama," in *By Way of Sainte-Beuve,* trans. Warner, p. 70.

129. *Jean Santeuil,* trans. Hopkins, p. 735.

130. Painter, *Marcel Proust,* p. 241.

131. On Ruskin, see Tadié, *Marcel Proust,* pp. 345–476.

132. Mona Ozouf, *Women's Words: Essay on French Singularity,* trans. Jane Marie Todd (Chicago: University of Chicago Press, 1997), p. 90.

133. E. Bizub, *La Venise intérieure: Proust et la poétique de la traduction* (Neuchâtel: A la Baconnière, 1991), p. 98, quoted by Tadié, *Marcel Proust,* p. 445.

134. Lauris, *Souvenirs d'une belle époque,* p. 127.

135. The following manuscripts can be consulted at the Bibliothèque nationale de France in Paris: NAF 1667 and 16618: *Bible d'Amiens;* 16622, f. 11 to 67, copy by Jeanne Proust and various texts of Ruskin; 16623: *Bible d'Amiens,* chapter 2; 16624 to 26: *Sésame et les Lys;* 16627: *Mornings in Florence;* 16630–16631: notes by Jeanne Proust concerning Ruskin.

136. See Cynthia Gamble, "Proust traducteur de *La Bible d'Amiens,*" *Bulletin d'Informations proustiennes* 28 (1997): 31–42.

137. Marcel to Jeanne, October 1899 (?), letter no. 225, *Correspondance,* 2:365.

138. Marcel to Jeanne, January 24, 1901 (?), letter no. 20, *Correspondance,* 2:414. See Kolb's notes on Ruskin's text, ibid.

139. Tadié, *Marcel Proust,* p. 281; translation modified.

140. Marcel to Jeanne, 1900 (?), letter no. 237, *Correspondance,* 2:383

141. To give a sense of the trip: in 1913, the Simplon line from Paris to Venice took twenty-two hours. It left Paris at 9:30 P.M., arriving in Venice at 7:30 P.M. by a direct line and for a roundtrip first-class fare of 206.85 francs.

142. Marcel to Leon Yeatman, May 3, 1900, letter no. 248, *Correspondance,* 2:397.

143. "Huit Lettres inédites à Maria de Madrazo par Marie Kiefenstahl-Nordlinger," *Bulletin de la Société des amis de Marcel Proust*, no. 3 (1953): 36. From the context it's clear that Marie Nordlinger is referring to Marcel's trip with his mother.

144. Marcel didn't stay at the Hôtel Europa until his second trip in October of the same year. The hotel was located across from the old customs house in what was then the Palazzo Giustiani; among its guests were Turner (who in 1842 painted *Customs House, San Giorgio*, and *Citadella from the Steps of the Europa)*, Claude Monet, and Richard Wagner.

145. *The Fugitive*, trans. Peter Collier, p. 590.

146. "Huit Lettres inédites" (see n. 143 above), p. 35.

147. *The Fugitive*, trans. Peter Collier, p. 590.

148. Marie Nordlinger to Maria de Madrazo in the *Bulletin de la Société des amis de Marcel Proust*, no. 3 (1953): 36; cf. notes 144 and 147.

149. Quoted in Tadié, *Marcel Proust*, p. 366.

150. *The Fugitive*, trans. Collier, p. 610.

151. *Swann's Way*, trans. Davis, pp. 86–87; cf. *The Fugitive*, trans. Collier, p. 612.

152. *The Fugitive*, trans. Collier, p. 596.

153. "Talking to Mama," in *By Way of Sainte-Beuve*, trans. Warner, pp. 67–68; *The Fugitive*, trans. Collier, pp.614–19; draft 15 for *Albertine Disparue* [*The Fugitive*], in *A la Recherche du temps perdu*, ed. Tadié, 4:694–96.

154. *The Fugitive*, trans. Collier, p. 615.

155. In a draft of *The Fugitive* (see note 154 above), more believable but less beautiful, he merely pretends to have left and stays out of his mother's sight "to make her sorrow last longer."

156. "Talking to Mama," in *By Way of Sainte-Beuve*, trans. Warner, p. 67; translation modified.

157. *Jean Santeuil*, trans. Hopkins, p. 552.

158. This establishment, which changed its name to the Hôtel Britannia and moved to the building next door, later was called the Hôtel Europa, the Hôtel Europa e Britannia, and finally the Hôtel Europa e Regina.

159. My thanks to Nathalie Mauriac, who enabled me to consult this document.

160. Madame Louis Tirman, for example, is listed without her husband, who died on August 2, 1899. Armand Fallières was elected president of the Senate on March 3, 1899, and is listed as such.

161. Marcel to Madame de Noailles, early August 1905, letter no. 161, *Correspondance*, 5:318.

162. *Swann's Way*, trans. Davis, p. 390; translation modified.

163. He died, as the saying goes, "in the arms of his mistress."—Trans.

164. C. Charle, *Les Elites de la République (1880–1900)* (Paris: Fayard, 1987), quoted by Panzac, in *Le Docteur Adrien Proust*, p. 102, who discusses the extent to which Adrien Proust corresponded to the stereotype of this elite.

165. *In the Shadow of Young Girls in Flower,* trans. Grieve, p. 17.

166. Cocteau, quoted by Claude Arnaud, *Jean Cocteau* (Paris: Gallimard, 2003), p. 88.

167. Albert Flament, *Le Bal du Pré-Catélan* (Paris: Fayard, 1946), p. 261.

168. Marcel to Jeanne, September 22, 1899, *Correspondance,* 2:341.

169. André Bénac was an administrative officer in the Banque de Paris et des Pays-Bas and a member of the administrative council of the national railroads. The Bénacs had a house in Beg-Meil, where Marcel visited them with Reynaldo Hahn in September 1895.

170. Monsieur and Madame Alvarès founded a school for young girls at the Cité Trévise, which Jeanne may have attended.

171. Marcel to Jeanne, September 22, 1899, *Marcel Proust: Selected Letters,* 1:206.

172. Jeanne to Marcel, August 14 or 15, 1900, letter no. 253, *Correspondance,* 2:402–3.

173. Jeanne to Marcel, August 19, 1903, letter no. 231, *Correspondance,* 3:402.

174. Jeanne to Marcel, August 14 or 15, 1900, letter no. 253, *Correspondance,* 1:402; "God, basin, or table" is a reference to La Fontaine's fable about the sculptor who must decide what to chisel out of a block of marble: a God, a basin, or a table.

175. Ibid.

176. Jeanne to Marcel, September 13, 1889, letter 19, *Correspondance,* 1:132.

177. Jeanne to Marcel, August 17, 1900, letter no. 255, *Correspondance,* 2:406.

178. Ibid.

179. Marcel to Jeanne, September 25 or 26, 1899, letter no. 217, *Correspondance,* 2:347.

180. Jeanne to Marcel, August 18, 1903, letter no. 229, *Correspondance,* 3:399.

181. Duplay, "Mon ami, Marcel Proust," 64–66.

182. The *agrégation* in medicine, a national competitive exam, was a prerequisite for teaching.—Trans.

183. Tadié, *Marcel Proust,* p. 408.

184. Francis and Gontier, *Marcel Proust et les siens,* p. 141.

185. Archives nationales, Minutier central, LXXXV 1235, Etude de maître Cottin.

186. Marcel to Madame Catusse, February 15, 1903, letter no. 221, *Marcel Proust: Selected Letters,* 1:302.

187. Marcel to Madame Alphonse Daudet, February 3, 1903, letter no. 126, *Correspondance,* 3:235.

188. *By Way of Sainte-Beuve,* trans. Warner, pp. 70–71. The quotations are from Racine.

189. Marcel to Jeanne, December 6, 1902, letter no. 206, *Marcel Proust: Selected Letters,* 1:281–82.

190. Proust, *Mon cher petit,* p. 165.

191. We find an echo of this conflict in Proust's *Sodom and Gomorrah,* trans. Sturrock, pp. 406–7.

192. Marcel to Jeanne, March 9, 1903, letter no. 228, *Marcel Proust: Selected Letters*, 1:309–12; translation modified.

193. Ibid.

194. Marcel to Jeanne, July 16, 2003, letter no. 249, *Marcel Proust: Selected Letters*, 1:340–41.

195. Marcel to Jeanne, spring 1903, letter no. 237, *Marcel Proust: Selected Letters*, 1:323–24.

196. Marcel to Jeanne, July 16, 2003, letter no. 249, *Marcel Proust: Selected Letters*, 1:340–41.

197. Marcel to Jeanne, May 1903, letter no. 240, *Marcel Proust: Selected Letters*, 1:327–28.

198. Marcel to Jeanne, date uncertain, letter no. 184, *Correspondance*, 3:328.

199. Marcel to Léon Radziwill, quoted by Painter in *Marcel Proust*, p. 362.

200. His father, the duc de Gramont, built the Château de Vaillières on land that had belonged to the baronne de Feuchères, using funds from his wife, Marguerite de Rothschild. Marguerite, who inspired the poet Gérard de Nerval, served as godmother to Adolphe Crémieux's daugher when his wife, Amélie Silny Crémieux, and her daughters converted to Catholicism.

201. Marcel to Antoine Bibesco, November 8, 1901, letter no. 178, *Marcel Proust: Selected Letters*, 1:229. Proust coined the euphemism *salaïste* from the surname "sala," after Count Sala. See Kolb's explanatory note 1 in ibid., p. 250

202. *Jean Santeuil*, trans. Hopkins, p. 735.

203. Reynaldo Hahn to Henri Massis, Bibliothèque Nationale de France, NAF, 25260.

204. For details, see Panzac, *Le Docteur Adrien Proust*.

205. We find this same detail in Proust's account of the grandmother's death in *The Guermantes Way*, trans. Treharne, p. 331.

206. Jeanne had insisted that the child be named Adrienne, after her husband. But Adrienne-Suzanne later chose to be called Suzy, much to the consternation of her uncle Marcel.

207. As told by Suzy Mante-Proust, in Francis and Gonthier, *Marcel Proust et les siens*, p. 135. Proust probably used this episode in writing about the grandmother's stroke in the public restroom on the Champs-Elysées; see note 206 above.

208. The monument was replaced in 1956 by a black marble tombstone, on which Marcel Proust's name is engraved in the center in large letters, while the names of his father, his mother, his brother, and his sisters-in-law are engraved on the sides. Instead of a cross, there is a rather unusual symbol in the form of a four-leafed clover.

209. Marcel to Madame de Noailles, December 3, 1903, letter no. 262, *Marcel Proust: Selected Letters*, 1:359.

210. Marcel to Maurice Barrès, January 19, 1906, letter no. 6, *Correspondance*, 6:28.

211. Marcel to Jeanne, December 1903, letter no. 261, *Marcel Proust: Selected Letters*, 1:358.

212. Marcel also would die at work.

213. Marcel to Jeanne, August 11, 1904, letter no. 55, *Marcel Proust: Selected Letters*, 2:68.

214. Marcel to Jeanne, September 23, 1904, letter no. 71, *Marcel Proust: Selected Letters*, 2:95.

215. Marcel to Jeanne, August 11, 1904, letter no. 55, *Marcel Proust: Selected Letters*, 2:68.

216. Marcel to Jeanne , September 23, 1904, letter no. 72, *Marcel Proust: Selected Letters*, 2:95.

217. Jeanne to Marcel, September 21, 1904, letter no. 70, *Marcel Proust: Selected Letters*, 2:91.

218. Marcel to Jeanne, September 21, 1904, letter no. 71, *Marcel Proust: Selected Letters*, 2:92.

219. Jeanne to Marcel, September 25, 1904, letter no. 75, *Marcel Proust: Selected Letters*, 2:102; translation modified.

220. August 23, 1906. Georges was buried on August 26.

221. Roger Duchêne, *L'Impossible Marcel Proust*, p. 464. Upon her death, Jeanne Proust left 1,734,573 gold francs (see footnote on p. 13 above) in addition to the building at 102, boulevard Haussmann, that she had inherited from Uncle Louis and owned together with Georges (ibid., p. 530).

222. Zola had died two years earlier.

223. Marcel to Maurice Le Blond, August 27 or 28, 1904, letter no. 61, *Marcel Proust: Selected Letters*, 2:77.

224. Marcel to Robert Dreyfus, mid-May 1905, letter no. 132, *Marcel Proust: Selected Letters*, 2:179.

225. Proust, *On Reading Ruskin*, trans. Autret, Burford, and Wolfe, pp. 128–29.

226. Marcel to Jeanne, June 15, 1905, letter no. 112, *Correspondance*, 5:219–20.

227. We're reminded here of Bergotte in *In Search of Lost Time*.

228. "Talking to Mamma," in *By Way of Sainte-Beuve*, trans. Warner, p. 68. This text, from Proust's notebooks, is the only place where Marcel directly evokes his mother's death.

229. One version of the story can be found in Valentine Thomson, "My Cousin Marcel Proust," *Harper's Magazine*, 164:714. The person at Jeanne's bedside could not have been Laure Neuburger, née Lazarus, as Philip Kolb claims, since she died in 1898. Laure Nathan, née Rodrigues-Ely, whom everyone called "Aunt Laure," was Jeanne's cousin and best friend.

230. Reynaldo Hahn, *Journal d'un musician* (Paris: Plon, 1933), p. 99.

231. Archives du Consistoire de Paris. The document specifies that this was a third-class burial, corresponding to the traditions of the grande bourgeoisie. The

presence of a rabbi—though confirmed by Philippe Landau, archivist of the Consistory—was not noted in the document. The newspapers noted among those in attendance: The marquis d'Albulfera, Madame Félix Faure, the comte and comtesse de Noailles, the comte and comtesse de Chevigné, the vicomte and vicomtesse de Grouchy, Monsieur and Madame R. de Madrázo, Charles Nathan, the baron Robert de Rothschild, Abel Hermant, Reynaldo Hahn, Lucien Daudet, Léon Brunschvicg, and Henri Bergson.

232. Marcel to Robert de Montesquiou, September 28, 1905, letter no. 152, *Marcel Proust: Selected Letters*, 2:208.

SELECTED BIBLIOGRAPHY

Translations or editions in English are given whenever possible.

Albaret, Céleste. *Monsieur Proust.* Edited by Georges Belmont. Translated by Barbara Bray. 1976. Reprinted with an introduction by André Alcimen. New York: New York Review of Books, 2003.

Amson, Daniel. *Adolphe Crémieux, l'oublié de la gloire.* Paris: Seuil, 1988.

Bauduin, Andrée, and Françoise Coblence. *Marcel Proust visiteur des psychanalystes.* Paris: Presses Universitaires de France/Quadrige, 2003.

Benbassa, Esther. *The Jews of France: A History from Antiquity to the Present.* Translated by M. B. DeBevoise. Princeton: Princeton University Press, 2001.

Berl, Emmanuel. *Interrogatoire par Patrick Modiano,* followed by *Il fait beau, allons au cimetière.* Paris: Gallimard, 1976.

Bernard Anne-Marie. *The World of Proust as Seen by Paul Nadar.* Translated by Susan Wise. Cambridge: MIT Press, 2002.

Billy, Robert de. *Marcel Proust: Lettres et conversations.* Paris: Editions des Portiques, 1930.

Bischoff, Chantal. *Geneviève Straus.* Paris: Balland, 1992.

Blanche, Jacques-Emile. *La Pêche aux souvenirs*. Paris: Flammarion, 1949.

Blum, Léon. *Souvenirs sur l'affaire*. Paris: Gallimard/Idées, 1981.

Blumenkrantz, Bernard. *Histoire des Juifs en France*. Paris: Privat, 1972.

Borrell, Anne. *Dining with Proust*. New York: Random House, 1996.

———. *Voyager avec Marcel Proust*. Paris: La Quinzaine Littéraire–Louis Vuitton, 1994.

Botton, Alain de. *How Proust Can Change Your Life: Not a Novel*. New York: Pantheon, 1997.

Bourdrel, Philippe. *Histoire des Juifs de France*, vol. 1: *Des origines à la Shoah*. Paris: Albin Michel, 2004.

Le Bulletin de la Société des amis de Marcel Proust.

Le Bulletin d'informations proustiennes.

Burns, Michael. *Dreyfus: A Family Affair 1789–1945*. New York: HarperCollins, 1991.

Les Cahiers Marcel Proust.

Carter, William. *Marcel Proust: A Life*. New Haven: Yale University Press, 2000.

Cattaui, Georges, ed. *Marcel Proust: Documents iconographiques*. Geneva: P. Cailler, 1956–57.

Citati, Pietro. *La Colombe poignardée*. Paris: Gallimard, 1997.

Cohen, David. *La Promotion des Juifs de France à l'époque du Second Empire*. Aix-en-Provence: Presses de l'Université de Provence, 1980.

Culot, Maurice. *Trouville*. Edited by Nada Jakovljevic. Institut français d'architecture. Liège: Mardaga, 1989.

Darmon, Pierre. *La vie quotidienne du médecin parisien en 1900*. Paris: Hachette/Pluriel, 2003.

Daudet, Lucien. *Autour de soixante lettres de Marcel Proust*. Paris: Gallimard (Cahiers Marcel Proust, no. 5), 1929.

Diesbach, Ghislain de. *Proust*. Paris: Perrin, 1991.

Dreyfus, Robert. *Souvenirs sur Marcel Proust*. Paris: Grasset/Les Cahiers rouges, 2001.

Duchêne, Roger. *L'Impossible Marcel Proust*. Paris: Laffont, 1994.

Fouquières, André de. *Mon Paris et ses Parisiens*. Paris: Horay, 1953.

Fraisse, Luc. *Proust au miroir de sa correspondance*. Paris: SEDES, 1996.

Francis, Claude, and Fernande Gontier. *Marcel Proust et les siens*. Paris: Plon, 1981.

Graetz, Michael. *The Jews in Nineteenth Century France: From the French Revolution to the Alliance israélite universelle*. Translated by Jane Marie Todd. Palo Alto: Stanford University Press, 1996.

Gregh, Fernand, *L'Age d'or*. Paris: Grasset, 1947.

Hassine, Juliette. *Marranisme et hébraïsme dans l'oeuvre de Proust*. Paris: Mignard, 1994.

Hermont-Belot, Rita. *L'Emancipation des Juifs en France*. Paris: Presses Universitaires de France, 1999.

Katz, Jacob. *Jews and Freemasons in Europe 1723–1939*. Translated by Leonard Oschry. Cambridge: Cambridge University Press, 1970.

Lauris, Georges de. *Souvenirs d'une belle époque*. Paris: Amiot-Dumont, 1948.

Marrus, Michael. *The Politics of Assimilation: A Study of the French-Jewish Community at the Time of the Dreyfus Affair.* New York: Oxford University Press, 1971.

Martin-Fugier, Anne. *Les Salons de la IIIe République.* Paris: Perrin, 2003.

———. *La Bourgeoise.* Paris: Grasset, 1983.

Maurois, André. *A la Recherche de Marcel Proust.* Paris: Hachette, 1949.

Miller, Milton L. *Nostalgia: A Psychoanalytic Study of Marcel Proust.* New York: Houghton Mifflin, 1956.

Muchawsky-Schnapper, Ester. *Les Juifs d'Alsace: Village, tradition, émancipation.* Jerusalem: Musée d'Israël, 1991.

Muhlstein, Anka. *Baron James: The Rise of the French Rothschilds.* New York: Viking, 1983.

Painter, George D. *Marcel Proust: A Biography.* London: Chatto and Windus, 1989.

Panzac, Daniel. *Le Docteur Adrien Proust.* Paris: L'Harmattan, 2003.

Péchenard, Christian. *Proust et les autres.* Paris: La Table ronde, 1999.

Perrot, Michèle, ed. *A History of Private Life,* vol. 4: *From the Fires of Revolution to the Great War.* Translated by Arthur Goldhammer. Cambridge: Cambridge University Press, 1990.

Proust, Marcel. *A la Recherche du temps perdu.* 4 vols. Edited by Jean-Yves Tadié. Paris: Gallimard/Editions de la Pléiade, 1987.

———. *Against Sainte-Beuve.* Translated by John Sturrock. London: Penguin, 1971.

———. *By Way of Sainte-Beuve.* Translated by Sylvia Townsend Warner. London: Chatto and Windus, 1958.

———. *Complete Stories of Marcel Proust.* Translated by J. Neusgroschel. New York: Cooper Square Press, 2001.

———. *Contre Sainte-Beuve.* Collection Idées. Paris: Gallimard, 1965. (See also *Against Sainte-Beuve; By Way of Sainte-Beuve.*)

———. *Contre Sainte-Beuve,* preceded by *Pastiches et mélanges* and followed by *Essais et articles.* Edited by Pierre Clarac and Yves Sandre. Paris: Gallimard, 1971.

———. *Contre Sainte-Beuve,* followed by *Nouveaux mélanges.* Preface by Bernard de Fallois. Paris: Gallimard, 1954.

———. *Correspondance de Marcel Proust.* 21 vols. Edited and annotated by Philip Kolb. Paris: Plon, 1970–93. (See also *Marcel Proust: Selected Letters.*)

———. *Ecrits de jeunesse, 1887–1895.* Edited by Anne Borrel. Paris: Institut Marcel Proust international, 1991.

———. *Finding Time Again.* Translated by Ian Patterson. London: Viking/Penguin, 2003.

———. *The Fugitive.* See *The Prisoner.*

———. *The Guermantes Way.* Translated by Mark Treharne. New York: Viking/Penguin, 2002.

———. "L'Indifférent." Translated by Alfred Corn. *Grand Street* 10, no. 4, pp. 52 ff.

———. *In the Shadow of Young Girls in Flower.* Translated by James Grieve. New York: Viking, 2004.

———. *Jean Santeuil.* Paris: Gallimard/Pléiade, 1971.

———. *Jean Santeuil.* Edited by Pierre Clarac and Yves Sandre, with a foreword by Jean-Yves Tadié. Paris: Gallimard/Quarto, 2001.

———. *Jean Santeuil.* Translated by Gerard Hopkins. New York: Simon and Schuster, 1956.

———. *Marcel Proust: Letters to His Mother.* Translated and edited with an introduction by George D. Painter. London: Rider, 1956.

———. *Marcel Proust: Selected Letters,* edited by Philip Kolb. Vol. 1: *1880–1903,* translated by Ralph Manheim, with an introduction by J. M. Cocking; New York: Doubleday, 1983. Vol. 2: *1904–1909,* translated with an introduction by Terence Kilmartin; London: Collins, 1989. Vol. 3: *1910–1917,* translated by Terence Kilmartin; London: HarperCollins, 1992. Vol. 4: *1918–1922,* translated by Joanna Kilmartin; London: HarperCollins, 2000.

———. *Mon cher petit: Lettre à Lucien Daudet.* Paris: Gallimard, 1991.

———. *On Reading Ruskin.* Translated by Jean Autret, William Burford, and Phillip J. Wolfe. New Haven: Yale University Press, 1987. (Includes "Preface to *Sésame et les Lys.*")

———. *Pleasures and Days.* Translated by Andrew Brown. London: Herperus Classics, 2004.

———. "Preface to *Sésame et les Lys.*" See *On Reading Ruskin.*

———. *The Prisoner,* translated by Carol Clark, followed by *The Fugitive,* translated by Peter Collier. New York: Viking/Penguin, 2003.

———. *Sodom and Gomorrah.* Translated by John Sturrock. New York: Viking/Penguin, 2002.

———. *Swann's Way.* Translated by Lydia Davis. New York: Viking/Penguin, 2002.

Raczymow, Henri. *Swan's Way.* Translated by Robert Bononno. Chicago: Northwestern University, Press, 2002.

———. *Le Paris littéraire et intime de Marcel Proust.* Paris: Parigramme, 1995.

Raphaël, Freddy, ed. *Regards sur la culture judéo-alsacienne.* Strasbourg: La Nuée bleue, 2001.

Récanati, Jean. *Profils juifs de Marcel Proust.* Paris: Buchet Chastel, 1979.

Rémusat, Madame de. *Memoirs of Madame de Rémusat 1802–1808.* Translated by Cashel Hoey and John Lilie. New York: Appleton, 1880.

Schneider, Michel. *Maman.* Paris: Gallimard/L'un et l'autre, 1999.

Schumann, Henry. *Mémoires des communautés juives de Moselle.* Metz: Editions Serpenoise, 1999.

Schwarzfuchs, Simon. *Du Juif à l'Israélite.* Paris: Fayard, 1989.

Soupault, Robert. *Marcel Proust du côté de la médecine.* Paris: Plon, 1967.

Tadié, Jean-Yves. *Marcel Proust.* Translated by Euon Cameron. New York: Viking, 2000.

Tamagne, Florence. *Mauvais genre? Une histoire des représentations de l'homosexualité.* Paris: La Martinière, 2001.

Urbain, Jean-Didier. *At the Beach.* Translated by Catherine Porter. Minneapolis: University of Minnesota Press, 2003.

Vergez-Chaignon, Bénédicte. *Les Internes des hôpitaux de Paris 1802–1952.* Paris: Hachette, 2002.

Wallon, Armand. *La Vie quotidienne dans les villes d'eaux 1850–1914.* Paris: Hachette, 1981.

White, Edmund. *Marcel Proust.* New York: Lipper/Viking, 1999.

Zeldin, Théodore. *A History of French Passions 1948–1945.* Vol. 1: *Ambition, Love and Politics.* Vol. 2: *Intellect, Taste and Anxiety.* Oxford: Clarendon Press, 1973.

INDEX